Foliage Plants

Prolonging Quality

Grateful acknowledgment for photos is given to Ball Seed Co. and Pan-American Seed Co., especially to Lisa Segroves and Will Healy; authors Dr. Thomas Blessington and Dr. Pamela Collins; Bali Hai for *Dieffenbachia amoena*; Dr. Marc Cathey, for *Aucuba japonica* 'Variegata'; the editors of GrowerTalks magazine for *Cissus rhombifolia, Chlorophytum comosum* and *Sansevieria trifasciata;*

Dr. Richard W. Henley, University of Florida, for *Adiantum, Araucaria heterophylla, Coffea arabica, Crassula argentea, Cyrtomium falcatum, Dracaena sanderana, Fittonia verschaffeltii, Gynura aurantiaca, Hedera helix, Hoya carnosa* 'Variegata', *Maranta leuconeura kerchoviana, Peperomia caperata, Peperomia obtusifolia, Pilea cadierei, Pilea microphylla, Pittosporum tobira, Plectranthus australis, Rhoeo spathacea* and *Saxifraga stolonifera;*

Eugene Memmler, Glendale, CA for *Aphelandra squarrosa, Asplenium nidus, Beaucarnea recurvata, Begonia x rex-cultorum* and *Brassaia actinophylla;* Oglesby Plant Laboratories, Inc./ Nursery, Inc. for *Spathiphyllum* 'Mauna Loa'; Tropical Ornamentals, Inc. for *Aspidistra elatior, Dizygotheca elegantissima, Dracaena deremensis* 'Janet Craig', *Dracaena deremensis* 'Warneckii', *Dracaena fragrans* 'Massangeana', *Howea forsterana, Monstera deliciosa, Philodendron selloum* and *Platycerium bifurcatum;*

Twyford Plant Laboratiories for *Calathea makoyana, Dieffenbachia maculata, Ficus benjamina, Ficus elastica* 'Decora' and *Syngonium podophyllum.*

Cover photo courtesy of North Carolina Zoo Aviary.

Foliage Plants

Prolonging Quality

Postproduction Care & Handling

Thomas M. Blessington

and

Pamela C. Collins

Ball Publishing

Batavia, Illinois USA

Ball Publishing
335 N. River St.
P.O. Box 9
Batavia, IL 60510 USA

Printed in the United States of America

98 97 96 95 94 93   5 4 3 2 1

Library of Congress Cataloging in Publication Data

Blessington, Thomas M. 1946–
    Foliage plants : prolonging quality : postproduction care & handling /
Thomas M. Blessington and Pamela C. Collins.
    p. cm.
Includes bibliographical references (p.   ) and index.

    ISBN 0-9626796-9-0 : $51.00
    1. Foliage plants—Handling.   2. Foliage plants—Postharvest
technology.   I. Collins, Pamela C., 1949–   .   II. Title.
SB423.7.B58   1993   92-45172
635.9'756--dc20   CIP

CONTENTS

Crops

FOREWORD

*F*oliage Plants: Prolonging Quality is one of a series of books about the care and handling of plants from grower to consumer. It's designed to give the entire marketing-user chain of grower, wholesaler, retailer and consumer the current recommendations on the most effective procedures for each postproduction stage—as each has its own specific considerations.

Nothing is more natural than having trees and shrubs in our living space. These green foliage plants remain season after season, some exhibiting dramatic leaf color changes and growth while others remain evergreen throughout their lives. Foliage plants today have benefited from extensive advances in exploration, breeding, culture, chemicals, media, supplemental lighting, containers and design principles, all of which have added new plants to grow, extended periods of performance and great flexibility in success-ful plant management. We are now able to purchase trees and shrubs shaped to many decorative forms that will thrive in dark, dry, stressful spaces.

Today, foliage plants, according to preliminary reports, also help remove pollutants from the air and reduce the impact of the "closed or sick building" syndrome. Research currently underway help explain how plants can survive toxic chemicals and lead to even wider acceptance of plants' usage. This book deals with the specific requirements for the postproduction care and handling of foliage plants. We hope you will find the successful practice of postpro-duction care begins here.

The Postproduction series includes the following four books: *Bedding Plants: Prolonging Shelf Performance* by Allan M. Armitage, the University of Georgia; *Cut Flowers: Prolonging Freshness (2nd ed.)* by John N. Sacalis, Rutgers University, and edited by Joseph L. Seals; *Flowering Potted Plants: Prolonging Shelf Performance* by Terril A. Nell, University of Florida; and *Foliage Plants: Prolonging Quality* by Thomas M. Blessington, University of Maryland, and Pamela C. Collins, landscape design and interior plantscaping consultant.

These four postproduction books origi-nated from the series produced through the Kiplinger Chair in Horticulture at The Ohio State University, Columbus, Ohio. During 1980-1981, I occupied the Kiplinger Chair, which is funded by businesses, foundations and individuals to support research and educational activities for floricultural excellence. The Chair honors Dr. D.C. Kiplinger, professor of floriculture, for his contributions as a teacher, researcher and extension specialist.

Recommendations for the Chair urged expanded research in production and distri-bution of high quality floral products, and postproduction books on bedding plants, cut flowers, flowering potted plants and foliage plants were subsequently planned and produced by the Kiplinger Chair.

Committee members during the creation of the guides were: Stanley F. Backman, Minneapolis, MN; Roger D. Blackwell, Columbus, OH; H. Marc Cathey, Beltsville, MD; for the Ohio Florists Association:

Willard H. Barco, Medina, OH, James F. Bridenbaugh, Kent, OH, and August J. Corso, Sandusky, OH; Paul Ecke Jr., Encinitas, CA; Harry K. Tayama, Columbus, OH; and for The Ohio State University: Robert A. Kennedy, Steven M. Still and Luther Waters Jr.

H. Marc Cathey
National Chair for Florist
    and Nursery Crops Review
U.S. Department of Agriculture
Washington, DC

INTRODUCTION

Choices. Decisions. Quality. Communication. You may wonder what these words have to do with a book on interior foliage plants. Growers, shippers, wholesalers, retailers and consumers make choices and decisions every day that affect keeping quality of foliage plants. Communication within this diverse group of people is important to identify the best techniques to produce healthy, high-quality products. Success of an indoor planting depends on good selection, production techniques sensitive to interior needs and delivery of undamaged material. Some interior spaces are designed with all the amenities to sustain abundant plant life, while others totally ignore basic needs. Therefore, initial selection by the retailer to match the environment is crucial for plant survival.

Choices are greatly increased when growers acclimatize, or condition, their plants to the indoor climate prior to sales release. Properly acclimatized plants retain quality better during shipping and storage than nonacclimatized plants. Physical protection and consideration of physiological needs by shippers and wholesalers assure safe delivery of perishable material to the consumer. Carefully selected, quality foliage plants require less maintenance and resist plant deterioration after installation.

This book's purpose is to provide information that promotes health and extended keeping quality of foliage plants under interior conditions. Currently available knowledge about production, postproduction handling and interior care is assembled together for use by all allied professionals. Some species' requirements are well documented by researchers and commercial interests, while others have received little substantial attention. Many species and cultivars still need additional study to provide recommendations from production through interior care.

Included in this guide is a wide range of plants based on popular use and availability in the industry. The selections include species and cultivars with considerable variety in size, growth habit, texture and response to environmental conditions. Most selections are readily available from production facilities. A few may be produced only in small quantities due to specialty forms, current market development or technical difficulties. Other species and cultivars are used in interiors but are not discussed here due to lack of information or other limitations. The foliage industry has many potentially useful plants from which to choose, and new species and cultivars are constantly being introduced.

Foliage plants have become an important part of the horticultural industry. They are found not only in homes but in offices, shops and major business complexes. They soften architectural surfaces, direct traffic and provide a feeling of life to otherwise sterile surroundings. But to maintain and increase consumer interest in foliage plants, the horticultural industry must provide good quality plants consistently from grower, shipper, wholesaler and retailer to the office desk or mall planter. Development of good production and postproduction techniques can also reduce costs due to loss of unsalable, damaged plants. Plants with good keeping quality and reasonable maintenance demands attract clients who carefully consider long-term upkeep and replacement expenses. Improved selections and quality control allow the foliage industry to evolve as building styles and interior environments change in response to social, economic and human needs. Availability of good plant variety in size, texture, color and environmental requirements provides flexibility for designers and steady market demand.

The final ingredient for continued interest in and success with foliage plants is consumer education about plant care. This service provides clients with a realistic view of a plant's needs and expected lifespan in a specific location. A little time and effort spent in this area can enhance respect for a professional industry and continue interest in using plants indoors.

POSTPRODUCTION FACTORS

The useful lifespan of a foliage plant can be broken down into four phases. *Production* is done by growers, including such specialists as tissue culture laboratories, plant propagators and plant finishers. *Postproduction* storage is carried out by shippers and wholesalers. *Retail handling* of plants is the responsibility of interior plantscapers, florists, garden centers and mass market distributors. *Consumer care* is the final phase, where interior keeping quality is determined by practices of the consumer alone or by a plant maintenance company. These phases are significantly distinct by function and chronological order within the plant's lifespan, but they are not independent of each other. Keeping quality of a plant is determined not only by conditions encountered during a single phase but is influenced by interactions with all preceding phases. Decisions made at each stage affect the potential to prolong quality.

Production factors

The production phase includes propagation and growth of the plant to a finished, salable condition. Healthy, high-quality plants at this point are not only attractive commodities, but also maintain quality better throughout the stresses of storage, transport and placement indoors. Production factors that influence interior keeping quality of a foliage plant are light, temperature, nutrition, water, media, disease or pest problems and cultural disorders.

Light. Production light levels are determined by genetic composition and by the interior light conditions to which a plant must adjust. Some species are naturally adapted to heavy shade of forest floors and perform well under low light. Others require high light to grow properly and are seldom used in interior settings unless sufficient direct sunlight is available. A third group of plants can adapt to reduced light if they are produced or acclimatized under specific light levels. As production light level is decreased, these plants become increasingly tolerant to marginal lighting. Physical changes such as growth habit, leaf size, leaf color and trunk caliper usually accompany the acclimatization process. These changes may or may not be desirable to the producer or designer/retailer. If major changes in growth habit are not acceptable, some plants can be produced under high light levels and then placed under shaded conditions until foliage is fully acclimatized. This process may take 6 weeks to 6 months or even longer, depending on species and size of specimen. Even then, these converted plants are not as fully conditioned to low light situations as those produced entirely under shade.

Temperature. Species chosen for use in interiors are mostly tropical plants, although a few subtropical and temperate climate plants also perform well indoors. Therefore, most recommended greenhouse minimum temperatures range from 60° to 70°F (16° to 21°C) to assure constant, uniform growth rates. The ability to sustain short periods of cool, nonfreezing temperatures without chilling injury varies considerably by species. Likewise, the ability to tolerate high temperatures without damage or reduction in

11

growth rate is quite variable. Careful selection of temperature-tolerant crop species can be important where economy in fuel consumption or lack of heat control is a major consideration. The acclimatization process itself is only minimally affected by production temperature.

Nutrition. Fertilization during the production phase definitely influences the interior keeping quality of foliage plants. Overfertilization decreases acclimatization effectiveness indoors, either by increasing respiration rate or by root damage from high soluble salts. Low levels of nutrition reduce plant growth and quality. The most efficient fertilizer rate and ratio depend on many factors. Extreme pH imbalances in potting media block the availability of essential elements. Where clay-containing soil is used as a potting medium, a 1:1:1 fertilizer ratio is recommended to assure adequate availability of phosphorous and potassium. In soilless media, a 3:1:2 ratio is suggested to decrease the soluble salt levels and costs of fertilizer components.

Most potting media require the addition of micronutrients. Incorporation of a micronutrient source into the medium prior to potting should provide good results. Alternatively, micronutrients can be applied in solution as part of a liquid fertilization program. Recent research reports recommend omitting superphosphate completely from the soil mix, as foliage plants do not show a specific need for the amendment. In fact, several important genera of foliage plants are sensitive to the fluoride present in superphosphate.

Fertilizer rates also depend on production light levels. Recommendations for fertilizer and light levels are based on a balance of good growth and acclimatization needs. Plants produced under high light levels may require increased fertilizer rates, while plants produced under heavy shade will need less fertilization to maintain a balanced growth. In addition, temperature affects fertilizer application decisions. Less fertilizer is needed during the cool seasons, and more fertilizer is required during warmer times of the year due to differences in growth rates. Temperature levels similarly affect the release rate of encapsulated fertilizers. Where heavy rainfall or overhead irrigation is a frequent occurrence, consider adjusting fertilizer applications upward.

Water. Perhaps the best general recommendation for irrigation practices is to avoid extremes. Plants experience stress when watered either too much or too little. Frequent irrigations stimulate fragile succulence, and excessive water retention in the media reduces root growth and resistance to soilborne diseases. Insufficient water or excessive drying of the media between waterings reduces growth and stimulates leaf abscission. Most plants maintain good growth and quality when irrigation schedules allow slight drying between thorough waterings. A few species require special considerations due to environmental adaptations to climates with high humidity and constant moisture or to climates with low humidity and dry soils.

Media. Water retention, cation exchange capacity and drainage characteristics of potting media all contribute to the health, growth and keeping quality of foliage plants. Many media components are now used, such as bark, peat, sand, vermiculite, perlite, styrofoam, cypress shavings, even clay soil. Mixtures of various components are designed for the special needs of a species and in response to the economics of component availability and transport costs. Soluble salts, fluoride levels and any other suspected elemental imbalance should be checked in all media components before incorporation into the finished mix. Most foliage plants require a pH of 5.5 to 6.5 to grow well. The potting medium usually requires micronutrient amendments as discussed under Nutrition. Pay careful attention to media preparation before planting to avoid costly cultural disorders caused by deficiencies, toxicities and poor root development.

Problems. All foliage plants show susceptibility to some disease or pest, although considerable variability exists among species. Use good cultural techniques, consistent sanitation practices and careful observation to reduce the need for heavy chemical control applications. Where chemical use is mandated, test a block of plants with the selected pesticide for symptoms of toxicity or for undesirable deposits on the foliage. Good disease and pest control during production not only provide a quality plant for sale but improve the probability that quality will be maintained during shipping. The crowded, enclosed environment imposed on plants during transit and storage is not only detrimental to an infested plant, but increases the likelihood of spreading problems to healthy plants and compounding economic losses.

Disorders. Some plant disfigurements are caused not by attacking organisms but by physiological responses to internal imbalances or environmental conditions. Susceptibility to injury varies considerably. Most ferns develop phytotoxic responses to a broad spectrum of pesticides, limiting the use of chemicals in production. Several important genera of foliage plants are sensitive to fluoride or boron in either the potting medium or atmosphere. Palms can display poor, stunted growth when deficient in manganese, iron or zinc. Production under light levels exceeding recommendations produces bleached, light green foliage color in some plants, while too much shade destroys normal variegation patterns and stimulates weak, elongated growth. Chilling injury is a major problem in several species. The final result of such disorders is an economic loss from unsalable, poor-quality plants. These plants hurt all of the foliage plant industry because they do not ship or store well, and they require extra regrowth time and maintenance attention in interior locations.

Postproduction factors

The postproduction phase exists from the time that plants leave the production ranges in shippers' vehicles and are possibly warehoused by wholesalers until they reach retail locations. The prime goal for shippers and wholesalers is to deliver plants with minimum quality deterioration. Factors that affect the plants' keeping quality during shipping and storage are storage light, temperature, exposure to gases, lasting qualities during storage and care and grooming of the plants prior to packing.

Light. Transport of plants under dark conditions is currently the most practical method of shipping. When plants travel a long distance, a recovery period is sometimes necessary to make up for the quality lost during the extended period of stress. In addition, wholesalers sometimes need to hold a shipment of plants for a time before distribution. Specially equipped greenhouses or environmental rooms are ideal places for plant holding. Recommended light levels for these locations are 500 to 1,000 fc (5.4 to 10.8 klx). Temperature, irrigation and relative humidity should approximate normal levels found indoors to retain acclimatization conditioning.

Temperature. Shipping temperature specifications have changed considerably with the development of guidelines for extended overseas transit. For many foliage plants, shipping durations can be increased when temperatures are reduced to levels that slow down physiological processes but do not cause chilling injury. Recommendations for some plants are very specific for different storage durations, depending on their sensitivity to injury over a long period of time. Where the new long-term guidelines are not available, existing recommendations are given.

Gases. Ethylene is the gas most frequently generated by plant material during transit; however, foliage plants are not particularly heavy producers. Avoid mixed shipments with fruits or vegetables, which release significant amounts during the ripening process. Plant damage is generally not a problem with storage below 65°F (18°C), as gas evolution and activity is inhibited by low temperature. Ethylene at levels greater than 1 to 2 ppm may cause damage if plants are held in storage for a long time above 65°F (18°C).

Lasting qualities. The key to plant keeping quality during shipping and storage is stress avoidance. Best quality retention is obtained with the shortest transit time. Most prepared and packaged plants tolerate 7 days of travel without significant quality loss. Ability to survive longer times depends on the species and shipping conditions. Some plants can be stored up to 4 weeks without significant deterioration when held under carefully controlled conditions of temperature, relative humidity and moisture. Keeping quality is also influenced by conditions encountered during the production phase. Plants produced within recommended ranges of light and fertilizer ship better than unacclimatized material. Winter- or spring-produced plants tolerate lower shipping temperatures better than summer-grown stock.

Care and grooming. Keeping quality during the postproduction phase can be improved if plants are well prepared and packaged before shipping. Fertilization should be discontinued at least a week prior to packing, especially when slow-release forms are used. Loose granules can shift during handling and fall between the soil ball and pot. Schedule the final irrigation so that the potting medium is moist or approximately 50% of soil capacity. Extremely wet or dry media conditions are detrimental to plant health during the storage period. Disease development can be reduced if foliage is dry during storage. When wet foliage is unavoidable at packing time, lower shipping temperatures help retard growth of organisms.

The shipping industry has developed advanced equipment and handling procedures designed to move delicate, perishable items such as plants. Growers improve protection of their commodity by using moisture-resistant boxes or specially developed shipping racks. Large specimens can be protected with sleeves that envelop the canopy and are closed at the top. High relative humidity levels of 80% to 90% reduce desiccation during storage time. These levels can be achieved by boxing or by placing the reefer (refrigerated van) air controller in the closed position. With such careful packing procedures, physical breakage and reduced desiccation can be avoided during transit.

Retail handling

The retail phase begins with delivery by shipper and wholesaler and continues until sale to the consumer or installation into a permanent interior location. Retailers can be interior plantscapers, florists, garden centers or mass market businesses. Shipping durations and provisions for poststorage care determine foliage plants' condition upon delivery. Length of stay on inventories depends largely on the retail businesses' nature. Regardless, plant care is based on environmental demands of an interior location.

Light. Plants may require a recuperative period upon arrival, and the ideal location is in a holding greenhouse or room with light levels of 500 to 1,000 fc (5.4 to 10.8 klx). Temperature, irrigation and relative humidity should approximate normal indoor levels to retain acclimatization conditioning. Where such facilities are not available, provide at least the minimum sustaining light levels given under each plant listing. Plants held under less than minimum light will be unable to maintain quality for very long.

Temperature. Most tropical foliage plants maintain good quality with temperature and relative humidity levels that are comfortable for humans. A few subtropical

Foliage Plants *Postproduction Factors*

and temperate climate species have special preferences for somewhat cooler night temperatures or higher humidities.

Water. Foliage plants usually perform best indoors when the potting medium is moist but well drained. Extremely wet or dry soil conditions stress plants and cause loss in quality. A few species require special moisture recommendations based on adaptations to native climates of high moisture and humidity or of dry soils and low humidity.

Disorders. The major problems with foliage plants at this stage are due to stress from shipping and storage. Most are temporary and correct themselves with a little recuperation time in a holding greenhouse or room. More severe losses happen when latent diseases or disorders from the production and postproduction phases are passed on to the retailer.

Consumer care

The useful lifespan of a foliage plant in its permanent interior location depends largely on successfully matching it to the environmental conditions of a space and caring for it by either the consumer or maintenance service. Any latent problems brought from earlier phases will reduce keeping quality under interior environmental stress and increase efforts needed to maintain an acceptable appearance. Factors that affect the keeping quality of foliage plants after interior installation are temperature, location, watering practices, grooming, disorders and cultivar selection.

Temperature. Most tropical foliage plants maintain good quality with temperature and relative humidity levels that are comfortable for humans. A few subtropical and temperate climate species have special preference for somewhat cooler night temperatures or higher humidities.

Locations. Success occurs when plants are matched carefully with interior locations. Some locations have severe environmental limitations, where plant choices are few. The limiting factor is usually inadequate lighting.

Plants with natural or acclimatized adaptation to low light levels are the most successful in these circumstances. The ability to tolerate minimum light levels varies within this group. Changes in growth habit can be expected in time as plants adjust to a location. Under marginal conditions durability and lifespan are significantly altered. Keeping quality potential improves where light can be increased. As lighting conditions approach the natural range of a plant, its growth and quality reach peak capabilities. At this level, maintenance becomes a matter of keeping growth in bounds rather than an effort to retard aging. Species and cultivar choice also increase as lighting approaches moderate levels. In locations that have direct sunlight, marginal interior plant selections requiring high light levels can be used with good keeping expectations. Specific guide recommendations list both optimum light ranges and minimum/maximum tolerances where the information is known.

Water. Foliage plants usually perform best indoors when the potting medium is moist but well drained. Extremely wet or dry soil conditions stress plants and cause loss in quality. A few species require special moisture recommendations based on adaptations to native climates of high moisture and humidity or of dry soils and low humidity.

Grooming. Under most interior conditions, maintenance to preserve existing quality levels is required more often than growth control. Plants are not static objects, and therefore growth or decline is inevitable. Specific recommendations attempt to identify trimming and repotting needs. Less fertilization is necessary under interior conditions, and specific recommendations are listed where known.

Disorders. Weak, damaged or diseased plants will not survive long if placed indoors. Healthy, high-quality plants tolerate interior conditions better. Problems that develop after installation are caused most often by low light, low humidity, drafty locations or air pollutants. Poor maintenance contributes to quality loss when plants are overwatered, underwatered, undusted, poorly fertilized and otherwise neglected. Stressed plants are most susceptible to attack by pests and diseases. Considerable variability exists between different foliage plant species.

Cultivars. The foliage plant industry has a wide range of species to provide variety in texture, color, size and cultural adaptability. In addition, numerous cultivars are available that have marketable attributes such as increased foliage color, interesting variegation or growth habit, disease or pest resistance, or improved ability to tolerate specific interior conditions. Plant introduction or breeding programs and tissue culture laboratories are continually adding new cultivars to the market. Each new cultivar should be thoroughly tested to develop guidelines that produce a high-quality plant with good interior keeping capabilities. All available cultivars cannot be discussed within this current guide, but where possible, commercially available related species and cultivars of the listed plants are briefly described.

ADDITIONAL READING

Conover, C.A. and R.T. Poole. 1984. Light and fertilizer recommendations for production of acclimatized potted foliage plants. *Foliage Digest* 7(8):1-6.

Conover, C.A. and R.T. Poole. 1984. Acclimatization of indoor foliage plants. *Horticultural Reviews* 6:119-154.

————. 1986. Factors influencing shipping of acclimatized foliage plants. *ARC-Apopka Research Rpt.* RH-86-11. Univ. of Florida.

————. 1983. Handling and overseas transportation of acclimatized foliage plants in reefers. *Foliage Digest* 6(5):3-4.

McConnell, D.B., R.W. Henley and R.L. Biamonte. 1981. Commercial foliage plants. J.N. Joiner, ed. *Foliage Plant Production.* Englewood Cliffs, NJ: Prentice-Hall Inc.

CROPS

Adiantum spp.

ad-ee-*an*-tum

Family Name: **Polypodiaceae**
Common Name: **Maidenhair Fern**

Originated in temperate North America, tropical America and eastern Asia.

ADIANTUM spp.

Production factors

Light. Use production light levels of 1,200 to 1,800 fc (13 to 19.4 klx) for acclimatized plants.

Temperature. To assure good growth, keep minimum greenhouse temperatures of 60° to 65°F (16° to 18°C).

Nutrition. At the recommended production light levels for acclimatized plants, fertilize with 18.4 to 23 pounds per 1000 square feet per year (lb/1000 sq. ft./yr) or 89.7 to 112.1 kilograms per 1000 square meters per year (kg/1000 sq. m/yr) of N-P-K.

Irrigation. Water plants sufficiently to keep the medium moist. Provide a minimum relative humidity of 50% for best results.

Media. Use a potting medium with good drainage characteristics. Check pH specifications as some species require a higher pH than others.

Problems.
Diseases: Leaf spot—*Corynespora cassiicola*, *Glomerella* sp., *Mycosphaerella* sp.
Pests: Mealybugs; mites; scales.

Disorders. Pesticide toxicity is common among ferns. Use good sanitation practices to avoid disease or insect problems. Wilting of foliage results in severe dieback of fronds. Avoid water stress.

Postproduction factors

Light. Transport of plants under dark conditions is currently the most common method of shipment. If extended holding is necessary before sale or installation, maintain maidenhair fern under 100 fc (1.1 klx) of light.

Temperature. Shipping temperatures of 60° to 70°F (16° to 21°C) are safe for maidenhair fern.

Gases. Leaf loss occurs with ethylene concentrations greater than 1 ppm.

Lasting qualities. Avoid storage exceeding 7 days, as ferns do not store well in dark.

Care and grooming. Maintain a relative humidity of 65% to 85%. Avoid low humidity.

Adiantum spp.

ad-ee-*an*-tum

A

Retail handling

Light. Provide plants with sufficient light after delivery to recuperate from the stresses of dark storage. Both shadowless north light and interior lighting provide appropriate illumination. Light levels of 75 to 150 fc (.8 to 1.6 klx) are best, although maidenhair fern tolerates a minimum of 50 fc (.5 klx) and a maximum of 200 fc (2.2 klx).

Temperature. Night temperatures can range from 50° to 60°F (10° to 16°C). Recommended day temperatures are 60° to 70°F (16° to 21°C). A high relative humidity of approximately 50% is preferred for best results.

Irrigation. Keep the potting medium evenly moist.

Disorders. Prolonged dark storage, ethylene toxicity or water stress can cause loss of leaflets.

Consumer care

Temperature. Night temperatures can range from 50° to 60°F (10° to 16°C), while recommended day temperatures are 60° to 70°F (16° to 21°C). A high relative humidity of approximately 50% provides best results.

Location. Maidenhair fern grows well under both shadowless light from a north window and interior lighting. Light levels of 75 to 150 fc (.8 to 1.6 klx) are best, although this genus tolerates a minimum of 50 fc (.5 klx) and a maximum of 200 fc (2.2 klx).

Irrigation. Keep soil moist during the growing season. Reduce water use during winter when plants are not actively growing. Water only enough during winter dormancy to prevent wilting, and locate plants under cool, humid conditions.

Grooming. Cut dead foliage back if fronds die from a missed watering. New fronds may emerge from the crown. Repot or divide if desired in late winter before spring growth begins. Fertilize every 6 months with a half-strength solution. Avoid high fertilizer levels and soluble salts.

Disorders. Maidenhair fern is not very durable when placed in an average interior environment because of its need for humid conditions and a winter rest period. However, it will flourish if carefully maintained under optimum conditions.

Cultivars. *Adiantum capillus-veneris* (Southern maidenhair fern) grows 18 to 24 inches (46 to 61 cm) tall and has very delicate fronds. It is found worldwide in warm-temperate and subtropical areas, including Virginia to Missouri, Florida, Texas and New Mexico. Fronds are two to three times pinnately divided into coarsely lobed, round to angular-ovate segments.

Adiantum raddianum (Delta maidenhair fern) is a native of the American tropics. It grows 6 to 15 inches (15 to 38 cm) tall and is the most cultivated of tropical maidenhair ferns. Cultivars of this species may be fertile or sterile, have crested or ruffled frond segments, large or small segments, dissected or skeletonized segments, united segments or variegated foliage.

Adiantum spp.

ad-ee-*an*-tum

A

ADDITIONAL READING

Bailey, L.H. and E.Z. Bailey. 1976. *Hortus Third.* New York: Macmillan Publishing Co. Inc.

Crockett, J.U. 1977. *Foliage house plants.* Revised. Alexandria, VA: Time-Life Books.

Everett, T.H. 1980. *The New York Botanical Garden Illustrated Encyclopedia of Horticulture.* New York: Garland Publishing Inc.

McConnell, D.B., R.W. Henley and R.L. Biamonte. 1981. Commercial foliage plants. J.N. Joiner, ed. *Foliage plant production.* Englewood Cliffs, NJ: Prentice-Hall Inc.

Staby, G.L., J.L. Robertson and D.C. Kiplinger. 1978. *Chain of Life.* Columbus, OH: Ohio Florists' Assn.

Sullivan, G.H., J.L. Robertson and G.L. Staby. 1980. Care and handling of foliage plants. *Management for retail florists with applications to nursery and garden centers.* San Francisco: W.H. Freeman and Co.

Aglaonema spp.

ag-luh-*nee*-muh

Family Name: **Araceae**
Common Name: **Chinese Evergreen**

Originated in the Philippine Islands.

AGLAONEMA 'SILVER QUEEN'

Production factors

Light. Production light levels of 1,000 to 2,500 fc (10.8 to 27 klx) are recommended for acclimatized plants.

Temperature. Maintain minimum night temperatures above 65°F (18°C). Avoid exposure to temperatures below 55°F (13°C) for 'Silver Queen' and 50°F (10°C) for other cultivars.

Nutrition. At the recommended produc-

tion light levels for acclimatized plants, fertilize with 34.5 pounds per 1000 square feet per year (lb/1000 sq. ft/yr) or 168.4 kilograms per 1000 square meters per year (kg/1000 sq. m/yr). A N-P-K ratio of 3:1:2 is suggested for use with soilless media, while 1:1:1 is recommended for soil-based media. Most media require the addition of micronutrients either by preplant incorporation of a granular source or as part of a liquid fertilization program. Select a micronutrient source with low boron concentration.

Irrigation. Allow the potting medium to dry slightly between waterings to avoid root rot and bacterial diseases.

Media. Use a potting medium with good drainage characteristics. Keep pH above 5.5 and avoid media components containing high levels of fluoride.

Problems.

Diseases: Anthracnose—*Colletotrichum* sp., *Glomerella cingulata*; blight—*Rhizoctonia solani, Sclerotium rolfsii, Xanthomonas vitians*; leaf spot—*Corynebacterium* sp., *Myrothecium roridum, Pseudomonas cichorii, Xanthomonas campestris* pv. *dieffenbachiae*; root rot—*Pythium splendens, Rhizoctonia solani*; soft rot—*Erwinia caratovora* subsp. *caratovora, E. dieffenbachiae;* stem rot—*Fusarium solani,* and virus—dasheen mosaic virus.

Pests: Mealybugs; mites.

Disorders. Bent-tip can occur during production, especially under conditions of

Aglaonema spp.

high light and water stress. Chinese evergreen is sensitive to fluoride and boron. Toxicity symptoms appear as necrotic spots on leaf margins and tips. Copper deficiency can develop when soil temperature falls below 65°F (18°C) especially in the cultivar 'Franscher.' New growth appears chlorotic, stunted and deformed. Avoid low temperatures or apply copper as a foliar spray or soil drench. Recommended rate for soil application is 1.5 pounds copper sulfate per 1,000 square feet (7.3 kilograms per 1000 square meters). Chilling injury appears as gray or yellow spots that develop into necrotic tissue.

Postproduction factors

Light. Transport of plants under dark conditions is currently the most common method of shipment. If holding is necessary before sale or installation, maintain plants under at least 50 fc (.5 klx) of light.

Temperature. Acclimatized plants can be shipped without damage for extended periods. 'Maria' travels well when held at 55° to 65°F (13° to 18°C). 'Fransher' can be held at 55° to 60°F (13° to 16°C) for up to 14 days but should be stored at 60° to 65°F (16° to 18°C) if additional time is required. 'Silver Queen' is more sensitive to chilling injury and should be shipped at 60° to 65°F (16° to 18°C).

Gases. Injury due to ethylene is generally not a problem when plants are shipped within the recommended temperature range. Ethylene may reach damaging levels if plants are shipped with produce or held in prolonged storage above the maximum listed temperature.

Lasting qualities. Under appropriate storage conditions, acclimatized plants retain good quality when shipped within 4 weeks. Maintain temperatures near the upper end of the recommended range when transport requires only 1 to 7 days.

Care and grooming. Good storage preparation improves quality retention during transit. Moisture content of the potting medium should approximate 50% of soil capacity when plants are packed. Maintain high humidity levels of 80% to 90% during storage to retard dessication, especially when shipping time exceeds 7 days.

Retail handling

Light. Provide plants with sufficient light upon delivery to recuperate from the stresses of dark storage. A specially designed holding greenhouse or room is ideal. When such a facility is unavailable, light levels near 150 fc (1.6 klx) are recommended. Chinese evergreen maintains quality well under poor lighting conditions and can tolerate a range of 25 to 250 fc (.3 to 2.7 klx).

Temperature. Good quality is maintained with day temperatures of 70° to 75°F (21° to 24°C) and night temperatures of 60° to 65°F (16° to 18°C). When a greenhouse is used to hold plants before installation, maintain 40% to 60% relative humidity for acclimatization to lower interior humidity levels.

Irrigation. Keep the potting medium slightly moist at all times.

Disorders. Chilling injury appears as gray to yellow spots that progress to necrosis. Some species of Chinese evergreen are less sensitive than others to chilling injury and may provide a means for improving hardiness in future cultivar selections.

Aglaonema spp.

ag-luh-*nee*-muh

A

Consumer care

Temperature. Maintain good quality with day temperatures of 70° to 75°F (21° to 24°C) and night temperatures of 60° to 65°F (16° to 18°C).

Location. Chinese evergreen thrives under shadowless light from a north window but also performs well under interior lighting. Light levels near 150 fc (1.6 klx) are recommended for best results. Chinese evergreen maintains quality well under poor light conditions and can tolerate a range of 25 to 250 fc (.3 to 2.7 klx).

Irrigation. Keep the potting medium slightly moist at all times.

Grooming. Prune or repot only if the plant becomes overcrowded. Fertilize every 2 to 4 months with a standard houseplant formula. Chinese evergreen is a very durable plant and will last indefinitely with proper care.

Cultivars. *Aglaonema* 'Silver Queen' is one of the most popular cultivars available in the trade. The leaves are mostly variegated silver green with a darker green margin, while the lower leaf surface is light green. Abundant basal branching forms a full foliaged plant. 'Silver Queen' is more cold sensitive than other cultivars; therefore, avoid temperatures below 55°F (13°C). Light levels of 100 to 150 fc (1.1 to 1.6 klx) prevent leggy, drooping growth patterns.

ADDITIONAL READING

Bailey, L.H. and E.Z. Bailey. 1976. *Hortus Third*. New York: Macmillan Publishing Co. Inc.

Chase, A.R. 1985. Diseases of foliage plants—revised list for 1985. *Foliage Digest* 8(6):3-8.

———— and R.T. Poole. 1986. Troubleshooting guide to foliage. *Greenhouse Grower* 4(4):54-55.

Conover, C.A. and R.T. Poole. 1981. Guide for fertilizing foliage plant crops. *ARC-Apopka Research Rpt.* RH-81-1. Univ. of Florida.

————. 1983a. Environmental factors influencing long-term shipping of tropical foliage plants. *Foliage Digest* 6(6):3-5.

————. 1983b. Handling and overseas transportation of acclimatized foliage plants in reefers. *Foliage Digest* 6(5):3-4.

————. 1984. Light and fertilizer recommendations for production of acclimatized potted foliage plants. *Foliage Digest* 7(8):1-6.

————. 1986. Factors influencing shipping of acclimatized foliage plants. *ARC-Apopka Research Rpt.* RH-86-11. Univ. of Florida.

————. 1987. Factors influencing shipping of acclimatized foliage plants. *Foliage Digest* 10(4):1-5.

Crockett, J.U. 1977. *Foliage house plants*. Revised. Alexandria, VA: Time-Life Books.

Everett, T.H. 1980. *The New York Botanical Garden Illustrated Encyclopedia of Horticulture*. New York: Garland Publishing Inc.

Holstead, C.L. 1985. *Care and handling of flowers and plants*. Floralife Inc. Society of American Florists. Alexandria, VA

Hummel, R.L. and R.J. Henny. 1986. Variation in sensitivity to chilling injury within the genus *Aglaonema*. *HortScience* 21:291-293.

McConnell, D.B., R.W. Henley and R.L. Biamonte. 1981. Commercial foliage plants. J.N. Joiner, ed. *Foliage plant production*. Englewood Cliffs, NJ: Prentice-Hall Inc.

Sullivan, G.H., J.L. Robertson and G.L. Staby. 1980. Care and handling of foliage plants. *Management for Retail Florists with Applications to Nursery and Garden Centers*. San Francisco: W.H. Freeman and Co.

Aphelandra squarrosa

a-fel-*an*-druh
squar-*oh*-suh

Family Name: **Acanthaceae**
Common Name: **Zebra Plant**

Originated in Brazil.

APHELANDRA SQUARROSA

Production factors

Light. Production light levels of 1,000 to 1,500 fc (10.8 to 16.2 klx) are recommended for acclimatized plants.

Temperature. Greenhouse temperatures of at least 65°F (18°C) keep plants actively growing. If winter fuel costs or supplies are a problem, however, zebra plant can be grown with a minimum temperature of 60°F (16°C).

Nutrition. At recommended production light levels for acclimatized plants, fertilize with 41.4 pounds per 1000 square feet per year (lb/1000 sq. ft/yr) or 202.1 kilograms per 1000 square meters per year (kg/1000 sq. m/yr) of N-P-K. A N-P-K ratio of 3:1:2 is suggested for use with soilless media, while 1:1:1 is recommended for soil-based media. Most media require the addition of micronutrients either by preplant incorporation of a granular source or as part of a liquid fertilization program.

Irrigation. Keep the medium evenly moist but not wet. These plants are very moisture sensitive and should be watched for wilting.

Media. Use a coarse and highly organic potting medium that drains well.

Problems.

Diseases: Blight—*Botrytis cinerea, Sclerotium rolfsii;* dieback—*Pseudomonas* sp.; stem gall—*Nectriella pironii;* leaf spot—*Corynespora cassiicola, Myrothecium roridum, Xanthomonas campestris*; soft rot—*Erwinia carotovora;* stem rot—*Phytophthora parasitica, Rhizoctonia solani;* virus—cucumber mosaic virus.

Pests: Mealybugs; scale; thrips.

Postproduction factors

Light. Transport of plants under dark conditions is currently the most common method of shipment. If extended holding is necessary before sale or installation, maintain zebra plant under 90 to 125 fc (1 to 1.4 klx) of fluorescent lighting for 16 hours a day.

Temperature. Recommended temperatures for shipping are 55° to 60°F (13° to 16°C). Do not hold plants at temperatures below 55°F (13°C).

Aphelandra squarrosa

a-fel-*an*-druh
squar-*oh*-suh

Gases. Injury due to ethylene is generally not a problem when plants are shipped within the recommended temperature range. Ethylene may reach damaging levels if plants are shipped with produce or held in prolonged storage above the maximum listed temperature.

Lasting qualities. Under appropriate storage conditions, acclimatized plants retain good quality when shipment does not exceed 2 weeks. Severe quality loss is expected when plants require more than 2 weeks to reach their destination. Maintain temperatures near the upper end of the recommended range when transport requires only 1 to 7 days.

Care and grooming. Good storage preparation improves quality retention during transit. Moisture content of the potting medium should approximate 50% of soil capacity when plants are packed. Maintain high humidity levels of 80% to 90% during storage to retard dessication, especially when shipping time exceeds 7 days.

Retail handling

Light. Provide plants with sufficient light upon delivery to recuperate from the stresses of dark storage. A specially designed holding greenhouse or room is ideal. Minimum light levels of 75 to 150 fc (.8 to 1.6 klx) are required for survival indoors. Retention of foliage and leaf color is improved with higher light levels of 250 to 500 fc (2.7 to 5.4 klx). Locations near south, east or west windows provide good natural lighting for zebra plant.

Temperature. Quality is best maintained with interior temperatures of 65° to 80°F (18° to 27°C). When a greenhouse is used to hold plants before installation, maintain 40%

to 60% relative humidity for acclimatization to lower interior humidity levels.

Irrigation. Keep the potting medium moist but not wet, and maintain a moderate humidity level.

Disorders. Plants that receive high fertilizer rates during production may develop symptoms of salt damage when placed under lower interior light. Soluble salt levels below 1,000 ppm are important for interior quality retention.

Consumer care

Temperature. Maintain plant quality with interior temperatures of 65° to 80°F (18° to 27°C).

Location. Minimum light levels of 75 to 150 fc (.8 to 1.6 klx) are required for survival indoors. Retention of foliage and leaf color is improved with higher light levels of 250 to 500 fc (2.7 to 5.4 klx). Locations near south, east or west windows provide good natural lighting for zebra plant.

Irrigation. Keep the potting medium moist but not wet, and maintain a moderate humidity level.

Grooming. Remove any dead leaves or inflorescences. The floral display should remain attractive for 4 to 8 weeks with good care and environmental conditions. This plant is normally used only for short-term display. Fertilize every 2 months with a standard houseplant formula if longer maintenance is desired. Soluble salt levels below 1,000 ppm are important for interior quality retention.

Disorders. Plants that receive high fertilizer rates during production may develop symptoms of salt damage when placed under lower interior light.

Foliage Plants *Aphelandra squarrosa*

Aphelandra squarrosa

a-fel-*an*-druh
squar-*oh*-suh

ADDITIONAL READING

Bailey, L.H. and E.Z. Bailey. 1976. *Hortus Third.* New York: Macmillan Publishing Co. Inc.

Chase, A.R. 1985. Diseases of foliage plants—revised list for 1985. *Foliage Digest* 8(6):3-8.

———. 1988. Diseases of foliage plants—1988 updated listing. *Foliage Digest* 11(6):5-8.

Conover, C.A. and R.T. Poole. 1977. Influence of fertilization and watering on acclimatization of *Aphelandra squarrosa*. Nees cv. 'Dania.' *Hort-Science* 12:569-570.

———. 1981. Guide for fertilizing foliage plant crops. *ARC-Apopka Research Rpt.* RH-81-l. Univ. of Florida.

———. 1983. Handling and overseas transportation of acclimatized foliage plants in reefers. *Foliage Digest* 6(5):3-4.

———. 1984. Light and fertilizer recommendations for production of acclimatized potted foliage plants. *Foliage Digest* 7(8):1-6.

———. 1986. Factors influencing shipping of acclimatized foliage plants. *ARC-Apopka Research Rpt.* RH-86-11. Univ. of Florida.

———. 1987. Factors influencing shipping of acclimatized foliage plants. *Foliage Digest* 10(4):1-5.

Everett, T.H. 1980. *The New York Botanical Garden Illustrated Encyclopedia of Horticulture.* New York: Garland Publishing Inc.

Florists' Transworld Delivery Association. 1985. *The Indoor Gardener.* Southfield, MI.

Kofranek, A.M. 1972. The maintenance of some indoor foliage plants under fluorescent lighting. *Florists' Review* 150(3895):19-20.

McConnell, D.B., R.W. Henley and R.L. Biamonte. 1981. Commercial foliage plants. J.N. Joiner, ed. *Foliage plant production.* Englewood Cliffs, NJ: Prentice-Hall Inc.

Orans, M. 1973. *Houseplants and Indoor Landscaping.* Barrington, IL: A.B. Morse Co.

Poole, R.T. and C.A. Conover. 1987. Foliage variety determines heat. *Greenhouse Grower* 5(1):21-22.

A

Araucaria heterophylla

ar-aw-*kay*-ree-uh
het-er-oh-*fil*-uh

Family Name: **Araucariaceae**
Common Name: **Norfolk Island Pine**

Originated on Norfolk Island.

ARAUCARIA HETEROPHYLLA

Production factors

Light. Use production light levels of 4,000 to 8,000 fc (43.2 to 86.4 klx) for acclimatized plants finished in 4- to 8-inch pots (10- to 20-cm). Larger trees can be produced under full sun conditions or light shade and then acclimatized under shade conditions for several weeks. This produces plants with stronger trunks and more compact foliage, however, foliage is lighter green than that of shade-produced plants.

Temperature. Norfolk Island pine is very tolerant of temperatures. Avoid temperatures above 95°F (35°C) or below 32°F (0°C), especially in windy weather. Provide production temperatures of 60° to 90°F (16° to 32°C) for seedlings and liners and 45° to 90°F (7° to 32°C) for potted trees to maintain active growth.

Nutrition. At recommended production light levels for acclimatized plants, fertilize with 34.5 pounds per 1000 square feet per year (lb/1000 sq. ft/yr) or 168.4 kilograms per 1000 square meters per year (kg/1000 sq. m/yr) of N-P-K. Increase the fertilizer rate 25% to 40% if plants are produced under 30% shade to full sun conditions. A N-P-K ratio of 3:1:2 is suggested for use with soilless media, while 1:1:1 is recommended for soil-based media. Most media require the addition of micronutrients either by preplant incorporation of a granular source or as part of a liquid fertilization program.

Irrigation. The medium should be allowed to dry slightly between waterings. Avoid extremely wet or dry soil conditions.

Media. Use a potting medium with good drainage characteristics, and provide support for a limited root system. A 3 parts peat to 1 part sand medium can hold heavy trunk growth upright and still maintain good water and fertilizer retention. Lighter mixes are recommended for initial establishment of seedling growth. Adjust the potting medium to a pH of 5.5 to 6.5.

Problems.
Diseases: Needle blight—*Colletotrichum*

derridis sp., *Gloeosporium* sp., *Macrophoma* sp., *Phyllosticta araucariae;* needle and stem blight—*Leptosphaeria* sp.; bleeding canker—*Dothiorella* sp.; twig dieback—*Cercospora thujina;* leaf spot—*Pestalotia sp.;* root rot—*Cylindrocladium* sp., *Pythium* sp., *Rhizoctonia solani.*

Pests: Mealybugs; scale; spider mites and thrips.

Disorders: Trees can become loose and lean in their pots. Crooked growth forms as terminal tips readjust to a vertical pattern. Micronutrient deficiencies cause chlorotic growth terminals. Plants develop poorly, and side branches droop unattractively when grown under inadequate light. Growth terminals can be damaged when exposed to temperatures above 95°F (35°C) or below 32°F (0°C), especially in windy weather. Iron deficiency occurs when pH levels rise above 7.0.

Postproduction factors

Light. Transport of plants under dark conditions is currently the most common method of shipment. If holding is necessary before sale or installation, maintain Norfolk Island pine under minimum light levels of 100 to 150 fc (1.1 to 1.6 klx).

Temperature. Acclimatized plants can be shipped without damage for extended periods when held at 50° to 65°F (10° to 18°C).

Gases. Injury due to ethylene is generally not a problem when plants are shipped within the recommended temperature range. Ethylene may reach damaging levels if plants are shipped with produce or held in prolonged storage above the maximum listed temperature.

Lasting qualities. Under appropriate storage conditions acclimatized plants retain good quality when shipped within 4 weeks. Maintain temperatures near the upper end of the recommended range when transport

requires only 1 to 7 days.

Care and grooming. Good storage preparation improves quality retention during transit. Moisture content of the potting medium should approximate 50% of soil capacity when plants are packed. Maintain high humidity levels of 80% to 90% during storage to retard dessication, especially when shipping time exceeds 7 days. Norfolk Island pine does not produce a strong root mass compared to top growth and may require staking in pot sizes of 3 gallons (11 l) or more to assure straight trunks.

Retail handling

Light. Provide plants with sufficient light to recuperate from the stresses of dark storage. A specially designed holding greenhouse or room is ideal. When such a facility is unavailable, maintain plants under at least 100 fc (1.1 klx) of light. Retailers should hold Norfolk Island pine under 200 fc (2.2 klx) or more if changes in growth habit are not desired. Choose locations with bright indirect or curtain-filtered sunlight to provide appropriate natural lighting.

Temperature. Norfolk Island pine tolerates cool interior temperatures, with a recommended range of 50° to 70°F (10° to 21°C). When a greenhouse is used to hold plants before installation, maintain 40% to 60% relative humidity for acclimatization to lower interior humidity levels.

Irrigation. Keep the potting medium moist but not wet. Allow the medium to dry slightly between waterings.

Disorders. Check for looseness of plants in the pots. Norfolk Island pine does not produce a strong root system compared to top growth and may require staking in pot

Araucaria heterophylla

ar-aw-*kay*-ree-uh
het-er-oh-*fil*-uh

sizes of 3 gallons (11 l) or more to assure straight trunks. Foliage droops when held under insufficient light.

Consumer care

Temperature. Norfolk Island pine tolerates cool interior temperatures, with a recommended range of 50° to 70°F (10° to 21°C).

Location. Installation under bright indirect or curtain-filtered sunlight is preferred. Light levels greater than 200 fc (2.2 klx) are recommended to preserve typical growth habit, although plants can be maintained under light levels as low as 100 fc (1.1 klx).

Irrigation. Keep the potting medium moist but not wet. Allow the medium to dry slightly between waterings.

Grooming. Fertilize every 3 to 4 months. Repot only if the plant becomes over-crowded. Leave the plant in a potbound condition as long as possible once the best size is reached for a location. Norfolk Island pine can be expected to grow 3 to 6 inches (8 to 15 cm) in height per year with ad-equate maintenance and light. Under good conditions, this plant may slowly but eventually outgrow its space.

Disorders. Norfolk Island pine does not produce a strong root mass compared to top growth and may require staking in pot sizes of 3 gallons (11 l) or more to assure straight trunks. Foliage droops when held under insufficient light.

ADDITIONAL READING

Bailey, L.H. and E.Z. Bailey. 1976. *Hortus Third.* New York: Macmillan Publishing Co. Inc.

Chase, A.R. 1985. Diseases of foliage plants—revised list for 1985. *Foliage Digest* 8(6):3-8.

Conover, C.A. and R.T. Poole. 1981. Guide for fertilizing foliage plant crops. *ARC-Apopka Research Rpt.* RH-81-1. Univ. of Florida.

———. 1983. Handling and overseas transportation of acclimatized foliage plants in reefers. *Foliage Digest* 6(5):3-4.

———. 1984. Light and fertilizer recommendations for production of acclimatized potted foliage plants. *Foliage Digest* 7(8):1-6.

———. 1986. Factors influencing shipping of acclimatized foliage plants. *ARC-Apopka Research Rpt.* RH-86-11. Univ. of Florida.

———. 1987. Factors influencing shipping of acclimatized foliage plants. *Foliage Digest* 10(4):1-5.

Crockett. J.U. 1977. *Foliage house plants.* Revised. Alexandria, VA: Time-Life Books.

Everett, T.H. 1980. *The New York Botanical Garden Illustrated Encyclopedia of Horticulture.* New York: Garland Publishing Inc.

Florists' Transworld Delivery Association. 1985. *The Indoor Gardener.* Southfield, MI.

Gaines, R.L. 1977. *Interior Plantscaping: Building Design for Interior Foliage Plants.* New York: Architectural Record Books.

Manaker, G.H. 1981. *Interior Plantscapes: Installa-tion, Maintenance, and Management.* Englewood Cliffs, NJ: Prentice-Hall Inc.

McConnell, D.B., R.W. Henley and R.L. Biamonte. 1981. Commercial foliage plants. J.N. Joiner, ed. *Foliage Plant Production.* Englewood Cliffs, NJ: Prentice-Hall Inc.

Orans, M. 1973. *Houseplants and Indoor Landscap-ing.* Barrington, IL: A.B. Morse Co.

Osborne, L.S., C.A. Conover and A.R. Chase. 1986. Norfolk Island pine. *Foliage Digest* 9(6):1-4.

Asparagus densiflorus 'Sprengeri'

as-*par*-uh-gus
den-sih-*flor*-us
spreng-er-eye

Family Name: **Liliaceae**
Common Name: **Sprenger Asparagus, Asparagus Fern**

Originated in South Africa.

ASPARAGUS DENSIFLORUS 'SPRENGERI'

Production factors

Light. Use production light levels of 2,500 to 4,500 fc (27 to 48.6 klx) for acclimatized plants.

Temperature. Greenhouse temperatures of at least 55°F (13°C) keep plants actively growing.

Nutrition. At recommended production light levels for acclimatized plants, fertilize with 27.6 pounds per 1000 square feet per year (lb/1000 sq ft/yr) or 134.8 kilograms per 1000 square meters per year (kg/1000 sq m/yr) of N-P-K. A N-P-K ratio of 3:1:2 is suggested for use with soilless media, while 1:1:1 is recom-mended for soil-based media. Most media require the addition of micronutrients either by preplant incorporation of a granular source or as part of a liquid fertilization program.

Irrigation. Keep the potting medium uniformly moist but not wet.

Media. Use a potting medium with good drainage characteristics.

Problems.

Diseases: Anthracnose—*Colletotrichum* sp.; canker—*Phoma asparagi, Fusarium oxysporum, Helminthosporium* sp.; stem canker —*Ascochytula asparagina*; crown gall—*Agrobacterium tumefaciens*; root rot—*Fusarium* sp.; root, stem and leaf rot—*Rhizoctonia solani;* rust—*Puccinia asparagi;* stem diseases—*Hendersonia asparagi, Leptosphaeria asparagina.*

Pests: Aphids; mealybugs; mites; nematodes; scale; thrips.

Disorders. Sprenger asparagus is very sensitive to airborne fluoride. Symptoms include chlorosis, bleaching and tanning of the needles followed by defoliation.

Postproduction factors

Light. Transport of plants under dark conditions is currently the most common method of shipment. If extended holding is necessary before sale or installation, maintain plants under at least 100 to 120 fc (1.1 to 1.3 klx) of light.

Asparagus densiflorus 'Sprengeri'

as-*par*-uh-gus
den-sih-*flor*-us
spreng-er-eye

A

Retail handling

Light. Provide plants with sufficient light upon delivery to recuperate from the stresses of dark storage. Sprenger asparagus prefers bright indirect or curtain-filtered sunlight but also performs well under interior lighting of 200 to 500 fc (2.2 to 5.4 klx). Plants require at least 100 fc (1.1 klx) of light for minimum growth maintenance.

Temperature. Sprenger asparagus tolerates cooler temperatures than many interior plants. Keep night temperatures of 50° to 65°F (10° to 18°C) and maintain day temperatures of 65° to 75°F (18° to 24°C).

Irrigation. Keep the potting medium uniformly moist.

Disorders. Plants are very sensitive to airborne fluoride. Chlorosis and needle drop develop if plants are held under insufficient light too long or if the medium becomes too wet or dry.

Consumer care

Temperature. Sprenger asparagus tolerates cooler temperatures than many interior plants. Keep night temperatures at 50° to 65°F (10° to 18°C) and day temperatures at 65° to 75°F (18° to 24°C).

Location. Plants thrive in areas with bright indirect or curtain-filtered sunlight but also perform well under interior lighting of 200 to 500 fc (2.2 to 5.4 klx). Provide at least 100 fc (1.1 klx) of light for minimum growth maintenance.

Irrigation. Keep the potting medium uniformly moist.

Grooming. Prune out old stems that die to make room for new emerging growth. Cut the entire canopy back if the plant loses all stems to a stressful situation. New growth should return from established tubers under good growing conditions. Overcrowded pots can be divided, repotted in fresh media, trimmed back and rejuvenated. Fertilize every 2 months. Sprenger asparagus can remain a quality plant indefinitely with good care.

Disorders. Air pollutants containing fluoride can cause sudden, severe defoliation. Chlorosis and needle drop develop if plants are held under insufficient light too long or if the medium becomes too wet or dry.

Cultivars. *Asparagus densiflorus* 'Myers' (Myers asparagus fern or foxtail fern) stems are stiffly ascending in a densely branched, plumelike form that suggests bushy tails. Foxtail ferns make nice specimen plants in pots or hanging baskets.

Asparagus setaceus (Asparagus fern) is tall-growing, with wiry stems holding up clusters of needlelike cladophylls in flatly arranged sprays. The evergreen foliage is texturally very fine and fernlike in appearance and is often used by florists for decorative greenery in arrangements.

Asparagus densiflorus 'Sprengeri'

as-*par*-uh-gus
den-sih-*flor*-us
spreng-er-eye

ADDITIONAL READING

Bailey, L.H. and E.Z. Bailey. 1976. *Hortus Third.* New York: Macmillan Publishing Co. Inc.

Conover, C.A. and R.T. Poole. 1981. Guide for fertilizing foliage plant crops. *ARC-Apopka Research Rpt.* RH-81-1. Univ. of Florida.

————. 1984. Light and fertilizer recommendations for production of acclimatized potted foliage plants. *Foliage Digest* 7(8):1-6.

Crockett, J.U. 1977. *Foliage house plants.* Revised. Alexandria, VA: Time-Life Books.

Everett, T.H. 1980. *The New York Botanical Garden Illustrated Encyclopedia of Horticulture.* New York: Garland Publishing Inc.

Florists' Transworld Delivery Association. 1985. *The Indoor Gardener.* Southfield, MI.

Gaines, R.L. 1977. *Interior Plantscaping: Building Design for Interior Foliage Plants.* New York: Architectural Record Books.

Holstead, C.L. 1985. *Care and Handling of Flowers and Plants.* Floralife Inc. Society of American Florists. Alexandria, VA.

Manaker G.H. 1981. *Interior Plantscapes: Installation, Maintenance and Management.* Englewood Cliffs, NJ: Prentice Hall, Inc.

McConnell, D.B., R.W. Henley and R.L. Biamonte. 1981. Commercial foliage plants. J.N. Joiner, ed. *Foliage Plant Production.* Englewood Cliffs, NJ: Prentice-Hall Inc.

Woltz, S.S. and W.E. Waters. 1978. Airborne fluoride effects on some foliage plants. *HortScience* 13:585-586.

A

Aspidistra elatior

ass-pih-*diss*-truh
ee-*lay*-tee-or

Family Name: **Liliaceae**
Common Name: **Cast-Iron Plant**

Originated in Japan.

ASPIDISTRA ELATIOR

Production factors

Light. Use production light levels of 3,000 to 5,000 fc (32.4 to 54 klx).

Temperature. This species can withstand freezing temperatures, but maintain a minimum greenhouse temperature above 50°F (10°C) to assure good growth.

Nutrition. At recommended production light levels, fertilize with 20.7 to 27.6 pounds per 1000 square feet per year (lb/ 1000 sq. ft/yr) or 100.9 to 134.8 kilograms per 1000 square meters per year (kg/1000 sq. m/yr) of N-P-K. Avoid fertilizers containing fluoride.

Irrigation. The medium should be evenly moist but not wet. Use a water source that is low in fluoride concentration.

Media. Choose a potting medium that drains well to avoid problems from overwatering. Screen potting media amendments for the presence of fluoride before using with cast iron plant. Maintain a pH of 6.9 to reduce availability of this element in the medium.

Problems.

Diseases: Leaf spot—*Ascochyta aspidistrae, Cercospora* sp., *Colletotrichum omnivorum, Gloeosporium* sp.; soft rot— *Erwinia carotovora.*

Pests: Scale; spider mites.

Disorders. Cast-iron plant is sensitive to fluoride. Symptoms of toxicity include tipburn and necrotic leaf margins.

Postproduction factors

Light. Transport of plants under dark conditions is currently the most common method of shipment. If extended holding is necessary before sale or installation, maintain plants under at least 50 fc (.5 klx) of light.

Temperature. Acclimatized plants can be shipped without damage for extended

Aspidistra elatior

ass-pih-*diss*-truh
ee-*lay*-tee-or

periods when held at 50° to 55°F (10° to 13°C).

Gases. Injury due to ethylene is generally not a problem when plants are shipped within the recommended temperature range. Ethylene may reach damaging levels if plants are shipped with produce or held in prolonged storage above the maximum listed temperature.

Lasting qualities. Under appropriate storage conditions acclimatized plants retain good quality when shipped within 4 weeks. Maintain temperatures near the upper end of the recommended range when transport requires only 1 to 7 days.

Care and grooming. Good storage preparation improves quality retention during transit. Potting medium moisture content should approximate 50% of soil capacity when plants are packed. Maintain high humidity levels of 80% to 90% during storage to retard dessication, especially when shipping time exceeds 7 days.

Retail handling

Light. Provide plants with sufficient light upon delivery to recuperate from the stresses of dark storage. A specially designed holding greenhouse or room is ideal. When such a facility is unavailable, provide lighting of 100 to 150 fc (1.1 to 1.6 klx) even though these plants can tolerate light levels as low as 50 fc (.5 klx). Light from a north window supports good growth and appearance.

Temperature. Cast-iron plant tolerates drafty locations and temperatures ranging from 45° to 85°F (7° to 29°C). However, interior temperatures of 70° to 75°F (21° to 24°C) are preferred for best plant health.

When a greenhouse is used to hold plants before installation, maintain 40% to 60% relative humidity for acclimatization to lower interior humidity levels.

Irrigation. Avoid overwatering by keeping the medium barely moist.

Disorders. Brown leaf margins and tips are symptoms of fluoride toxicity.

Consumer care

Temperature. Plants tolerate drafty locations and temperatures ranging from 45° to 85°F (7° to 29°C). Interior temperatures of 70° to 75°F (21° to 24°C), however, are preferred for best plant health.

Location. Cast-iron plant thrives when installed under light from a north window. Provide minimum lighting of 100 to 150 fc (1.1 to 1.6 klx) for quality retention, although these plants tolerate light levels as low as 50 fc (.5 klx).

Irrigation. Avoid overwatering by keeping the medium barely moist.

Grooming. This is a very durable plant and will last indefinitely with good care. Dust leaves occasionally, or wash with clean water. Avoid leaf cleaning agents. Cast-iron plant tolerates potbound conditions very well and can remain in the same pot for a long time without damage. Early spring is the best time for division and repotting if desired. Fertilize every 4 months.

Disorders. Leaves develop brown margins and tips if exposed to fluoride.

Cultivars. *Aspidistra elatior* 'Variegata' (Variegated cast-iron plant) has a growth habit like the parent species, but leaves are green and white striped. This variegation tends to disappear with excessive fertilization.

A

ADDITIONAL READING

Arthurs, Kathryn, ed. 1974. *How to Grow House Plants.* Menlo Park, CA: Lane Publishing Co.

Bailey, L.H. and E.Z. Bailey. 1976. *Hortus Third.* New York: Macmillan Publishing Co. Inc.

Conover, C.A. and R.T. Poole. 1983. Environmental factors influencing long-term shipping of tropical foliage plants. *Foliage Digest* 6(6):3-5.

———. 1983. Handling and overseas transportation of acclimatized foliage plants in reefers. *Foliage Digest* 6(5):3-4.

———. 1986. Factors influencing shipping of acclimatized foliage plants. *ARC-Apopka Research Rpt.* RH-86-11. Univ. of Florida.

———. 1987. Factors influencing shipping of acclimatized foliage plants. *Foliage Digest* 10(4):1-5.

Crockett, J.U. 1977. *Foliage house plants.* Revised. Alexandria, VA: Time-Life Books.

Everett, T.H. 1980. *The New York Botanical Garden Illustrated Encyclopedia of Horticulture.* New York: Garland Publishing Inc.

Florists' Transworld Delivery Association. 1985. *The Indoor Gardener.* Southfield, MI.

Manaker, G.H. 1981. *Interior Plantscapes: Installation, Maintenance and Management.* Englewood Cliffs, NJ: Prentice-Hall Inc.

McConnell, D.B., R.W. Henley and R.L. Biamonte. 1981. Commercial foliage plants. J.N. Joiner, ed. *Foliage Plant Production.* Englewood Cliffs, NJ: Prentice-Hall Inc.

Wright, M., ed. 1979. *The Complete Indoor Gardener.* Rev. ed. New York: Random House.

Asplenium nidus

as-*pleen*-ee-um
nye-dus

Family Name: **Polypodiaceae**
Common Name: **Bird's-Nest Fern**

Originated in tropical Asia and Polynesia.

ASPLENIUM NIDUS

Production factors

Light. Use production light levels of 1,500 to 2,000 fc (16.2 to 21.6 klx).

Temperature. Provide a minimum night temperature of 60°F (16°C) for optimum growth.

Nutrition. At recommended production light levels fertilize with 13.8 to 23 pounds per 1000 square feet/per year (lb/1000 sq. ft/yr) or 67.3 to 112.1 kilograms per 1000 square meters per year (kg/1000 sq. m/yr) of N-P-K.

Irrigation. Keep the potting medium evenly moist. Avoid accumulation of water in plant crown to prevent onset of crown rot.

Media. Choose a highly organic potting medium that drains well for good growth.

Problems.

Diseases: Blight—*Rhizoctonia solani* AG1; leaf spot—*Cercospora asplenii, Pseudomonas asplenii (P. cichorii), Pseudomonas gladioli.*

Pests: Mealybugs; foliar nematodes—*Aphelenchoides fragariae;* scale; slugs.

Postproduction factors

Light. Transport of plants under dark conditions is currently the most common method of shipment. If extended holding is necessary before sale or installation, maintain bird's-nest fern under at least 50 fc (.5 klx) of light.

Temperature. Acclimatized plants can be shipped without damage for extended periods when held at 50° to 65°F (10° to 18°C).

Gases. Injury due to ethylene is generally not a problem when plants are shipped within the recommended temperature range. Ethylene may reach damaging levels if plants are shipped with produce or held in prolonged storage above the maximum listed temperature.

Asplenium nidus

as-*pleen*-ee-um
nye-dus

Lasting qualities. Under appropriate storage conditions plants retain good quality when shipped within 4 weeks. Maintain temperatures near the upper end of the recommended range when transport requires only 1 to 7 days.

Care and grooming. Good storage preparation improves quality retention during transit. Moisture content of the potting medium should approximate 50% of soil capacity when plants are packed. Maintain high humidity levels of 80% to 90% during storage to retard dessication, especially when shipping time exceeds 7 days.

Retail handling

Light. Provide plants with sufficient light upon delivery to recuperate from the stresses of dark storage. A specially designed holding greenhouse or room is ideal. When such a facility is unavailable, provide minimum light levels of 75 to 150 fc (.8 to 1.6 klx). Bird's-nest fern tolerates light ranging from 50 to 250 fc (.5 to 2.7 klx). A north window exposure with indirect light is the best natural light location.

Temperature. This fern prefers night temperatures of 55° to 60°F (13° to 16°C) and day temperatures of 60° to 70°F (16° to 21°C). When a greenhouse is used to hold plants before installation, maintain 40% to 60% relative humidity for acclimatization to lower interior humidity levels.

Irrigation. Maintain evenly moist soil conditions.

Disorders. Soluble salt levels above 1,000 ppm can affect interior quality retention.

Consumer care

Temperature. Bird's-nest fern prefers night temperatures of 55° to 60°F (13° to 16°C) and day temperatures of 60° to 70°F (16° to 21°C).

Location. Bird's-nest fern thrives when installed under indirect light from north windows. Use minimum light levels of 75 to 150 fc (.8 to 1.6 klx), although plants tolerate light ranging from 50 fc to 250 fc (.5 to 2.7 klx).

Irrigation. Maintain evenly moist soil conditions.

Grooming. Trim out dead fronds. Schedule repotting of overcrowded plants for late winter before new growth begins. Fertilize every 3 to 4 months.

Disorders. Soluble salt levels above 1,000 ppm can affect interior quality retention.

Cultivars. *Asplenium bulbiferum* (Mother fern) has arching fronds that can grow up to 4 feet long and 1 foot wide (120 cm long and 30 cm wide). The highly divided fronds and leaflets appear lacy and develop plantlets on the upper surfaces when mature. Mother fern reproduces by these plantlets as well as by spore formation.

Asplenium nidus

as-*pleen*-ee-um
nye-dus

ADDITIONAL READING

Bailey, L.H. and E.Z. Bailey. 1976. *Hortus Third.* New York, NY: Macmillan Publishing Co. Inc.

Chase, A.R. 1985. Diseases of foliage plants— Revised list for 1985. *Foliage Digest* 8(6):3-8.

———. 1988. Diseases of foliage plants—1988 updated listing. *Foliage Digest* 11(6):5-8.

Conover C.A. and R.T. Poole. 1983. Handling and overseas transportation of acclimatized foliage plants in reefers. *Foliage Digest* 6(5):3-4.

———. 1986. Factors influencing shipping of acclimatized foliage plants. *ARC-Apopka Research Rpt.* RH-86-11. Univ. of Florida.

———. 1987. Factors influencing shipping of acclimatized foliage plants. *Foliage Digest* 10(4):1-5.

Crockett, J.U. 1977. *Foliage house plants.* Revised. Alexandria, VA: Time-Life Books.

Everett, T.H. 1980. *The New York Botanical Garden Illustrated Encyclopedia of Horticulture.* New York: Garland Publishing Inc.

Florists' Transworld Delivery Association. 1985. *The Indoor Gardener.* Southfield, MI.

Holstead, C.L. 1985. *Care and Handling of Flowers and Plants.* Floralife Inc. Society of American Florists. Alexandria, VA.

McConnell, D.B., R.W. Henley and R.L. Biamonte. 1981. Commercial foliage plants. J.N. Joiner, ed. *Foliage Plant Production.* Englewood Cliffs, NJ: Prentice-Hall Inc.

Orans, M. 1973. *Houseplants and Indoor Landscaping.* Barrington, IL: A.B. Morse Co.

Staby, G.L., J.L. Robertson and D.C. Kiplinger. 1978. *Chain of Life.* Columbus, OH: Ohio Florists' Assn.

Sullivan, G.H., J.L. Robertson and G.L. Staby. 1980. Care and handling of foliage plants. *Management for Retail Florists with Applications to Nursery and Garden Centers.* San Francisco: W.H. Freeman and Co.

A

Aucuba japonica 'Variegata'

aw-*kew*-buh
jap-*on*-ih-kuh
vare-ee-*gay*-tuh

Family Name: **Cornaceae**
Common Name: **Gold-Dust Plant**

Originated in temperate Asia from the Himalayas to Japan.

AUCUBA JAPONICA 'VARIEGATA'

Retail handling

Light. Provide plants with sufficient light to recuperate from the stresses of dark storage. Interior lighting of 400 fc (4.3 klx) or more maintains a quality appearance. Bright indirect or curtain-filtered sunlight produce adequate natural light.

Temperature. Provide cooler temperatures in winter, although this temperate climate shrub adapts well to interior conditions. Use night temperatures of 40° to 55°F (4° to 13°C) and day temperatures of 65°F (18°C). Plants prefer locations with at least 40% relative humidity.

Irrigation. Keep the potting medium barely moist.

Consumer care

Temperature. Provide cooler temperatures in winter, although this temperate climate shrub adapts well to interior conditions. Use night temperatures of 40° to 55°F (4° to 13°C) and day temperatures of 65°F (18°C). Plants prefer locations with at least 40% relative humidity.

Location. Gold-dust plant thrives when installed under bright indirect or curtain-filtered sunlight. Interior light levels of 400 fc (4.3 klx) or more preserve good quality.

Irrigation. Keep the potting medium barely moist.

Grooming. Spray foliage occasionally with clean water to keep down both dust and spider mites—this plant's most common indoor pest problem. Fertilize at 3 to 4 month intervals. If the plant becomes potbound, repot in early spring before new growth emerges. Large plants can be pruned to desired size at that time.

Aucuba japonica 'Variegata'

aw-*kew*-buh
jap-*on*-ih-kuh
vare-ee-*gay*-tuh

A

ADDITIONAL READING
Bailey, L.H. and E.Z. Bailey. 1976. *Hortus Third.*
    New York: Macmillan Publishing Co. Inc.
Crockett, J.U. 1977. *Foliage House Plants.* Revised.
    Alexandria, VA: Time-Life Books.
Everett, T.H. 1980. *The New York Botanical Garden
    Illustrated Encyclopedia of Horticulture.* New
    York: Garland Publishing Inc.
Orans, M. 1973. *Houseplants and indoor landscaping.*
    Barrington, IL: A.B. Morse Co.

Beaucarnea recurvata

boh-*kar*-nee-uh
ree-kur-*vay*-tuh

B

Family Name: **Agavaceae**
Common Name: **Ponytail, Elephant Foot Tree**

Originated in Mexico.

BEAUCARNEA RECURVATA

Production factors

Light. Use production light levels of 4,000 to 6,000 fc (43.2 to 64.8 klx).

Temperature. Maintain greenhouse temperatures above 55°F (13°C) for best plant growth.

Nutrition. At recommended production light levels, fertilize with 20.7 to 27.6 pounds per 1000 square feet per year (lb/1000 sq. ft/yr) or 100.9 to 134.8 kilograms per 1000 square meters per year (kg/1000 sq. m/yr) of N-P-K.

Irrigation. Plants should be watered moderately. Allow the potting medium to dry somewhat between irrigations.

Media. Use a potting medium with good drainage for this desert native.

Problems.

Diseases: Leaf spot—*Phyllosticta* sp.; root rot—*Fusarium, Pythium* spp.; soft rot—*Erwinia carotovora;* stem rot—*Fusarium* sp.

Pests: Mealybugs; mites; scale.

Disorders. The small root system suffers from rot when overwatered.

Postproduction factors

Light. Transport of plants under dark conditions is currently the most common method of shipment. If extended holding is necessary before sale or installation, maintain ponytail under at least 100 fc (1.1 klx) of light. Provide light levels above 200 fc (2.2 klx) for best quality retention.

Temperature. Acclimatized plants can be shipped without damage for extended periods when held at 55° to 60°F (13° to 16°C).

Gases. Injury due to ethylene is generally not a problem when plants are shipped within the recommended temperature range. Ethylene may reach damaging levels if plants are shipped with produce or held in prolonged storage above the maximum listed temperature.

Lasting qualities. Under appropriate storage conditions acclimatized plants retain good quality when shipped within 4 weeks. Maintain temperatures near the upper end of the recommended range when transport requires only 1 to 7 days.

Care and grooming. Good storage preparation improves quality retention during transit. Moisture content of the potting medium should approximate 50% of soil capacity when plants are packed. Maintain high humidity levels of 80% to 90% during storage to retard dessication, especially when shipping time exceeds 7 days.

Retail handling

Light. Provide plants with sufficient light upon delivery to recuperate from the stresses of dark storage. A specially designed holding greenhouse or room is ideal. When such a facility is unavailable, maintain ponytail under at least 100 fc (1.1 klx) of light. Use light levels above 200 fc (2.2 klx) for best quality retention.

Temperature. Keep moderate interior temperatures of 60° to 75°F (16° to 24°C) for best performance, although ponytail tolerates temperatures ranging from 40° to 90°F (4° to 32°C). When a greenhouse is used to hold plants before installation, maintain 40% to 60% relative humidity for acclimatization to lower interior humidity levels.

Irrigation. Allow the potting medium to dry somewhat between irrigations to prevent root rot.

Consumer care

Temperature. Keep moderate interior temperatures of 60° to 75°F (16° to 24°C) for best performance, although ponytail tolerates temperatures ranging from 40° to 90°F (4° to 32°C).

Location. Ponytail grows best in high-light areas (800 fc [8.6 klx] for 12 hours per day), but good quality retention is possible in locations that receive bright indirect light (500 fc; 5.4 klx). A minimum light level of 100 fc (1.1 klx) is required for survival.

Irrigation. Allow the potting medium to dry somewhat between irrigations to prevent root rot.

Grooming. This plant grows slowly and can thrive for years in containers barely larger than the bulbous trunk. Repot in early spring before new growth begins if overcrowding does occur. Fertilize every 3 to 4 months. Ponytail is a very durable interior plant and will retain a high quality appearance for many years with good care.

ADDITIONAL READING

Bailey, L.H. and E.Z. Bailey. 1976. *Hortus Third.* New York: Macmillan Publishing Co. Inc.

Conover, C.A. and R.T. Poole. 1983. Handling and overseas transportation of acclimatized foliage plants in reefers. *Foliage Digest* 6(5):3-4.

————. 1986. Factors influencing shipping of acclimatized foliage plants. *ARC-Apopka Research Rpt.* RH-86-11. Univ. of Florida.

————. 1987. Factors influencing shipping of acclimatized foliage plants. *Foliage Digest* 10(4):1-5.

Crockett, J.U. 1977. *Foliage House Plants.* Revised. Alexandria, VA: Time-Life Books.

Gaines, R.L. 1977. Interior Plantscaping: Building Design for Interior Foliage Plants. New York: Architectural Record Books.

Beaucarnea recurvata

boh-*kar*-nee-uh
ree-kur-*vay*-tuh

Florists' Transworld Delivery Association. 1985. *The Indoor Gardener*. Southfield, MI.

Manaker G.H. 1981. *Interior Plantscapes: Installation, Maintenance and Management*. Englewood Cliffs, NJ: Prentice-Hall Inc.

McConnell, D.B., R.W. Henley and R.L. Biamonte. 1981. Commercial foliage plants. J.N. Joiner, ed. *Foliage Plant Production*. Englewood Cliffs, NJ: Prentice-Hall Inc.

Orans, M. 1973. *Houseplants and Indoor Landscaping*. Barrington, IL: A.B. Morse Co.

B

Begonia X *rex-cultorum*

bi-*goh*-nyah
rehx-kul-*tor*-um

Family Name: **Begoniaceae**
Common Name: **Rex Begonia**

B

Of complex hybrid origin, *Begonia* X *rex-cultorum* was created by crosses of various rhizomatous begonia and begonia rex. The parent species are naturally distributed worldwide in tropical and subtropical regions.

BEGONIA X *REX-CULTORUM*

Production factors

Light. Use production light levels of 2,000 to 3,000 fc (21.6 to 32.4 klx).

Temperature. Maintain greenhouse temperatures above 60°F (16°C) for continuous growth.

Nutrition. At recommended production light levels, fertilize with 20.7 to 27.6 pounds per 1000 square feet per year (lb/1000 sq. ft/yr) or 100.9 to 134.8 kilograms per 1000 square meters per year (kg/1000 sq. m/yr) of N-P-K.

Irrigation. Keep the potting medium uniformly moist from spring through fall. All varieties require some reduction in water during the winter. Winter watering needs depend on the variety, however, because some become more dormant than others.

Media. Use an organic potting medium with good drainage characteristics.

Problems.

Diseases: Anthracnose—*Colletotrichum* sp., *Gloeosporium* sp., *Glomerella cingulata;* blight—*Botrytis cinerea;* crown gall—*Agrobacterium tumefaciens;* leaf spot—*Alternaria* sp., *Cercospora begoniae, Corynespora cassiicola, Myrothecium roridum, Macrophoma* sp., *Phyllosticta* sp., *Xanthomonas campestris;* powdery mildew—*Erysiphe cichoracearum, Oidium* sp.; leaf rot—*Rhizoctonia solani;* root rot—*Pythium splendens;* soft rot—*Erwinia carotovora;* stem rot—*Phytophthora* sp.

Pests: Mites; scale.

Disorders. Rex begonia is highly susceptible to injury by airborne fluoride. Watery leaf scorch develops, then turns light and transparent. The injured leaf tissue dries and rolls up. Necrosis may begin anywhere on

45

Foliage Plants *Begonia* X *rex-cultorum*

Begonia x rex-cultorum

bi-*goh*-nyah
rehx-kul-*tor*-um

the leaf and spread quickly. Blooms become watersoaked, desiccate and abscise.

Postproduction factors

Temperature. Avoid cold temperatures during storage. Rex begonia subjected to 35°F (2°C) for 24 hours displays severe chilling damage. Plants produced with high rates of fertilizer are more sensitive to chilling injury. Watch fertilization carefully if exposure to cool temperatures during shipping is a possibility.

Retail handling

Light. Provide plants with sufficient light upon delivery to recuperate from the stresses of dark storage. Bright indirect or curtain-filtered sunlight preserves good quality. Provide at least 400 fc (4.3 klx) of light.

Temperature. Plants require fairly warm temperatures of 60° to 65°F (16° to 18°C) at night and 70° to 75°F (21° to 24°C) during the day.

Irrigation. Keep the potting medium barely moist and avoid overwatering. A humid atmosphere, however, is beneficial even though wet roots are not.

Disorders. Rex begonia is highly susceptible to injury by airborne fluoride. Foliage and blooms are both affected. Exposure to low temperatures during transit can cause chilling injury, particularly in plants produced under a high fertility program.

Consumer care

Temperature. Plants require fairly warm temperatures of 60° to 65°F (16° to 18°C) at night and 70° to 75°F (21° to 24°C) during the day.

Location. Rex begonia thrives in areas with bright indirect or curtain-filtered sunlight. Provide at least 400 fc (4.3 klx) of light.

Irrigation. Keep the potting medium barely moist and avoid overwatering. A humid atmosphere, however, is beneficial even though wet roots are not.

Grooming. Fertilize from midwinter to fall at 2-month intervals with half-strength houseplant formula. Do not fertilize during periods of winter dormancy. Repot over-crowded plants in spring. Remove any dead foliage and divide if necessary. Wide, shallow azalea pots are recommended because of the spreading rhizomatous nature of the roots.

Disorders. Rex begonia is highly susceptible to injury by airborne fluoride. Foliage and blooms are both affected.

Cultivars. *Begonia* x *erythrophylla* (Beefsteak begonia) possesses thick, fleshy rhizomes from which large, kidney-shaped to nearly round leaves emerge on long, hairy petioles. The leaves are dark green on the top surface and maroon-red underneath. Light pink flowers are held in dainty sprays above the foliage in winter and spring. This begonia is more adaptable to dry interior atmospheres than Rex hybrids.

Begonia X *rex-cultorum*

bi-*goh*-nyah
rehx-kul-*tor*-um

B

Begonia masoniana —Iron-cross begonia is a rhizomatous begonia with obliquely broad-cordate leaves. Thick leaves are highly wrinkled and hairy on the upper surface. Leaf coloration consists of a dark chocolate brown cross- or star-shaped blotch with light green edges. This species prefers high humidity like *B.* X *rex-cultorum* hybrids.

ADDITIONAL READING

Bailey, L.H. and E.Z. Bailey. 1976. *Hortus Third*. New York: Macmillan Publishing Co. Inc.

Chase, A.R. 1985. Diseases of foliage plants—revised list for 1985. *Foliage Digest* 8(6):3-8.

Crockett, J.U. 1977. *Foliage house plants*. Revised. Alexandria, VA: Time-Life Books.

Everett, T.H. 1980. *The New York Botanical Garden Illustrated Encyclopedia of Horticulture*. New York: Garland Publishing Inc.

McConnell, D.B., R.W. Henley and R.L. Biamonte. 1981. Commercial foliage plants. J.N. Joiner, ed. *Foliage plant production*. Englewood Cliffs, NJ: Prentice-Hall Inc.

Poole, R.T. and C.A. Conover. 1983. Factors influencing chilling damage of foliage plants. *Foliage Digest* 6(8):3-4.

Woltz, S.S. and W.E. Waters. 1978. Airborne fluoride effects on some flowering and landscape plants. *HortScience* 13:430-432.

Brassaia actinophylla

brass-eye-uh
ak-tin-oh-*fil*-uh

Family Name: **Araliaceae**
Common Name: **Australian Umbrella Tree, Queensland Umbrella Tree**

Originated in Queensland. This plant was previously named *Schefflera actinophylla*.

BRASSAIA ACTINOPHYLLA

Production factors

Light. Use production light levels of 3,000 to 5,000 fc (32.4 to 54 klx) for acclimatized plants. Allow for a minimum of 5 weeks acclimatization of Australian umbrella tree produced under full sun conditions before installing in an interior environment.

Temperature. This species tolerates short exposures to temperatures below 40°F (4°C); however, avoid temperatures below 50°F (10°C) for best plant health. Provide greenhouse temperatures of at least 60°F (16°C) for continuous growth.

Nutrition. At recommended production light levels for acclimatized plants, fertilize with 48.3 pounds per 1000 square feet per year (lb/1000 sq. ft/yr) or 235.8 kilograms per 1000 square meters per year (kg/1000 sq. m/yr) of N-P-K. A N-P-K ratio of 3:1:2 is suggested for use with soilless media, while 1:1:1 is recommended for soil-based media. A ratio of 5:1:2 can also be used with production of Australian umbrella tree. The 3:1:2 and 5:1:2 fertilizer ratios decrease fertilizer costs and reduce soluble salts in soilless media. Both slow-release and liquid fertilizer sources produce quality plants when compared at equivalent ratios. Most media require the addition of micronutrients either by preplant incorporation of a granular source or as part of a liquid fertilization program.

Irrigation. Allow the potting medium to dry somewhat between waterings. Water thoroughly when irrigating but avoid a constantly wet condition.

Media. Provide a potting medium with good drainage characteristics to avoid root rot. Australian umbrella tree does not benefit from hydrophilic soil amendments that are used to reduce intervals between irrigations.

Problems.
Diseases: Anthracnose—*Colletotrichum*

Brassaia actinophylla

brass-eye-uh
ak-tin-oh-*fil*-uh

sp., *Gloeosporium* sp.; blight—*Sclerotium rolfsii;* leaf spot—*Alternaria* sp., *Cephaleuros virescens, Cercospora* sp., *Corynespora* sp., *Erwinia chrysanthemi, Phytophthora parasitica* var. *nicotianae, Pseudomonas cichorii; Xanthomonas campestris* pv. *hederae;* root rot—*Pythium* sp.; stem rot—*Rhizoctonia solani.*

Pests: Leaf miners; root rot nematode—*Meloidogyne;* scale; spider mites; thrips.

Disorders. Necrotic areas on mature foliage and death of tender new growth are symptoms of chilling injury. Adventitious roots form when the roots are poorly developed or destroyed due to disease, poor soil aeration or overwatering.

Postproduction factors

Light. Transport of plants under dark conditions is currently the most common method of shipment. If extended holding is necessary before sale or installation, Australian umbrella tree can be maintained indefinitely under interior lighting of 150 fc (1.6 klx) or more.

Temperature. Australian umbrella tree ships well at reduced temperatures of 50° to 55°F (10° to 13°C) for extended periods without loss of quality.

Gases. Injury due to ethylene is generally not a problem when plants are shipped within the recommended temperature range. Ethylene may reach damaging levels if plants are shipped with produce or held in prolonged storage above the maximum listed temperature.

Lasting qualities. Under appropriate storage conditions acclimatized plants retain good quality when shipped within 4 weeks. Maintain temperatures near the upper end of

the recommended range when transport requires only 1 to 7 days.

Care and grooming. Good storage preparation improves quality retention during transit. Moisture content of the potting medium should approximate 50% of soil capacity when plants are packed. Maintain high humidity levels of 80% to 90% during storage to retard dessication, especially when shipping time exceeds 7 days.

Retail handling

Light. Provide plants with sufficient light upon delivery to recuperate from the stresses of dark storage. A specially designed holding greenhouse or room is ideal. When such a facility is unavailable, maintain Australian umbrella tree under at least 75 to 100 fc (.8 to 1.1 klx) of light. Better growth and quality retention can be expected if lighting is increased to 200 fc (2.2 klx). Do not extend the lighting period beyond 16 hours a day. Plants prefer natural light locations with partial shade to bright indirect light.

Temperature. Provide interior temperatures of 65° to 80°F (18° to 27°C) for optimum growth and quality. Australian umbrella tree tolerates low interior temperatures for a short time, but avoid prolonged exposures below 50°F (10°C). When a greenhouse is used to hold plants before installation, maintain 40% to 60% relative humidity for acclimatization to lower interior humidity levels.

Irrigation. Water plants thoroughly at each irrigation but allow the potting medium to dry somewhat between waterings. Avoid very dry soil conditions.

Disorders. Cold-damaged plants display necrotic areas on older leaves and death of

Brassaia actinophylla

tender new growth. Plants perform poorly when given continuous light; therefore, do not extend lighting period beyond 16 hours/day. Australian umbrella tree responds to continuous light by losing its deep green leaf color. Leaves become light green or even completely yellow in extreme cases. Shade-produced foliage will sunburn if not protected from strong light during the shipping period or after delivery. Adventitious roots indicate destruction of the roots from disease, overwatering or poor media aeration. Australian umbrella tree under water stress is susceptible to attack by spider mites. Cultivars possessing thicker leaves are tolerant but not totally resistant to spider mites; therefore, proper watering procedures are very important.

Consumer care

Temperature. Provide interior temperatures of 65° to 80°F (18° to 27°C) for optimum growth and quality. Plants tolerate low interior temperatures for a short time, but avoid prolonged exposures below 50°F (10°C).

Location. Australian umbrella tree prefers natural light locations with partial shade to bright indirect light. Maintain plants under at least 75 to 100 fc (.8 to 1.1 klx) of light. Better growth and quality retention can be expected if lighting is increased to 200 fc (2.2 klx). Do not extend the lighting period beyond 16 hours a day.

Irrigation. Water plants thoroughly at each irrigation, but allow the potting medium to dry somewhat between waterings. Avoid very dry soil conditions.

Grooming. Remove dead or damaged growth when needed. Sponging or spraying with clean water removes dust and reduces any existing spider mite population. Prune as needed to control plant size in relation to its location. Fertilization every 3 months with a standard water soluble houseplant formula is generally sufficient. The need for fertilization, however, is dependent on the growing conditions of the plant. Australian umbrella tree responds less to fertilizer when maintained under low light conditions of 100 fc (1.1 klx) than when receiving 200 fc (2.2 klx) or more. This is a durable and long-lived interior plant that will retain excellent quality with good care.

Disorders. Cold-damaged plants display necrotic areas on older leaves and death of tender new growth. Continuous lighting causes leaves to become light green or even yellow. Development of adventitious roots are signs of root destruction from disease, overwatering or poor media aeration. Shade-produced foliage will sunburn if placed in a bright-to-sunny location. Australian umbrella tree under water stress is susceptible to attack by spider mites. Cultivars possessing thicker leaves are tolerant but not totally resistant to spider mites; therefore, proper watering procedures are very important.

Brassaia actinophylla

brass-eye-uh
ak-tin-oh-*fil*-uh

ADDITIONAL READING

Bailey, L.H. and E.Z. Bailey. 1976. *Hortus Third.* New York: Macmillan Publishing Co. Inc.

Ben-Jaacov, J., R.T. Poole and C.A. Conover. 1982. Effects of long-term dark storage on quality of Schefflera. *HortScience* 17:347-349.

Chase, A.R. 1985. Diseases of foliage plants— Revised list for 1985. *Foliage Digest* 8(6):3-8.

——— and R.T. Poole. 1986. Troubleshooting guide to foliage. *Greenhouse Grower* 4(10):68-69.

Colijn, A.C. and R.K. Lindquist. 1986. Effects of moisture stress on two spotted spider mite populations, *Tetranychus urticae* Koch (Acari: Tetranychidae) in Schefflera (*Brassaia actinophylla* Endl.). *J. Environ. Hort.* 4:130-133.

Conover, C.A. and R.T. Poole. 1975. Acclimatization of tropical trees for interior use. *HortScience* 10:600-601.

———. 1981. Guide for fertilizing foliage plant crops. *ARC-Apopka Research Rpt.* RH-81-1. Univ. of Florida.

———. 1981. Influence of light and fertilizer levels and fertilizer sources on foliage plants maintained under interior environments for one year. *J. Amer. Soc. Hort. Sci.* 106:571-574.

———. 1983. Handling and overseas transportation of acclimatized foliage plants in reefers. *Foliage Digest* 6(5):3-4.

———. 1984. Light and fertilizer recommendations for production of acclimatized potted foliage plants. *Foliage Digest* 7(8):1-6.

———. 1985. Comparison of a liquid fertilizer source with several slow-release fertilizers on *Brassaia actinophylla* and *Ficus benjamina*. *Foliage Digest* 8(6):1-3.

———. 1986. Factors influencing shipping of acclimatized foliage plants. *ARC-Apopka Research Rpt.* H-86-11. Univ. of Florida.

———. 1987. Factors influencing shipping of acclimatized foliage plants. *Foliage Digest* 10(4):1-5.

Conover, C.A., R.T. Poole and T.A. Nell. 1982. Influence of intensity and duration of cool white fluorescent lighting and fertilizer on growth and quality of foliage plants. *J. Amer. Soc. Hort. Sci.* 107:817-822.

Crockett, J.U. 1977. *Foliage house plants.* Revised. Alexandria, VA: Time-Life Books.

Everett, T.H. 1980. *The New York Botanical Garden Illustrated Encyclopedia of Horticulture.* New York: Garland Publishing Inc.

Florists' Transworld Delivery Association. 1985. *The Indoor Gardener.* Southfield, MI.

Gaines, R.L. 1977. *Interior Plantscaping: building design for interior foliage plants.* New York: Architectural Record Books.

Holstead, C.L. 1985. *Care and handling of flowers and plants.* Floralife Inc. Society of American Florists. Alexandria, VA.

McConnell, D.B., R.W Henley and R.L. Biamonte. 1981. Commercial foliage plants. J.N. Joiner, ed. *Foliage Plant Production.* Englewood Cliffs, NJ: Prentice-Hall Inc.

Poole, R.T. and C.A. Conover. 1985. Nitrogen, phosphorus and potassium fertilization of *Brassaia actinophylla, Calathea mahoyana* and *Chrysalidocarpus lutescens. J. Environ. Hort.* 3(1):1-3.

———. 1986. Response of Schefflera to variations in irrigation procedure. *Foliage Digest* 9(7):7-8.

———. 1987. Foliage variety determines heat. *Greenhouse Grower* 5(1):21-22.

Staby, G.L., J.L. Robertson and D.C. Kiplinger. 1978. *Chain of Life.* Columbus, OH: Ohio Florists' Assn.

Sullivan, G.H., J.L. Robertson and G.L. Staby. 1980. Care and handling of foliage plants. *Management for Retail Florists with Applications to Nursery and Garden Centers.* San Francisco: W.H. Freeman and Co.

B

Calathea makoyana

kal-uh-*thee*-uh mak-oy-*an*-uh

Family Name: **Marantaceae**
Common Name: **Peacock Plant**

Originated in Brazil.

CALATHEA MAKOYANA

Production factors

Light. Use production light levels of 1,000 to 2,000 fc (10.8 to 21.6 klx) for good foliage variegation.

Temperature. Provide greenhouse temperatures above 55°F (13°C) to assure continuous growth. Control of maximum greenhouse temperatures is also important. Small plants tolerate high temperatures (100°F/38°C maximum) better than large plants. Keep greenhouse temperatures below 90°F (32°C) to avoid damage to large specimens.

Nutrition. At recommended production light levels for acclimatized plants, fertilize with 34.5 pounds per 1000 square feet per year (lb/1000 sq. ft/yr) or 168.4 kilograms per 1000 square meters per year (kg/1000 sq. m/yr) of N-P-K. A N-P-K ratio of 3:1:2 is suggested for use with soilless media, while 1:1:1 is recommended for soil-based media. Peacock plant prefers a nitrogen source containing at least 50% urea or ammonia. Use fertilizers with low potassium and fluoride content. Most media require the addition of micronutrients either by preplant incorporation of a granular source or as part of a liquid fertilization program.

Irrigation. Keep the potting medium uniformly moist but not wet. Use a water source that is low in fluoride.

Media. Choose a well-aerated, organic potting medium such as 3 peat:1 sand (by volume). Maintain pH near 6.5. Amendments should be screened for fluoride contamination before use in the medium.

Problems.

Diseases: Leaf spot—*Alternaria alternata, Bipolaris setariae, Drechslera setariae, Phyllosticta* sp.; root rot—*Fusarium oxysporum;* virus—cucumber mosaic virus.

Pests: Caterpillars; mealybugs; nematodes; scale; slugs; snails; spider mites.

Disorders. Pale leaves with reduced

C

variegation develop when plants are produced under light levels below 1000 fc (10.8 klx). Conversely, high light levels above 2,000 fc (21.6 klx) bleach leaves and cause tip necrosis. Large specimens can be damaged by temperatures above 90°F (32°C). Peacock plant is sensitive to fluoride. Chlorosis appears when either nitrogen or iron is deficient. Leaf spotting and reduced foliage color are symptoms of potassium toxicity.

Postproduction factors

Light. Transport of plants under dark conditions is currently the most common method of shipment. If extended holding is necessary before sale or installation, peacock plant can be sustained under 75 to 100 fc (.8 to 1.1 klx) of light for some time. Increase light levels to at least 150 to 250 fc (1.6 to 2.7 klx) for long-term holding.

Retail handling

Light. Provide plants with sufficient light upon delivery to recuperate from the stresses of dark storage. Maintain under at least 150 to 250 fc (1.6 to 2.7 klx) of light. Light levels of 400 fc (4.3 klx) or more improve retention of the striking foliage color. Areas with bright indirect or curtain filtered sunlight provide appropriate natural illumination.

Temperature. Use temperatures of 65° to 85°F (18° to 29°C). Avoid drafty locations.

Irrigation. Keep the potting medium evenly moist but not wet. Plants prefer high humidity that can be provided by misting or placing the pot on a moist gravel bed or in a terrarium.

Disorders. Water stress from poor watering practices or low humidity causes browning of leaf margins, tipburn, loss of leaf color and drooping of foliage.

Consumer care

Temperature. Keep temperatures between 65° and 85°F (18° and 29°C). Avoid drafty locations.

Location. Provide at least 150 to 250 fc (1.6 to 2.7 klx) of light. Light levels of 400 fc (4.3 klx) or more improve retention of the striking foliage color. Areas with bright indirect or curtain-filtered sunlight maintain good plant quality.

Irrigation. Keep the potting medium evenly moist but not wet. Plants prefer high humidity that can be provided by misting or placing the pot on a moist gravel bed or in a terrarium.

Grooming. Fertilize every 2 months with a standard houseplant formula. Repot plants as needed to prevent crowding of roots. Division and repotting is recommended in early spring before new growth begins. Peacock plant requires regular attention and special environmental conditions; however, with good care this plant can be a spectacular accent.

Disorders. Poor watering practices and low humidity reduce foliage quality.

Calathea makoyana

C

ADDITIONAL READING

Arthurs, Kathryn, ed. 1974. *How to Grow House Plants.* Menlo Park, CA: Lane Publishing Co.

Bailey, L.H. and E.Z. Bailey. 1976. *Hortus Third.* New York: Macmillan Publishing Co. Inc.

Chase, A.R., L.S. Osborne and R.T. Poole. 1986. Calathea. *Foliage Digest* 9(12):1-4

Conover, C.A. and R.T. Poole. 1981. Guide for fertilizing foliage plant crops. *ARC-Apopka Research Rpt.* RH-51-1. Univ. of Florida.

———. 1984. Light and fertilizer recommendations for production of acclimatized potted foliage plants. *Foliage Digest* 7(8):1-6.

Crockett, J.U. 1977. *Foliage House Plants.* Revised. Alexandria, VA: Time-Life Books.

Everett, T.H. 1980. *The New York Botanical Garden Illustrated Encyclopedia of Horticulture.* New York: Garland Publishing Inc.

Florists' Transworld Delivery Association. 1985. *The Indoor Gardener.* Southfield, MI.

McConnell, D.B., R.W. Henley and R.L. Biamonte. 1981. Commercial foliage plants. J.N. Joiner, ed. *Foliage Plant Production.* Englewood Cliffs, NJ: Prentice-Hall Inc.

Wright, M., ed. 1979. *The Complete Indoor Gardener.* Rev. ed. New York: Random House.

Chamaedorea elegans

ka-mee-*dor*-ee-uh
ay-le-gahnz

Family Name: **Palmae**
Common Name: **Parlor Palm**

Originated in Mexico and Guatemala.

CHAMAEDOREA ELEGANS

Production factors

Light. Use production light levels of 1,500 to 3,000 fc (16.2 to 32.4 klx) for acclimatized plants.

Temperature. Keep greenhouse temperatures above 60°F (16°C) to promote continu-ous growth. Maintain minimum temperatures above 45°F (7°C).

Nutrition. At recommended production light levels for acclimatized plants, fertilize with 34.5 pounds per 1000 square feet per year (lb/1000 sq. ft/yr) or 168.4 kilograms per 1000 square meters per year (kg/1000 sq. m/yr) of N-P-K. A N-P-K ratio of 3:1:2 is suggested for use with soilless media, while 1:1:1 is recommended for soil-based media. Do not exceed recommended fertilizer rates. Incorporate 1.5 pounds per cubic yard (.9 kg per cubic m) Micromax or another equivalent source into the potting medium prior to planting. Avoid fertilizers containing fluoride or boron. Also, micronutrient sources containing copper or iron should not be applied to foliage.

Irrigation. Keep the potting medium uniformly moist but not wet. Use a water source that is low in fluoride and boron.

Media. Choose a potting medium with good drainage characteristics, and maintain pH values within 6.0 to 6.5. Amendments should be screened for toxic levels of fluoride or boron before use in the medium.

Problems.

Diseases: Blight—*Gliocladium vermosceni, Phytophthora* sp.; leaf spot—*Bipolaris setariae, Drechslera setariae, Exserohilum rostratum, Phaeotrichoconis crotalariae;* seedling root rot—*Fusarium, Pythium* spp.

Pests: Burrowing nematodes—*Radopholus similis;* lesion nematodes—*Paratylen-*

Chamaedorea elegans

ka-mee-*dor*-ee-uh
ay-le-gahnz

chus spp.; spider mites; thrips.

Disorders. Parlor palm is sensitive to high levels of soluble salts. Symptoms of salt damage include tip and marginal necrosis and destruction of root hairs. Plants may exhibit manganese deficiency symptoms of chlorosis and stunted growth without incorporation of a micronutrient fertilizer. Foliar-applied micronutrients and other chemicals containing copper or iron produce necrotic spots on foliage. Fluoride and boron reduce plant quality. Symptoms of fluoride toxicity include tip necrosis and necrotic interveinal spotting of foliage. Boron toxicity also causes tip necrosis and spotting, but necrotic areas are lighter brown with a yellow band between necrotic and healthy tissues.

Postproduction factors

Light. Transport of plants under dark conditions is currently the most common shipping method. If extended holding is necessary before sale or installation, maintain parlor palm under 150 fc (1.6 klx) of light.

Temperature. Acclimatized plants can be shipped without damage for extended periods when held at 50° to 60°F (10° to 16°C).

Gases. Injury due to ethylene is generally not a problem when plants are shipped within the recommended temperature range. Ethylene may reach damaging levels if plants are shipped with produce or held in prolonged storage above the maximum listed temperature.

Lasting qualities. Under appropriate storage conditions acclimatized plants retain good quality when shipped within 4 weeks. Maintain temperatures near the upper end of the recommended range when transport

requires only 1 to 7 days.

Care and grooming. Good storage preparation improves quality retention during transit. Moisture content of the potting medium should approximate 50% of soil capacity when plants are packed. Maintain high humidity levels of 80% to 90% during storage to retard desiccation, especially when shipping time exceeds 7 days.

Retail handling

Light. Provide plants with sufficient light upon delivery to recuperate from the stresses of dark storage. A specially designed holding greenhouse or room is ideal. When such a facility is unavailable, maintain light levels at 75 to 150 fc (.8 to 1.6 klx) for quality retention. Parlor palm performs well in locations with low light. Direct sunlight actually fades leaf color; therefore, use filtered light or light from a north window if natural light is available.

Temperature. Keep temperatures of 60° to 85°F (16° to 29°C) for optimum growth and quality. Parlor palm tolerates low interior temperatures for a short time but avoid drafty locations and prolonged exposure below 50°F (10°C). When a greenhouse is used to hold plants before installation, maintain 40% to 60% relative humidity for acclimatization to lower interior humidity levels.

Irrigation. Keep the potting medium evenly moist but not wet to avoid root rot.

Disorders. Symptoms of salt damage include tip and marginal necrosis and destruction of root hairs. Foliage develops necrotic lesions in response to fluoride or boron toxicity and to foliar application of chemicals containing copper or iron.

Chamaedorea elegans

ka-mee-*dor*-ee-uh
ay-le-gahnz

Consumer care

Temperature. Keep temperatures of 60° to 85°F (16° to 29°C) for optimum growth and quality. Parlor palm tolerates low interior temperatures for a short time, but avoid drafty locations and prolonged exposure below 50°F (10°C).

Location. Plants perform well in locations with low light. Direct sunlight actually fades leaf color; therefore, filtered light or light from a north window is preferred. Light levels near 50 fc (.5 klx) are tolerated, but 75 to 150 fc (.8 to 1.6 klx) are recommended for quality retention.

Irrigation. Keep the potting medium evenly moist but not wet to avoid root rot.

Grooming. Fertilize every 4 to 5 months. Do not overfertilize. Periodically wash foliage with a tepid water shower or damp sponge to remove dust and dirt. Regular cleaning of foliage also aids in the control of spider mite populations. Repot in early spring only when plant becomes quite rootbound. Parlor palm is a durable and versatile plant material for interiors. This tough plant tolerates low interior humidity and light and will maintain good quality indefinitely with reasonable care.

Disorders. Root loss occurs when plants are overfertilized and overwatered. Foliage develops necrotic lesions in response to fluoride or boron toxicity and to foliar application of chemicals containing copper or iron.

Cultivars. *Chamaedorea erumpens* (bamboo palm) forms clumps of shoots that can grow to 10 feet (3 m) under ideal conditions. Leaves are shorter than those of parlor palm, and the general growth habit is more upright and columnar. This plant is suitable for vertical definition and screening needs.

C

ADDITIONAL READING

Arthurs, Kathryn (ed.). 1974. *How to Grow House Plants.* Menlo Park, CA: Lane Publishing Co.

Bailey, L.H. and E.Z. Bailey. 1976. *Hortus Third.* New York: Macmillan Publishing Co. Inc.

Chase, A.R. 1985. Diseases of foliage plants—Revised list for 1985. *Foliage Digest* 8(6):3-8.

Chase, A.R. and R.T. Poole. 1986. Troubleshooting guide to foliage. *Greenhouse Grower* 4(11):24-27.

Conover, C.A. and R.T. Poole. 1981. Guide for fertilizing foliage plant crops. *ARC-Apopka Research Rpt.* RH-81-1. University of Florida.

———. 1983. Handling and overseas transportation of acclimatized foliage plants in reefers. *Foliage Digest* 6(5):3-4.

———. 1984. Light and fertilizer recommendations for production of acclimatized potted foliage plants. *Foliage Digest* 7(8):1-6.

———. 1986. Factors influencing shipping of acclimatized foliage plants. *ARC-Apopka Research Rpt.* RH-86-11. University of Florida.

———. 1987. Factors influencing shipping of acclimatized foliage plants. *Foliage Digest* 10(4):1-5.

Crockett, J.U. 1977. *Foliage House Plants.* Revised. Alexandria, VA: Time-Life Books.

Everett, T.H. 1980. *The New York Botanical Garden Illustrated Encyclopedia of Horticulture.* New York: Garland Publishing Inc.

Florists' Transworld Delivery Association. 1985. *The Indoor Gardener.* Southfield, MI.

Gaines, R.L. 1977. *Interior Plantscaping: building design for interior foliage plants.* New York: Architectural Record Books.

Holstead, C.L. 1985. *Care and Handling of Flowers and Plants.* Floralife Inc. Society of American Florists. Alexandria, VA.

McConnell, D.B., R.W. Henley and R.L. Biamonte. 1981. Commercial foliage plants. J.N. Joiner (ed.). *Foliage Plant Production.* Englewood Cliffs, NJ: Prentice-Hall Inc.

Orans, M. 1973. *Houseplants and Indoor Landscaping.* Barrington, IL: A.B. Morse Co.

Poole, R.T. and C.A. Conover. 1986. Boron and fluoride toxicity of foliage plants. *Foliage Digest* 9(3):3-6.

Staby, G.L., J.L. Robertson and D.C. Kiplinger. 1978. *Chain of Life.* Columbus, OH: Ohio Florists' Association.

Chamaedorea elegans

ka-mee-*dor*-ee-uh
ay-le-gahnz

Sullivan, G.H., J.L. Robertson and G.L. Staby. 1980. Care and handling of foliage plants. *Management for Retail Florists with Applications to Nursery and Garden Centers.* San Francisco: W.H. Freeman and Co.

Woltz, S.S. and W.E. Waters. 1978. Airborne fluoride effects on some flowering and landscape plants. *HortScience* 13:430-432.

Wright, M. (ed.). 1979. *The Complete Indoor Gardener.* Rev. ed. New York: Random House.

C

Chlorophytum comosum 'Variegatum'

klo-ro-*fi*-tum
ko-*mo*-sum
vare-ee-*gay*-tum

Family Name: **Liliaceae**
Common Name: **Spider Plant**

Originated in South Africa.

C

CHLOROPHYTUM COMOSUM 'VITTATUM'

Production factors

Light. Production light levels of 1,000 to 2,500 fc (10.8 to 27 klx) are recommended for acclimatized plants.

Temperature. Spider plant tolerates cool temperatures down to 45°F (7°C), but greenhouse temperatures of at least 55°F (13°C) assure good growth.

Nutrition. At recommended production light levels for acclimatized plants, fertilize with 34.5 pounds per 1000 square feet per year (lb/1000 sq. ft/yr) or 168.4 kilograms per 1000 square meters per year (kg/1000 sq m/yr) of N-P-K. A N-P-K ratio of 3:1:2 is suggested for use with soilless media, while 1:1:1 is recommended for soil-based media. Avoid use of super or treble phosphate or of any fertilizer containing fluoride or boron. Most media require the addition of micronutrients either by preplant incorporation of a granular source or as part of a liquid fertilization program.

Irrigation. Keep the potting medium uniformly moist but not wet. Use a water source that is low in fluoride and boron.

Media. Choose a potting medium with good drainage characteristics and maintain pH values within 6.0 to 6.5. Amendments should be screened for toxic levels of fluoride or boron before addition to the medium.

Problems.

Diseases: Blight—*Sclerotium rolfsii;* root rot—*Pythium* sp.; soft rot—*Erwinia carotovora.*

Pests: Aphids; mealybugs; scale; spider mites; whitefly.

Disorders. Tipburn and marginal browning develop if the medium dries out between waterings. Spider plant is very sensitive to fluoride and boron in water, media or fertilizer. This species also reacts strongly to atmospheric fluoride. Symptoms of fluoride toxicity include tip and marginal necrosis of

Chlorophytum comosum 'Variegatum'

klo-ro-*fi*-tum
ko-*mo*-sum
vare-ee-*gay*-tum

older and mid-aged leaves. With continued exposure, damage progresses from inter-veinal spotting and streaking to necrosis that spreads down the leaf. A thin, light red-brown area separates the shriveling leaf tip from live tissue. Symptoms of boron toxicity are similar, but necrotic tissue is a uniform brown with distinct parallel veins.

Postproduction factors

Light. Transport under dark conditions is currently the most common shipping method. If extended holding is necessary before sale or installation, provide at least 75 to 100 fc (.8 to 1.1 klx) of light.

Gases. Spider plant develops epinasty when exposed to 5 ppm ethylene for a prolonged time. Symptoms disappear after removal from gas source.

Retail handling

Light. Provide plants with sufficient light upon delivery to recuperate from stresses of dark storage. Spider plant survives under 75 to 100 fc (.8 to 1.1 klx) of light, but 150 to 250 fc (1.6 to 2.7 klx) are recommended to preserve expected appearance. Bright indirect or curtain-filtered sunlight provides the best natural lighting for growth and quality maintenance.

Temperature. Plants tolerate periods of cool temperatures to 45°F (7°C), but average interior temperatures of 60° to 80°F (16° to 27°C) maintain growth and quality.

Irrigation. Keep the potting medium evenly moist but not wet. Do not allow the medium to dry completely.

Disorders. Spider plant develops foliage necrosis upon exposure to atmospheric fluoride. Damage also occurs when toxic levels of fluoride or boron are present in the medium, fertilizer or water source. Epinasty develops when plants are exposed to 5 ppm ethylene for an extended time. Symptoms disappear after removal from gas source. Water stress causes foliage tipburn and marginal browning.

Consumer care

Temperature. Plants tolerate periods of cool temperatures to 45°F (7°C), but average interior temperatures of 60° to 80°F (16° to 27°C) maintain growth and quality.

Location. Spider plant thrives when installed under bright indirect or curtain-filtered sunlight. Plants survive under 75 to 100 fc (.8 to 1.1 klx) of light, but 150 to 250 fc (1.6 to 2.7 klx) are recommended for best results.

Irrigation. Keep the potting medium evenly moist but not wet. Do not allow the medium to dry completely.

Grooming. Wash foliage periodically with a tepid water shower or damp sponge to remove dust and dirt. Divide and repot at any season when root mass compacts the potting medium and moisture maintenance becomes difficult. Fertilize every 2 months. Spider plant is a sturdy plant that tolerates occasional abuse and neglect. Specimens will maintain excellent quality with good care.

Disorders. Foliage necrosis characterizes fluoride or boron toxicity. Water stress causes foliage tipburn and marginal browning.

Cultivars. *Chlorophytum comosum* (spider plant) is the species type with solid green leaves instead of the white-margined

C

Chlorophytum comosum 'Variegatum'

klo-ro-*fi*-tum
ko-*mo*-sum
vare-ee-*gay*-tum

foliage of 'Variegatum.' All other characteristics are similar to 'Variegatum.'

Chlorophytum comosum 'Mandaianum' is smaller in growth habit. Variegated foliage is green on the margins with a bright yellow stripe in the leaf center.

Chlorophytum comosum 'Vittatum' is similar in size to the species type, but foliage is recurved with a central white stripe and green margins.

C

ADDITIONAL READING
Bailey, L.H. and E.Z. Bailey. 1976. Hortus Third. New York: Macmillan Publishing Co. Inc.

Conover, C.A. and R.T. Poole. 1981. Guide for fertilizing foliage plant crops. *ARC-Apopka Research Rpt.* RH-81-1. University of Florida.

————. 1984. Light and fertilizer recommendations for production of acclimatized potted foliage plants. *Foliage Digest* 7(8):1-6.

Crockett, J.U. 1977. *Foliage House Plants.* Revised. Alexandria, VA: Time-Life Books.

Everett, T.H. 1980. *The New York Botanical Garden Illustrated Encyclopedia of Horticulture.* New York: Garland Publishing Inc.

Florists' Transworld Delivery Association. 1985.*The Indoor Gardener.* Southfield, MI.

Gaines, R.L. 1977. *Interior Plantscaping: building design for interior foliage plants.* New York: Architectural Record Books.

Marousky, F.J. and B.K. Harbaugh. 1978. Deterioration of foliage plants during transit. *Proc. 1978 Natl. Tropical Foliage Short Course.* University of Florida, IFAS Coop. Ext. Serv., Orlando, FL.

McConnell, D.B., R.W. Henley and R.L. Biamonte. 1981. Commercial foliage plants. J.N. Joiner (ed.). *Foliage Plant Production.* Englewood Cliffs, NJ: Prentice-Hall Inc.

Orans, M. 1973. *Houseplants and Indoor Landscaping.* Barrington, IL: A.B. Morse Co.

Poole, R.T. and C.A. Conover. 1986. Boron and fluoride toxicity of foliage plants. *Foliage Digest* 9(3):3-6.

Woltz, S.S. and W.E. Waters. 1978. Airborne fluoride effects on some foliage plants. *HortScience* 13:585-586.

Chrysalidocarpus lutescens

kri-sah-li-do-*kar*-pus
loo-*tes*-enz

Family Name: **Palmae**
Common Name: **Areca Palm**

Originated in Madagascar.

CHRYSALIDOCARPUS LUTESCENS

Production factors

Light. Production light levels of 5,000 to 6,000 fc (54 to 64.8 klx) are recommended for acclimatized plants.

Temperature. Areca palm tolerates brief exposure to 32°F (0°C); however best growth is obtained when root zones are maintained at 70° to 80°F (21° to 27°C) and air temperatures do not exceed 95°F (35°C).

Nutrition. At recommended production light levels for acclimatized plants, fertilize with 41.4 pounds per 1000 square feet per year (lb/1000 sq. ft/yr) or 202.1 kilograms per 1000 square meters per year (kg/1000 sq. m/yr) of N-P-K. A N-P-K ratio of 3:1:2 is suggested for use with soilless media, while 1:1:1 is recommended for soil-based media. Do not exceed the recommended fertilizer rate. Incorporate 1.5 pound per cubic yard (.9 kg per cubic m) Micromax or another equivalent source into the potting medium prior to planting. Avoid phosphate amendments, fertilizers containing fluoride and foliar-applied micronutrient sources containing copper or iron.

Irrigation. Keep the potting medium uniformly moist but not wet. Use a water source that is low in fluoride.

Media. Choose a potting medium with good drainage characteristics, and maintain pH values within 6.0 to 6.5. Amendments should be screened for toxic levels of fluoride before adding to the medium.

Problems.

Diseases that commonly attack areca palm: Blight—*Sclerotinia homeocarpa;* leaf spot—*Drechslera setariae, Exserohilum rostratum, Phaeotrichoconis crotalariae;* root rot and damping off—*Fusarium, Phytophthora, Pythium, Rhizoctonia* spp.;

stem rot—*Gliocladium vermosceni.*

Other diseases that attack palms, including areca palm: Anthracnose—*Gloeosporium* sp., *Glomerella cingulata (Colletotrichum gloeosporioides);* black spot—*Catacauma palmicola*; leaf spot—*Alternaria* sp., *Cercospora* sp., *Curvularia lunata, Cylindrocladium scoparium, Cytospora* sp., *Didymella phacidiomorpha, Didymopleella* sp., *Diplodia* sp., *Exosporium palmivorum, Gloeosporium* sp., *Helminthosporium* sp., *Leptothyrium* sp., *Monilochaetes* sp., *Pestalotia palmarum; Phomopsis* sp., *Phyllachora* sp., *Phyllosticta* sp., *Physalospora rhodina, Stigmina palmivora;* microplasma—lethal yellowing; bud rot—*Cytospora palmarum;* root rot—*Ceratocystis paradoxa, Clitocybe tabescens, Endoconidiophora paradoxa, Ganoderma sulcatum;* wood rot—*Ganoderma* spp.; false smut—*Graphiola phoenicis.*

Pests that commonly attack areca palm: Caterpillars; mealybugs; scales; spider mites; thrips.

Other pests that attack palms, including areca palm: Chewing beetles; leaf skeletonizer; nematodes; seed weevils.

Disorders. Areca palm is sensitive to high levels of soluble salts. Salt damage symptoms include tip and marginal necrosis and destruction of root hairs. Plants may exhibit iron, manganese or zinc deficiency symptoms of chlorosis and stunted growth when a micronutrient fertilizer is not used. Foliar-applied micronutrient fertilizers and other chemicals containing copper or iron produce necrotic spots on foliage. Fluoride in the air, water, media or fertilizers reduces plant quality. Foliage initially develops necrotic spots that progress to streaked interveinal chlorosis, and total necrosis follows.

Postproduction factors

Light. Transport under dark conditions is currently the most common shipping method. If extended holding is necessary before sale or installation, provide at least 100 fc (1.1 klx) of light.

Temperature. Acclimatized plants can be shipped without damage for 1 to 14 days when held at 55° to 65°F (13°C to 18°C). Provide temperatures of 60° to 65°F (16° to 18°C) for longer shipping durations of 15 to 28 days.

Gases. Injury due to ethylene is generally not a problem when plants are shipped within the recommended temperature range. Ethylene may reach damaging levels if plants are shipped with produce or held in prolonged storage above the maximum listed temperature.

Lasting qualities. Under appropriate storage conditions acclimatized plants retain good quality when shipped within 2 weeks. Maintain temperatures near the upper end of the recommended range when transport requires only 1 to 7 days. Quality loss of 25% per week is expected when areca palm is stored for more than 2 weeks.

Care and grooming. Good storage preparation improves quality retention during transit. Moisture content of the potting medium should approximate 50% of soil capacity when plants are packed. Maintain high humidity levels of 80% to 90% during storage to retard desiccation, especially when shipping time exceeds 7 days.

Retail handling

Light. Provide plants with sufficient light upon delivery to recuperate from stresses of

Chrysalidocarpus lutescens

kri-sah-li-do-*kar*-pus
loo-*tes*-enz

C

dark storage. A specially designed holding greenhouse or room is ideal. When such a facility is unavailable, place areca palm under at least 100 fc (1.1 klx) of light. Higher light levels of 150 to 400 fc (1.6 to 4.3 klx) improve quality retention. Bright indirect or curtain-filtered sunlight renders the best natural lighting to preserve plant appearance.

Temperature. Keep average interior temperatures of 60° to 80°F (16° to 27°C). When a greenhouse is used to hold plants before installation, maintain 40% to 60% relative humidity for acclimatization to lower interior humidity levels.

Irrigation. Keep the potting medium evenly moist but not wet to avoid root rot.

Disorders. Progressive foliage necrosis is a symptom of fluoride toxicity. High soluble salts from overfertilization cause both foliage and root damage. Soluble salt levels below 1,000 ppm are important for interior quality retention. Necrotic spotting of foliage develops in response to toxic levels of copper or iron. Avoid spray compounds containing these elements.

Consumer care

Temperature. Maintain average interior temperatures of 60° to 80°F (16° to 27°C).

Location. Areca palm thrives in areas with bright indirect or curtain-filtered sunlight. Plants survive under light levels of 100 fc (1.1 klx) but 150 to 400 fc (1.6 to 4.3 klx) improve quality retention.

Irrigation. Keep the potting medium evenly moist but not wet to avoid root rot.

Grooming. Fertilize every 4 months. Do not overfertilize since soluble salt levels

below 1,000 ppm are important for interior quality retention. Periodically wash foliage with a tepid water shower or damp sponge to remove dust and dirt. Regular cleaning of foliage improves control of spider mite populations. Avoid spray compounds containing copper or iron. Repotting should be scheduled for early spring only when the plant becomes quite rootbound. Areca palm is a durable plant that retains quality well with reasonable care. Under good growth conditions this plant may eventually exceed its space and require replacement with a smaller specimen.

Disorders. Progressive foliage necrosis is a symptom of fluoride toxicity. High soluble salts from overfertilization cause both foliage and root damage. Necrotic spotting of foliage develops in response to toxic levels of foliar-applied copper or iron.

ADDITIONAL READING

Bailey, L.H. and E.Z. Bailey. 1976. *Hortus Third.* New York: Macmillan Publishing Co. Inc.

Chase, A.R. 1985. Diseases of foliage plants—Revised list for 1985. *Foliage Digest* 8(6):3-8.

Chase, A.R. 1988. Diseases of foliage plants—1988 updated listing. *Foliage Digest* 11(6):5-8.

Chase, A.R. and R.T. Poole. 1986. Troubleshooting guide to foliage. *Greenhouse Grower* 4(11):24-27.

Chase, A.R., R.T. Poole and L.S. Osborne. 1985. Areca palm. *Foliage Digest* 8(10):6-8.

Conover C.A. and R.T. Poole. 1981. Guide for fertilizing foliage plant crops. *ARC-Apopka Research Rpt.* RH-81-1. University of Florida.

———. 1983. Handling and overseas transportation of acclimatized foliage plants in reefers. *Foliage Digest* 6(5):3-4.

———. 1984. Light and fertilizer recommendations for production of acclimatized potted foliage plants. *Foliage Digest* 7(8):1-6.

———. 1986. Factors influencing shipping of acclimatized foliage plants. *ARC-Apopka Research Rpt.* RH-86-11. University of Florida.

Chrysalidocarpus lutescens

kri-sah-li-do-*kar*-pus
loo-*tes*-enz

C

———. 1987. Factors influencing shipping of acclimatized foliage plants. *Foliage Digest* 10(4):1-5

Crockett, J.U. 1977. *Foliage House Plants.* Revised. Alexandria, VA: Time-Life Books.

Florists' Transworld Delivery Association. 1985. *The Indoor Gardener.* Southfield, MI.

Gaines, R.L. 1977. *Interior Plantscaping: building design for interior foliage plants.* New York: Architectural Record Books.

Holstead, C.L. 1985. Care and Handling of Flowers and Plants. Floralife Inc. Society of American Florists. Alexandria, VA.

Manaker G.H. 1981. *Interior Plantscapes: Installation, Maintenance and Management.* Englewood Cliffs, NJ: Prentice-Hall Inc.

McConnell, D.B., R.W. Henley and R.L. Biamonte. 1981. Commercial foliage plants. J.N. Joiner (ed.). *Foliage Plant Production.* Englewood Cliffs, NJ: Prentice-Hall Inc.

Poole, R.T. and C.A. Conover. 1986. Boron and fluoride toxicity of foliage plants. *Foliage Digest* 9(3):3-6.

Staby, G.L., J.L. Robertson and D.C. Kiplinger. 1978. *Chain of Life.* Columbus, OH: Ohio Florists' Association.

Sullivan, G.H., J.L. Robertson and G.L. Staby. 1980. Care and handling of foliage plants. *Management for Retail Florists with Applications to Nursery and Garden Centers.* San Francisco: W.H. Freeman and Co.

Woltz, S.S. and W.E. Waters. 1978. Airborne fluoride effects on some flowering and landscape plants. *HortScience* 13:430-432.

Cissus rhombifolia

siss-us
rom-bi-*fo*-lee-a

C

Family Name: **Vitaceae**
Common Name: **Grape Ivy, Venezuela Treebine Vine**

Originated in Mexico to Columbia, Brazil, West India.

CISSUS RHOMBIFOLIA

Production factors

Light. Use production light levels of 1,200 to 2,000 fc (13 to 21.6 klx) for acclimatized plants.

Temperature. Maintain greenhouse temperatures of 68° to 82°F (20° to 28°C) to promote good growth. Higher temperatures suppress propagation and growth production.

Nutrition. At recommended production light levels for acclimatized plants, fertilize with 34.5 pounds per 1000 square feet per year (lb/1000 sq. ft/yr) or 168.4 kilograms per 1000 square meters per year (kg/1000 sq. m/yr) of N-P-K. A N-P-K ratio of 3:1:2 is suggested for use with soilless media. Most media require the addition of micronutrients either by preplant incorporation of a granular source or as part of a liquid fertilization program.

Irrigation. Keep the potting medium uniformly moist but not wet.

Media. Use a potting medium with good drainage and aeration characteristics. Coarse media components such as bark, perlite, styrofoam and calcined clay are often mixed with fibrous peat to provide both good drainage and water retention. Maintain pH values within 5.5 to 6.2.

Problems.

Diseases: Anthracnose—*Colletotricum* sp.; blight—*Botrytis cinerea, Rhizoctonia solani, Sclerotium rolfsii;* dieback—*Pestalotiopsis menezesiana;* leaf spot—*Cercospora* sp.; downy mildew—*Plasmopara* sp.; powdery mildew—*Oidium* sp.; root rot—*Pythium* sp.; rust—*Endophyllum circumscriptum;* smut—*Mykosyrinx cissi, Ustilago cissi.*

Pests: Aphids; caterpillars, mealybugs; broad mites; two-spotted spider mites; scale; thrips.

Cissus rhombifolia

siss-us
rom-bi-fo-lee-a

C

Postproduction factors

Light. Transport of plants under dark conditions is currently the most common shipping method. Provide at least 75 to 100 fc (.8 to 1.1 klx) of light if extended holding is necessary before sale or installation.

Retail handling

Light. Provide plants with sufficient light upon delivery to recuperate from stresses of dark storage. Grape ivy tolerates minimum lighting of 75 to 100 fc (.8 to 1.1 klx), but light levels of 150 to 400 fc (1.6 to 4.3 klx) improve quality retention and growth potential. Bright indirect or curtain-filtered sunlight give the best natural lighting to preserve plant appearance.

Temperature. Interior temperatures of 65° to 75°F (18° to 24°C) are recommended for best quality retention. Plants tolerate somewhat cooler temperatures, but powdery mildew is more troublesome under such conditions.

Irrigation. Keep the potting medium evenly moist but not wet to avoid root rot problems.

Consumer care

Temperature. Interior temperatures of 65° to 75°F (18° to 24°C) are recommended for best quality retention. Plants tolerate somewhat cooler temperatures, but powdery mildew is more troublesome under such conditions.

Location. Grape ivy thrives in areas with bright indirect or curtain-filtered sunlight. Plants tolerate minimum lighting of 75 to 100 fc (.8 to 1.1 klx), but light levels of 150 to 400 fc (1.6 to 4.3 klx) improve quality retention and growth potential.

Irrigation. Keep the potting medium evenly moist but not wet to avoid root rot problems.

Grooming. Wash foliage periodically with a tepid water shower or damp sponge to remove dust and dirt. Regular cleaning of foliage also improves spider mite control. Repot whenever plant becomes over-crowded. Fertilize every 3 months. Grape ivy is a dependable plant that will retain quality indefinitely with good care.

Cultivars. *Cissus rhombifolia* 'Ellen Danica' is a selection of grape ivy with lobed leaves resembling oaks or maples.

Cissus rhombifolia 'Fionia' leaves have large, wide leaflets and short lateral leaflet stalks, giving a compact, full appearance.

Cissus rhombifolia 'Mandaiana' is a selection of grape ivy with more compact growth habit than the species type. The leaf is also smaller, darker and more leathery.

Cissus rhombifolia 'Mandaiana Compacta' is even more compact than 'Madaiana' with short internodes and wide, closely associated leaflets.

ADDITIONAL READING

Arthurs, Kathryn (ed.). 1974. *How to Grow House Plants.* Menlo Park, CA: Lane Publishing Co.

Bailey, L.H. and E.Z. Bailey. 1976. *Hortus Third.* New York: Macmillan Publishing Co. Inc.

Chase. A.R. 1985. Diseases of foliage plants—Revised list for 1985. *Foliage Digest* 8(6):3-8.

Chase, A.R., L.S. Osborne and R.W. Henley. 1985. Grape ivy. *Foliage Digest* 8(8):5-8.

Conover, C.A. and R.T. Poole. 1981. Guide for fertilizing foliage plant crops. *ARC-Apopka Research Rpt.* RH-81-1. University of Florida.

67

C

————. 1984. Light and fertilizer recommendations for production of acclimatized potted foliage plants. *Foliage Digest* 7(8):1-6.

Crockett, J.U. 1977. *Foliage House Plants.* Revised. Alexandria, VA: Time-Life Books.

Florists' Transworld Delivery Association. 1985. *The Indoor Gardener.* Southfield, MI.

Gaines, R.L. 1977. *Interior Plantscaping: building design for interior foliage plants.* New York: Architectural Record Books.

McConnell, D.B., R.W. Henley and R.L. Biamonte. 1981. Commercial foliage plants. J.N. Joiner (ed.). *Foliage Plant Production.* Englewood Cliffs, NJ: Prentice-Hall Inc.

Orans, M. 1973. *Houseplants and Indoor Landscaping.* Barrington, IL: A.B. Morse Co.

Wright, M. (ed.). 1979. *The Complete Indoor Gardener.* Rev. ed. New York: Random House.

Codiaeum variegatum pictum

ko-dee-*ie*-um
va-ree-a-*gah*-tum
pik-tum

Family Name: **Euphorbiaceae**
Common Name: **Garden Croton**

C

Originated in the Malay Peninsula and Pacific Islands. Previously called *Croton pictum.*

CODIAEIUM VARIEGATUM PICTUM

Production factors

Light. Use production light levels of 4,000 to 8,000 fc (43.2 to 86.4 klx) for acclimatized plants.

Temperature. Provide greenhouse temperatures above 60°F (16°C) to assure good growth. Maintain temperatures above 40°F (5°C) for quality retention.

Nutrition. At recommended production light levels for acclimatized plants, fertilize with 48.3 pounds per 1000 square feet per year (lb/1000 sq. ft/yr) or 235.8 kilograms per 1000 square meters per year (kg/1000 sq. m/yr) of N-P-K. A N-P-K ratio of 3:1:2 is suggested for use with soilless media, while 1:1:1 is recommended for soil-based media. Most media require the addition of micronutrients either by preplant incorporation of a granular source or as part of a liquid fertilization program.

Irrigation. Keep the potting medium uniformly moist but not wet.

Media. Use a potting medium with good water retention and drainage characteristics.

Problems.

Diseases: Anthracnose—*Colletotrichum gloeosporioides, Gloeosporium* sp., *Glomerella cingulata*; blight—*Sclerotium rolfsii;* stem canker—*Coniothyrium* sp., *Leptosphaeria* sp.; crown gall—*Agrobacterium tumefaciens;* stem gall—*Nectriella pironii;* leaf spot—*Cercospora stevensonii, Helminthosporium* sp., *Macrophoma* sp., *Phomopsis* sp., *Phyllosticta* sp., *Xanthomonas campestris* pv. *poinsettiae*; root rot—*Phytophthora* sp., *Rhizoctonia solani;* stem and root rot—*Fusarium* sp.; rust—*Puccinia crotonia;* scab—*Sphaceloma venezuelanus.*

Pests: Mealybugs; mites; lesion nematode—*Paratylenchus coffea*; scale; thrips.

Codiaeum variegatum pictum

ko-dee-*ie*-um
va-ree-a-*gah*-tum
pik-tum

Disorders. Garden croton tolerates fairly cool temperatures but loses leaves when exposed to temperatures below 40°F (5°C).

Postproduction factors

Light. Transport of plants under dark conditions is currently the most common shipping method. Provide at least 150 to 200 fc (1.6 to 2.2 klx) of light if extended holding is necessary before sale or installation.

Temperature. Acclimatized plants can be shipped without damage for extended periods when held at 60° to 65°F (16° to 18°C). (Results reported on cultivar 'Norma.') Garden croton is more resistant to brief cold exposure than many foliage plants. It tolerates exposure during storage to temperatures of 35°F (2°C) for 48 hours without symptoms of chilling injury. (Results reported on cultivar 'Gold Dust.')

Gases. Injury due to ethylene is generally not a problem when plants are shipped within the recommended temperature range. Ethylene may reach damaging levels if plants are shipped with produce or held in prolonged storage above the maximum listed temperature.

Lasting qualities. Under appropriate storage conditions acclimatized plants retain good quality when shipped within 4 weeks. Maintain temperatures near the upper end of the recommended range when transport requires only 1 to 7 days.

Care and grooming. Good storage preparation improves quality retention during transit. Moisture content of the potting medium should approximate 50% of soil capacity when plants are packed. Maintain high humidity levels of 80% to 90% during storage to retard desiccation, especially when shipping time exceeds 7 days.

Retail handling

Light. Provide plants with sufficient light upon delivery to recuperate from the stresses of dark storage. A specially designed holding greenhouse or room is ideal. Garden croton retains quality best when held under high light levels. The best foliage color and growth patterns are obtained when plants receive 4 or more hours of direct sun each day or 500 to 1,000 fc (5.4 to 10.8 klx) of interior lighting for 12 hours per day. However, some cultivars tolerate lower light levels. 'Bravo' retains good quality indoors when produced under 1,750 fc (18.9 klx) and then held under 100 fc (1.1 klx) of light for 12 hours per day. Careful cultivar selection and precise production and post-production technique will allow more successful use of these colorful plants under a wider range of interior conditions.

Temperature. Hold plants at temperatures of 65° to 85°F (18° to 29°C) for optimum quality retention. Avoid drafty locations. When a greenhouse is used to hold plants before installation, maintain 40% to 60% relative humidity to acclimatize plants to lower interior humidity levels.

Irrigation. Garden croton requires more water during warmer seasons than during winter. Keep the potting medium moist but not wet.

Disorders. Leaf drop occurs if temperatures fall suddenly or if plants are placed in a drafty location.

Codiaeum variegatum pictum

ko-dee-*ie*-um
va-ree-a-*gah*-tum
pik-tum

Consumer care

Temperature. Hold plants at temperatures of 65° to 85°F (18° to 29°C) for optimum quality retention. Avoid drafty locations.

Location. Garden croton retains quality best when placed in areas receiving bright light. The best foliage color and growth patterns are obtained when plants receive 4 or more hours of direct sun each day or 500 to 1,000 fc (5.4 to 10.8 klx) of interior lighting for 12 hours per day. However, some cultivars tolerate lower light levels. 'Bravo' retains good quality indoors when produced under 1,750 fc (18.9 klx) and then held under 100 fc (1.1 klx) of light for 12 hours a day.

Irrigation. Garden croton requires more water during the warmer seasons than during winter. Keep the potting medium moist but not wet.

Grooming. Wash foliage periodically with a tepid water shower or damp sponge to remove dust and dirt. Regular cleaning of foliage also aids in control of spider mite populations. Repot in early spring only when the plant becomes quite rootbound. Pruning in early spring keeps plants at a desired size and promotes compact growth habit. Fertilize every 2 months during the growing season. Garden croton can be durable under good maintenance and environmental conditions. This colorful plant has potential to tolerate typical interior environments with careful cultivar selection, production and postproduction technique.

Disorders. Leaf drop occurs if temperatures fall suddenly or if plants are placed in a drafty location.

Cultivars. Many cultivars exist.

ADDITIONAL READING

Arthurs, Kathryn (ed.). 1974. *How to Grow House Plants.* Menlo Park, CA: Lane Publishing Co.

Bailey, L.H. and E.Z. Bailey. 1976. *Hortus Third.* New York: Macmillan Publishing Co. Inc.

Bequette, B.L., T.M. Blessington and J.A. Price. 1985. Influence of lighting systematics on the interior performance of two croton cultivars. *HortScience* 20:927-929.

Chase, A.R. 1985. Diseases of foliage plants— Revised list for 1985. *Foliage Digest* 8(6):3-8.5.

Conover, C.A. and R.T. Poole. 1981. Guide for fertilizing foliage plant crops. *ARC-Apopka Research Rpt.* RH-81-1. University of Florida.

————. 1983. Handling and overseas transportation of acclimatized foliage plants in reefers. *Foliage Digest* 6(5):3-4.

————. 1984. Light and fertilizer recommendations for production of acclimatized potted foliage plants. *Foliage Digest* 7(8):1-6.

————. 1986. Factors influencing shipping of acclimatized foliage plants. *ARC-Apopka Research Rpt.* RH-86-11. University of Florida.

————. 1987. Factors influencing shipping of acclimatized foliage plants. *Foliage Digest* 10(4):1-5.

Crockett. J.U. 1977. *Foliage House Plants.* Revised. Alexandria, VA: Time-Life Books.

Everett, T.H. 1980. *The New York Botanical Garden Illustrated Encyclopedia of Horticulture.* New York: Garland Publishing Inc.

Florists' Transworld Delivery Association. 1985. *The Indoor Gardener.* Southfield, MI.

Gaines, R.L. 1977. *Interior Plantscaping: building design for interior foliage plants.* New York: Architectural Record Books.

McConnell, D.B., R.W. Henley and R.L. Biamonte. 1981. Commercial foliage plants. J.N. Joiner (ed.). *Foliage Plant Production.* Englewood Cliffs, NJ: Prentice-Hall Inc.

Poole, R.T. and C.A. Conover. 1983. Factors influencing chilling damage of foliage plants. *Foliage Digest* 6(8):3-4.

————. 1987. Foliage variety determines heat. *Greenhouse Grower* 5(1):21-22.

Wright, M. (ed.). 1979. *The Complete Indoor Gardener.* Rev. ed. New York: Random House.

C

71

Coffea arabica

kof-ee-a a-*ra*-bi-ka

Family Name: **Rubiaceae**
Common Name: **Arabian Coffee, Common Coffee**

C

Originated in tropical Africa.

COFFEA ARABICA

Production factors

Light. Use production light levels of 1,000 to 2,500 fc (10.8 to 27 klx) for acclimatized plants.

Temperature. Keep greenhouse temperatures above 60°F (16°C) to sustain continuous growth.

Nutrition. At recommended production light levels for acclimatized plants, fertilize with 34.5 pounds per 1000 square feet per year (lb/1000 sq. ft/yr) or 168.4 kilograms per 1000 square meters per year (kg/1000 sq. m/yr) of N-P-K. A N-P-K ratio of 3:1:2 is suggested for use with soilless media, while 1:1:1 is recommended for soil-based media. Most media require the addition of micronutrients either by preplant incorporation of a granular source or as part of a liquid fertilization program.

Irrigation. Keep the potting medium uniformly moist but not wet.

Media. Use a potting medium with good drainage characteristics.

Problems.

Diseases: Anthracnose—*Colletotrichum coffeanum*; damping off—*Rhizoctonia solani;* leaf spot—*Cercospora coffeicola, Glomerella cingulata;* pink mold—*Trichothecium roseum;* neck rot—*Fusarium* sp.

Pests: Aphids; mealybugs; scale; whitefly.

Disorders. Leaf drop is a problem at temperatures below 55°F (13°C). Leaf desiccation and leaf drop occur if the medium becomes dry between irrigations. Arabian coffee is highly sensitive to atmospheric fluoride exposure. Symptoms of fluoride toxicity include marginal foliage scorch, marginal leaf curl and new growth chlorosis.

Coffea arabica *kof*-ee-a a-*ra*-bi-ka

Postproduction factors

Light. Transport of plants under dark conditions is currently the most common shipping method. Maintain Arabian coffee under at least 75 to 100 fc (.8 to 1.1 klx) of light if extended holding is necessary before sale or installation.

Retail handling

Light. Provide plants with sufficient light upon delivery to recuperate from stresses of dark storage. A south or west window with bright filtered light provides the best natural light location for Arabian coffee. Plants tolerate minimum lighting of 75 to 100 fc (.8 to 1.1 klx), but growth and quality retention are improved with higher light levels to 500 fc (5.4 klx).

Temperature. Maintain interior temperatures of 65° to 80°F (18° to 27°C).

Irrigation. Keep the potting medium evenly moist but not wet. Locations with moderate to high humidity levels are recommended for best plant health.

Disorders. Water stress promotes leaf loss. Arabian coffee develops marginal foliage scorch, marginal leaf curl and chlorotic new growth when exposed to atmospheric fluoride.

Consumer care

Temperature. Maintain interior temperatures of 65° to 80°F (18° to 27°C).

Location. A south or west window with bright filtered light provides the best natural

light location for Arabian coffee. Plants tolerate minimum lighting of 75 to 100 fc (.8 to 1.1 klx), but growth and quality retention are improved with higher light levels to 500 fc (5.4 klx).

Irrigation. Keep the potting medium evenly moist but not wet. Locations with moderate to high humidity levels are recommended for best plant health.

Grooming. Prune to control size, and repot if needed in early spring. Pinching helps to keep the foliage canopy compact. Fertilize every 2 months. Arabian coffee prospers where good environmental conditions and regular care are provided.

Disorders. Water stress promotes leaf loss. Check for toxic levels of airborne fluoride if quality deteriorates even with good care.

ADDITIONAL READING

Arthurs, Kathryn (ed.). 1974. *How to Grow House Plants.* Menlo Park, CA: Lane Publishing Co.

Bailey, L.H. and E.Z. Bailey. 1976. *Hortus Third.* New York: Macmillan Publishing Co. Inc.

Conover C.A. and R.T. Poole. 1981. Guide for fertilizing foliage plant crops. *ARC-Apopka Research Rpt.* RH-81-1. University of Florida.

————. 1984. Light and fertilizer recommendations for production of acclimatized potted foliage plants. *Foliage Digest* 7(8):1-6.

Everett, T.H. 1980. *The New York Botanical Garden Illustrated Encyclopedia of Horticulture.* New York: Garland Publishing Inc.

Florists' Transworld Delivery Association. 1985. *The Indoor Gardener.* Southfield, MI.

Gaines, R.L. 1977. *Interior Plantscaping: building design for interior foliage plants.* New York: Architectural Record Books.

Manaker, G.H. 1981. *Interior Plantscapes: installation, maintenance and management.* Englewood Cliffs, NJ: Prentice-Hall Inc.

McConnell, D.B., R.W. Henley and R.L. Biamonte. 1981. Commercial foliage plants. J.N. Joiner (ed.). *Foliage Plant Production.* Englewood Cliffs, NJ: Prentice-Hall Inc.

C

Coffea arabica

kof-ee-a a-*ra*-bi-ka

Orans, M. 1973. *Houseplants and Indoor Landscaping.* Barrington, IL: A.B. Morse Co.

Woltz, S.S. and W.E. Waters. 1978. Airborne fluoride effects on some foliage plants. *HortScience* 13:585-586.

C

Cordyline terminalis

kor-*di*-li-nee
ter-min-*ah*-lis

Family Name: **Agavaceae**
Common Name: **Ti Plant, Hawaiian Good-Luck Plant**

Originated in Eastern Asia. This plant was previously named *Dracaena terminalis*.

C

CORDYLINE TERMINALIS

Production factors

Light. Production light levels of 3,000 to 3,500 fc (32.4 to 37.8 klx) are recommended for acclimatized plants with good foliage color.

Temperature. Maintain temperatures of 65° to 95°F (18° to 35°C) for best growth and quality control. Extreme temperatures are tolerated, but growth is reduced.

Nutrition. At recommended production light levels for acclimatized plants, fertilize with 34.5 pounds per 1000 square feet per year (lb/1000 sq. ft/yr) or 168.4 kilograms per 1000 square meters per year (kg/1000 sq. m/yr) of N-P-K. A N-P-K ratio of 3:1:2 is suggested for use with soilless media, while 1:1:1 is recommended for soil-based media. Avoid fertilizers containing fluoride. Incorporate micronutrients at a lower than average rate of 1 pound per cubic yard (.6 kg per cubic m) Micromax or another equivalent source into the potting medium prior to planting. When liquid fertilizer is injected through an overhead irrigation system, follow with clear water for several minutes to flush solution out of growth terminals.

Irrigation. Keep the potting medium uniformly moist but not wet. Use a water source that is low in fluoride.

Media. Choose a potting medium with good water retention and drainage characteristics, and maintain pH values within 5.5 to 6.5. Amendments should be screened for toxic concentrations of fluoride before addition to the medium.

Problems.

Diseases: Anthracnose—*Colletotrichum* sp., *Glomerella cingulata;* blight—*Sclerotium rolfsii;* leaf spot—*Cercospora cordylines, Cladosporium dracaenatum, Fusarium moniliforme, Phyllosticta dracaenae, Phytophthora parasitica;* crown rot—*Phytophthora* sp.; root rot—*Rhizoctonia solani;* soft rot—*Erwinia caratovora* subsp.

caratovora, Erwinia chrysanthemi; root and stem rot—*Fusarium* sp.

Pests: Fungus gnats; lesion nematode—*Paratylenchus* spp.; mealybugs; two-spotted mites; root mealybugs; scale; thrips.

Disorders. Ti plant is highly sensitive to fluoride exposure by air, water, media or fertilizer. Symptoms include tipburn and marginal necrosis followed by mottling and death of the entire leaf in severe cases. 'Baby Doll' is particularly prone to injury. Foliage color intensity is affected by light, temperature and fertility. Low light levels and high fertilizer rates during summer reduce leaf color. Terminal growing points die when leaf shine compound or excess fertilizer collects in the area.

Postproduction factors

Light. Transport of plants under dark conditions is currently the most common shipping method. If extended holding is necessary before sale or installation, maintain ti plant under at least 50 to 100 fc (.5 to 1.1 klx) of light. Long-term maintenance at this light level produces elongated growth and reduces foliage color. Provide more light if this change in appearance is not desired.

Temperature. Acclimatized plants can be shipped without damage for at least 2 weeks. Some cultivar variation exists. Shipping temperature recommendations for 'Baby Doll' are 55° to 60°F (13° to 16°C) for 1 to 14 days and 50° to 55°F (10° to 13°C) for 15 to 28 days. Shipping temperature recommendations for 'Dragon Tongue' are 60° to 65°F (16° to 18°C) for 1 to 14 days.

Gases. Injury due to ethylene is generally not a problem when plants are shipped within recommended temperature range. Ethylene may reach damaging levels if plants are shipped with produce or held in prolonged storage above maximum listed temperature.

Lasting qualities. Under appropriate storage conditions acclimatized plants retain good quality when shipped within 2 weeks. Maintain temperatures near the upper end of the recommended range when transport requires only 1 to 7 days. Quality loss of approximately 25% per week is expected when 'Baby Doll' is stored for more than 2 weeks.

Care and grooming. Good storage preparation improves quality retention during transit. The potting medium moisture content should approximate 50% of soil capacity when plants are packed. Maintain high humidity levels of 80% to 90% during storage to retard desiccation, especially when shipping time exceeds 7 days.

Retail handling

Light. Provide plants with sufficient light upon delivery to recuperate from stresses of dark storage. A specially designed holding greenhouse or room is ideal. Ti plant is very adaptable to light levels. Sites with as little as 50 fc (.5 klx) of light are tolerated, although elongated growth becomes more pronounced and foliage variegation is reduced. Plants maintain quality for longer durations when held under 75 to 150 fc (.8 to 1.6 klx). Foliage color and quality retention improve as light increases to 800 fc (8.6 klx). Natural light locations with at least 4 hours of direct sunlight stimulate the brightest foliage display.

Temperature. Hold plants at temperatures of 65° to 85°F (18° to 29°C) for

Cordyline terminalis

kor-*di*-li-nee
ter-min-*ah*-lis

optimum growth and quality. When a greenhouse is used to hold plants before installation, maintenance of 40% to 60% relative humidity is desired for acclimatization to lower interior humidity levels.

Irrigation. Keep the potting medium evenly moist but not wet. Locations with high humidity are recommended for best plant health.

Disorders. Symptoms of tipburn, marginal necrosis, mottling or total leaf necrosis indicate exposure to fluoride. Excessive drying between waterings causes tipburn and marginal necrosis.

Consumer care

Temperature. Provide interior temperatures of 65° to 85°F (18° to 29°C) for optimum growth and quality.

Location. Ti plant is very adaptable to light levels. Interior sites with as little as 50 fc (.5 klx) are tolerated, although elongated growth becomes more pronounced and foliage variegation is reduced. Plants maintain quality for longer durations when held under 75 to 150 fc (.8 to 1.6 klx). Foliage color and quality retention improve as light increases to 800 fc (8.6 klx). Sites that provide at least 4 hours of direct sunlight make the brightest foliage displays possible.

Irrigation. Keep the potting medium evenly moist but not wet. Locations with high humidity are recommended for best plant health.

Grooming. Fertilize every 3 to 4 months. Prune to control size and repot as needed at any season. Ti plant is a very exciting and colorful specimen under ideal environmental conditions. Under low light durability is reduced, foliage color is subdued and the growth habit becomes more elongated. However, with good care this species can still display interesting color, texture and form under low light.

Disorders. Check for toxic levels of fluoride if quality deteriorates even with good care. Excessive drying between waterings causes tipburn and marginal necrosis.

Cultivars. Many cultivars are available.

ADDITIONAL READING

Bailey, L.H. and E.Z. Bailey. 1976. *Hortus Third*. New York: Macmillan Publishing Co. Inc.

Chase, A.R. 1985. Diseases of foliage plants—Revised list for 1985. *Foliage Digest* 8(6):3-8.

Conover, C.A. and R.T. Poole. 1981. Guide for fertilizing foliage plant crops. *ARC-Apopka Research Rpt.* RH-81-1. University of Florida.

———. 1983. Handling and overseas transportation of acclimatized foliage plants in reefers. *Foliage Digest* 6(5):34

———. 1986. Factors influencing shipping of acclimatized foliage plants. *ARC-Apopka Research Rpt.* RH-86-11. University of Florida.

———. 1987. Factors influencing shipping of acclimatized foliage plants. *Foliage Digest* 10(4):1.5.

Crockett, J.U. 1977. *Foliage House Plants*. Revised. Alexandria, VA: Time-Life Books.

Everett, T.H. 1980. *The New York Botanical Garden Illustrated Encyclopedia of Horticulture*. New York: Garland Publishing Inc.

Gaines, R.L. 1977. *Interior Plantscaping: building design for interior foliage plants*. New York: Architectural Record Books.

Manaker, G.H. 1981. *Interior Plantscapes: installation, maintenance, and management*. Englewood Cliffs, NJ: Prentice-Hall Inc.

McConnell, D.B., R.W Henley and R.L. Biamonte. 1981. Commercial foliage plants. J.N. Joiner (ed.). *Foliage Plant Production*. Englewood Cliffs, NJ: Prentice-Hall Inc.

Osborne, L.S., C.A. Conover and A.R. Chase. 1985. *Cordyline* (ti plant). *Foliage Digest* 8(9):4-7.

Poole, R.T. and C.A. Conover. 1986. Boron and fluoride toxicity of foliage plants. *Foliage Digest* 9(3):3-6.

Cordyline terminalis

kor-*di*-li-nee
ter-min-*ah*-lis

Woltz, S.S. and W.E. Waters. 1978. Airborne fluoride effects on some foliage plants. *HortScience* 13:585-586.

Wright, M. (ed.). 1979. *The Complete Indoor Gardener.* Rev. ed. New York: Random House.

C

Crassula argentea

krass-*yew*-luh
ar-*jen*-tee-uh

Family Name: **Crassulaceae**
Common Name: **Jade plant**

Originated in South Africa.

C

CRASSULA ARGENTEA

Production factors

Irrigation. Keep the potting medium dry between irrigations.

Media. Use a potting medium with very good drainage characteristics.

Disorders. Overwatering injures delicate fibrous roots.

Postproduction factors

Light. Transport of plants under dark conditions is currently the most common shipping method. If extended holding is necessary before sale or installation, main-tain jade plant under at least 75 to 100 fc (.8 to 1.1 klx) of light. Long-term maintenance under low light produces elongated, lax growth. Provide more light if this is not desired.

Temperature. Acclimatized plants can be shipped without damage for extended periods when held at 50° to 65°F (10° to 18°C).

Gases. Jade plant suffers leaf loss upon extended exposure to 5 ppm ethylene. Injury due to ethylene is generally not a problem when plants are shipped within the recom-mended temperature range. Ethylene may reach damaging levels if plants are shipped with produce or held in prolonged storage above the maximum listed temperature.

Lasting qualities. Under appropriate storage conditions acclimatized plants retain good quality when shipped within 4 weeks. Maintain temperatures near upper end of the recommended range when transport requires only 1 to 7 days.

Care and grooming. Good storage preparation improves quality retention during transit. Moisture content of the potting medium should approximate 50% of soil capacity when plants are packed. Maintain high humidity levels of 80% to 90% during storage to retard desiccation, especially when shipping time exceeds 7 days.

Foliage Plants *Crassula argentea*

Crassula argentea

krass-*yew*-luh
ar-*jen*-tee-uh

Retail handling

Light. Provide plants with sufficient light upon delivery to recuperate from stresses of dark storage. A specially designed holding greenhouse or room is ideal. When such a facility is unavailable, maintain jade plant under at least 75 to 100 fc (.8 to 1.1 klx) of light. Long-term maintenance under low light produces elongated, lax growth; provide more light if this is not desired.

Temperature. Good growth and quality are sustained with interior temperatures of 55° to 75°F (13° to 24°C), although jade plant tolerates a wide range of temperatures from 40° to 100°F (4° to 38°C). When a greenhouse is used to hold plants before installation, maintain 40% to 60% relative humidity for acclimatization to lower interior humidity levels.

Irrigation. Allow the medium to become almost dry between thorough waterings.

Disorders. Leaf loss is a symptom of exposure to toxic ethylene levels during transit. Overwatering injures delicate fibrous roots.

Consumer care

Temperature. Good growth and quality are sustained with interior temperatures of 55° to 75°F (13° to 24°C), although jade plant tolerates a wide range of temperatures from 40° to 100°F (4° to 38°C).

Location. Jade plant maintains quality and interest in many areas. Low interior light levels of 75 to 100 fc (.8 to 1.1 klx) are tolerated, but over time the growth habit assumes a looser, more open and rather elongated appearance, with branches draping over the edge of the pot. Higher light improves quality retention and enables the plant to produce a more sturdy, compact growth habit. Recommendations for light range up to 1,000 fc (10.8 klx) for 12 hours a day, or 4 hours of direct sun. Intense sunlight may cause leaf scorch.

Irrigation. Allow the medium to become almost dry between thorough waterings.

Grooming. Fertilize every 3 to 4 months. Prune to control size and shape. Repot at any season only when plants become quite potbound. Installation sites protected from heavy traffic are desirable since stems are brittle. Jade plant is a durable plant that will retain quality with good care.

Disorders. Overwatering injures delicate fibrous roots.

ADDITIONAL READING

Bailey, L.H. and E.Z. Bailey. 1976. *Hortus Third.* New York: Macmillan Publishing Co. Inc.

Conover, C.A. and R.T. Poole. 1983. Handling and overseas transportation of acclimatized foliage plants in reefers. *Foliage Digest* 6(5):3-4.

———. 1986. Factors influencing shipping of acclimatized foliage plants. *ARC-Apopka Research Rpt.* RH-86-11. University of Florida.

———. 1987. Factors influencing shipping of acclimatized foliage plants. *Foliage Digest* 10(4): 1-5.

Crockett, J.U. 1977. *Foliage House Plants.* Revised. Alexandria, VA: Time-Life Books.

Everett, T.H. 1980. *The New York Botanical Garden Illustrated Encyclopedia of Horticulture.* New York: Garland Publishing Inc.

Florists' Transworld Delivery Association. 1985. *The Indoor Gardener.* Southfield, MI.

Gaines, R.L. 1977. *Interior Plantscaping: building design for interior foliage plants.* New York: Architectural Record Books.

C

Crassula argentea

krass-*yew*-luh
ar-*jen*-tee-uh

Marousky, F.J. and B.K. Harbaugh. 1978. Deterioration of foliage plants during transit. *Proc. 1978 Natl. Tropical Foliage Short Course,* University of Florida, IFAS Coop. Ext. Serv., Orlando, FL.

Orans, M. 1973. *Houseplants and Indoor Landscaping.* Barrington, IL: A.B. Morse Co.

C

Cyrtomium falcatum

ser-*toh*-mee-um
fal-*kay*-tum

Family Name: **Polypodiaceae**
Common Name: **Holly Fern**

Originated in Asia, South Africa and Polynesia.

CYRTOMIUM FALCATUM

Production factors

Light. Use production light levels of 1,800 to 2,400 fc (19.4 to 25.9 klx) for acclimatized plants.

Nutrition. At recommended production light levels for acclimatized plants, fertilize with 18.4 to 27.5 pounds per 1000 square feet per year (lb/1000 sq. ft/yr) or 89.7 to 134.5 kilograms per 1000 square meters per year (kg/1000 sq. m/yr) of N-P-K.

Irrigation. Keep the potting medium uniformly moist but not wet.

Media. Use an organic potting medium with good drainage characteristics.

Problems.
Pests: Mealybugs; scale.

Postproduction factors

Light. Transport of plants under dark conditions is currently the most common shipping method. Maintain holly fern under at least 75 to 100 fc (.8 to 1.1 klx) of light if extended holding is necessary before sale or installation.

Retail handling

Light. Maintain plants under sufficient light upon delivery to recuperate from the stresses of dark storage. At least 75 to 100 fc (.8 to 1.1 klx) of light are required for survival. Quality retention is improved with higher light levels of 150 to 250 fc (1.6 to 2.7 klx). A shadowless north window exposure provides appropriate natural lighting for holly fern.

Temperature. Plants tolerate cool temperatures to 35°F (2°C), but interior temperatures of 50° to 72°F (10° to 22°C) maintain good growth and quality.

Irrigation. Keep the potting medium barely moist.

Cyrtomium falcatum

ser-*toh*-mee-um
fal-*kay*-tum

Consumer care

Temperature. Plants tolerate cool temperatures to 35°F (2°C), but interior temperatures of 50° to 72°F (10° to 22°C) maintain good growth and quality.

Location. Holly fern thrives in areas with shadowless north light. Although 75 to 100 fc (.8 to 1.1 klx) is sufficient for survival, light levels of 150 to 250 fc (1.6 to 2.7 klx) improve quality retention.

Irrigation. Keep the potting medium barely moist.

Grooming. Fertilize every 6 months with half-strength houseplant formula. Repot overcrowded plants in early spring, carefully setting the crown no deeper than the previous level. Holly fern is a durable plant that tolerates low light, low humidity and drafty locations. This tough fern will maintain good quality indefinitely with reasonable care.

Cultivars. *Cyrtomium falcatum* 'Rochfordianum' (Rocheford's holly fern) is a robust selection of the species type that has fronds with broad, distinctly toothed edges.

ADDITIONAL READING

Bailey, L.H. and E.Z. Bailey. 1976. *Hortus Third.* New York: Macmillan Publishing Co. Inc.

Crockett, J.U. 1977. *Foliage House Plants.* Revised. Alexandria, VA: Time-Life Books.

Everett, T.H. 1980. *The New York Botanical Garden Illustrated Encyclopedia of Horticulture.* New York: Garland Publishing Inc.

Gaines, R.L. 1977. *Interior Plantscaping: building design for interior foliage plants.* New York: Architectural Record Books.

McConnell, D.B., R.W. Henley and R.L. Biamonte. 1981. Commercial foliage plants. J.N. Joiner (ed.). *Foliage Plant Production.* Englewood Cliffs, NJ: Prentice-Hall Inc.

C

Dieffenbachia amoena

dee-fan-*bahk*-ee-a
a-*moyn*-a

Family Name: **Araceae**
Common Name: **Dumb Cane**

Originated in tropical America.

D

DIEFFENBACHIA AMOENA

Production factors

Light. Production light levels of 1,500 to 2,500 fc (16.2 to 27 klx) are recommended for acclimatized plants.

Temperature. Maintain a minimum greenhouse temperature of 65°F (18°C) for steady growth production at an economical fuel consumption level.

Nutrition. At recommended production light levels for acclimatized plants, fertilize with 34.5 pounds per 1000 square feet per year (lb/1000 sq.ft/yr) or 168.4 kilograms per 1000 square meters per year (kg/1000 sq. m/yr) of N-P-K. A N-P-K ratio of 3:1:2 is suggested for use with soilless media, while 1:1:1 is recommended for soil-based media. Most media require the addition of micronutrients either by preplant incorporation of a granular source or as part of a liquid fertilization program.

Irrigation. Allow the potting medium to dry moderately between thorough waterings.

Media. Use a potting medium with good drainage characteristics.

Problems.

Diseases: Blight—*Fusarium moniliforme, Rhizoctonia solani, Sclerotium rolfsii;* blight and stem rot—*Erwinia carotovora* subsp. *carotovora, Erwinia chrysanthemi, Erwinia dieffenbachiae;* leaf spot—*Cephalosporium cinnamomeum, Cercospora* sp., *Colletotrichum* spp., *Gloeosporium* sp., *Glomerella cingulata, Leptosphaeria* sp., *Myrothecium roridum, Phaeosphaeria eustoma, Phyllosticta* sp., *Phytophthora parasitica* var. *nicotianae, Pseudomonas cichorii, Volutella* sp., *Xanthomonas campestris* pv. *dieffenbachiae;* root rot—*Pythium* spp.; stem rot—*Fusarium oxysporum, Fusarium solani, Pythium splendens, Phytophthora palmivora;* virus—Cucumber mosaic virus, Dasheen mosaic virus.

Pests: Mites; mealybugs; lesion nematodes—*Pratylenchus* spp.; thrips.

Dieffenbachia amoena

dee-fan-*bahk*-ee-a a-*moyn*-a

Disorders. Temperatures below 65°F (18°C) reduce plant growth and root development. Overwatering encourages crown and root rot, while severe water stress increases leaf drop.

Postproduction factors

Light. Transport of plants under dark conditions is currently the most common shipping method. If extended holding is necessary before sale or installation, maintain dumb cane under at least 75 to 100 fc (.8 to 1.1 klx) of light.

Temperature. Acclimatized plants can be safely shipped when held at 55° to 65°F (13° to 18°C). Exposure to lower temperatures during transport should be avoided. Dumb cane develops moderate to severe symptoms of chilling injury when temperatures fall to 35°F (2°C) for 24 hours. Plants receiving frequent production irrigation suffer even greater damage when chilled, so irrigation frequency should be carefully monitored if exposure to cool temperatures during shipping is a possibility.

Gases. Injury due to ethylene is generally not a problem when plants are shipped within recommended temperature range. Ethylene may reach damaging levels if plants are shipped with produce or held in prolonged storage above maximum listed temperature.

Lasting qualities. Under appropriate storage conditions acclimatized plants retain good quality when shipped within 2 weeks. Maintain temperatures near upper end of recommended range when transport requires only 1 to 7 days. Lower foliage turns yellow with extended storage time. Quality loss of approximately 25% per week is expected when dumb cane is stored for more than 2 weeks.

Care and grooming. Good storage preparation improves quality retention during transit. Moisture content of the potting medium should approximate 50% of soil capacity when plants are packed. Maintain high humidity levels of 80% to 90% during storage to retard desiccation, especially when shipping time exceeds 7 days.

Retail handling

Light. Provide plants with sufficient light upon delivery to recuperate from the stresses of dark storage. A specially designed holding greenhouse or room is ideal. When such a facility is unavailable, maintain dumb cane under at least 75 to 100 fc (.8 to 1.1 klx) of light. Quality retention is improved with higher light levels of 150 to 250 fc (1.6 to 2.7 klx). Bright indirect or curtain-filtered sunlight provides excellent natural lighting.

Temperature. Maintain temperatures of 65° to 80°F (18° to 27°C) for optimum growth and quality. Avoid drafty locations. When a greenhouse is used to hold plants before installation, maintain 40% to 60% relative humidity for acclimatization to lower interior humidity levels.

Irrigation. Allow the potting medium to dry moderately between thorough waterings.

Disorders. Chilling injury occurs if plants are exposed to low temperatures during transit. Lower foliage begins to turn yellow when plants require more than 2 weeks of storage. Test media for high soluble salts if roots become damaged. Soluble salt levels below 1,500 ppm are important for interior quality retention.

D

Overwatering encourages crown and root rot, while severe water stress increases leaf drop.

Consumer care

Temperature. Maintain temperatures of 65° to 80°F (18° to 27°C) for optimum growth and quality. Avoid drafty locations.

Location. Dumb cane thrives in areas with bright indirect or curtain-filtered sunlight. Plants tolerate 75 to 100 fc (.8 to 1.1 klx) of light, but maintain quality better with 150 to 250 fc (1.6 to 2.7 klx).

Irrigation. Allow the potting medium to dry moderately between thorough waterings.

Grooming. Wash foliage periodically with a tepid water shower or damp sponge to remove dust and dirt. Regular cleaning of foliage also aids spider mite control. Fertilize every 2 to 3 months or on a schedule that maintains soluble salts below 1,500 ppm. Repot dumb cane whenever roots become too crowded. Overgrown plants can be pruned back in spring to stimulate new growth and to control size. Dumb cane is a durable, decorative plant for interiors and will maintain quality indefinitely with good care. It tolerates heavy traffic areas well, but avoid accessibility to small children due to calcium oxalate in plant tissue.

Disorders. Test media for high soluble salts if roots begin to deteriorate. Overwatering encourages crown and root rot, while severe water stress increases leaf drop.

Cultivars. Commercial propagating companies have recently developed procedures to produce dumb cane using tissue culture techniques. This new propagating method facilitates mass production of new cultivars.

Dieffenbachia amoena

dee-fan-*bahk*-ee-a
a-*moyn*-a

ADDITIONAL READING

Bailey, L.H. and E.Z. Bailey 1976. *Hortus Third.* New York: Macmillan Publishing Co. Inc.

Chase, A.R. 1985a. Diseases of foliage plants—Revised list for 1985. *Foliage Digest* 8(6):3-8.

———. 1985b. You can prevent foliage diseases. *Greenhouse Grower* 3(12):36-45.

Conover. C.A. and R.T. Poole. 1981. Guide for fertilizing foliage plant crops. *ARC-Apopka Research Rpt.* RH-81-1. University of Florida.

———. 1983. Handling and overseas transportation of acclimatized foliage plants in reefers. *Foliage Digest* 6(5):3-4.

———. 1984. Light and fertilizer recommendations for production of acclimatized potted foliage plants. *Foliage Digest* 7(8):1-6.

———. 1986. Factors influencing shipping of acclimatized foliage plants. *ARC-Apopka Research Rpt.* RH-86-11. University of Florida.

———. 1987. Factors influencing shipping of acclimatized foliage plants. *Foliage Digest* 10(4):1-5.

Crockett, J.U. 1977. Foliage House Plants. Revised. Alexandria, VA: Time-Life Books.

Everett, T.H. 1980. *The New York Botanical Garden Illustrated Encyclopedia of Horticulture.* New York: Garland Publishing Inc.

Gaines, R.L. 1977. *Interior Plantscaping: building design for interior foliage plants.* New York: Architectural Record Books.

Henny, R.J., C.A. Conover and R.T. Poole. 1986. New hybrid Dieffenbachia released by AREC-Apopka for Florida foliage growers. *Florida Foliage* 12(11):17-20.

Howle, L. 1987. Foliage varieties sharpen your competitive edge. *Greenhouse Manager* 5(9):50-69.

Florists' Transworld Delivery Association. 1985. *The Indoor Gardener.* Southfield, MI.

Manaker, G.H. 1981. *Interior Plantscapes: installation, maintenance, and management.* Englewood Cliffs, NJ: Prentice-Hall Inc.

McConnell, D.B., R.W. Henley and R.L. Biamonte. 1981. Commercial foliage plants. J.N. Joiner (ed.). *Foliage Plant Production.* Englewood Cliffs, NJ: Prentice-Hall Inc.

Orans, M. 1973. *Houseplants and Indoor Landscaping.* Barrington, IL: A.B. Morse Co.

Peppler, K.Z. 1986. New varieties for 1986. *Greenhouse Manager* 4(1):14-32.

Poole, R.T. and C.A. Conover. 1983. Factors influencing chilling damage of foliage plants. *Foliage Digest* 6(8):3-4.

———. 1987. Foliage variety determines heat. *Greenhouse Grower* 5(1):21-22.

Staby, G.L., J.L. Robertson and D.C. Kiplinger. 1978. *Chain of Life.* Ohio Florists' Association, Columbus, OH.

Sullivan, G.H., J.L. Robertson and G.L. Staby. 1980. Care and handling of foliage plants. *Management for Retail Florists with Applications to Nursery and Garden Centers.* San Francisco: W.H. Freeman and Co.

Wright, M. (ed.). 1979. *The Complete Indoor Gardener.* Rev. ed. New York: Random House.

Dieffenbachia maculata

dee-fan-*bahk*-ee-a
mak-ew-*lah*-ta

Family Name: **Araceae**
Common Name: **Spotted Dumb Cane**

Originated in Central America and northern South America.

DIEFFENBACHIA MACULATA

Production factors

Light. Use production light levels of 1,500 to 2,500 fc (16.2 to 27 klx) for acclimatized plants.

Temperature. Maintain a minimum greenhouse temperature of 65°F (18°C) for steady growth production at an economical fuel consumption level. Many foliage plants can tolerate occasional nights below recommended minimum temperatures without loss in quality or growth rate, but spotted dumb cane needs consistent night temperatures for best results.

Nutrition. At recommended production light levels for acclimatized plants, fertilize with 34.5 pounds per 1000 square feet per year (lb/1000 sq.ft/yr) or 168.4 kilograms per 1000 square meters per year (kg/1000 sq. m/yr) of N-P-K. A N-P-K ratio of 3:1:2 is suggested for use with soilless media, while 1:1:1 is recommended for soil-based media. Most media require addition of micronutrients either by preplant incorporation of a granular source or as part of a liquid fertilization program. Fertilizer applications significantly greater than the recommended rate do not improve plant quality and, in fact, increase sensitivity to at least one fungal disease, *Myrothecium roridum.*

Irrigation. Allow the potting medium to dry moderately between thorough waterings.

Media. Use a potting medium with good drainage characteristics.

Problems.

Diseases: Blight—*Fusarium moniliforme, Rhizoctonia solani, Sclerotium rolfsii;* blight and stem rot—*Erwinia carotovora* subsp. *carotovora, Erwinia chrysanthemi, Erwinia dieffenbachiae;* leaf spot—*Cephalosporium cinnamomeum, Cercospora* sp., *Colletotrichum* spp., *Gloeosporium* sp., *Glomerella cingulata, Leptosphaeria* sp., *Myrothecium roridum, Phaeosphaeria eustoma, Phyllosticta* sp., *Phytophthora parasitica* var. *nicotianae, Pseudomonas cichorii, Volutella* sp., *Xanthomonas campestris* pv. *dieffenba-*

Dieffenbachia maculata dee-fan-*bahk*-ee-a mak-ew-*lah*-ta

chiae; root rot—*Pythium* spp.; stem rot—*Fusarium oxysporum, Fusarium solani, Pythium splendens, Phytophthora palmivora;* virus—Cucumber mosaic virus, Dasheen mosaic virus.

Pests: Mites; mealybugs; lesion nematodes—*Paratylenchus* spp.; thrips.

Disorders. Temperatures below 65°F (18°C) reduce plant growth and root development. Overwatering encourages crown and root rot, while severe water stress increases leaf drop.

Postproduction factors

Light. Transport of plants under dark conditions is currently the most common shipping method. Maintain spotted dumb cane under at least 75 to 100 fc (.8 to 1.1 klx of light if extended holding is necessary before sale or installation.

Temperature. Maintain temperatures of 60° to 68°F (16° to 20°C) during transport. Plants are very sensitive to chilling temperatures; therefore, keep storage containers above 55°F (13°C) at all times.

Gases. Foliage becomes chlorotic when exposed to high levels of ethylene (5 ppm for 3 days).

Lasting qualities. Spotted dumb cane retains quality best when shipment can be completed within 7 days. Lower foliage turns yellow with extended dark storage.

Care and grooming. Plants should be well established at time of sale with healthy roots showing on the outside of the soil ball. Soluble salt levels below 1,500 ppm are important for interior quality retention.

Retail handling

Light. Provide plants with sufficient light upon delivery to recuperate from the stresses of dark storage. Spotted dumb cane tolerates 75 to 100 fc (.8 to 1.1 klx) of light but maintains quality better under 150 to 250 fc (1.6 to 2.7 klx). Natural lighting with bright indirect or curtain-filtered sunlight preserves good appearance. Long-term, continuous illumination actually reduces plant quality. Light durations of 12 hours per day are sufficient for maintenance.

Temperature. Optimum growth and quality are obtained at temperatures of 65° to 80°F (18° to 27°C). Avoid drafty locations.

Irrigation. Allow the potting medium to dry moderately between thorough waterings.

Disorders. Chilling injury occurs if plants are exposed to low temperatures during transit. Excessive dark storage or ethylene toxicity can cause chlorosis during transit. Test media for soluble salts above 1,500 ppm if roots become damaged. Continuous lighting reduces plant quality. Overwatering encourages crown and root rot, while severe water stress increases leaf drop.

Consumer care

Temperature. Maintain temperatures of 65° to 80°F (18° to 27°C) for optimum growth and quality. Avoid drafty locations.

Location. Spotted dumb cane thrives in areas with bright indirect or curtain-filtered sunlight. Plants tolerate 75 to 100 fc (.8 to 1.1 klx) of light but maintain quality better

D

with 150 to 250 fc (1.6 to 2.7 klx). Long-term, continuous illumination actually reduces plant quality. Light durations of 12 hours per day are sufficient for maintenance.

Irrigation. Allow the potting medium to dry moderately between thorough waterings.

Grooming. Wash foliage periodically with a tepid water shower or damp sponge to remove dust and dirt. Regular cleaning of foliage also aids in the control of spider mite populations. Careful monitoring for spider mite outbreaks is important as spotted dumb cane is quite susceptible to these pests. Fertilize every 2 to 3 months or on a schedule that maintains soluble salts below 1,500 ppm. Repot whenever roots become too crowded. Overgrown plants can be pruned back in spring to stimulate new growth and to control size. Spotted dumb cane is a durable and decorative plant for interiors and will maintain quality indefinitely with good care. It tolerates heavy traffic areas well, but avoid accessibility to small children due to presence of calcium oxalate in plant tissue.

Disorders. Test media for high soluble salts if roots begin to deteriorate. Continuous lighting reduces plant quality. Overwatering encourages crown and root rot, while severe water stress increases leaf drop.

Cultivars. Commercial propagating companies have recently developed procedures to produce spotted dumb cane using tissue culture techniques. This new propagating method greatly facilitates mass production development of new cultivars.

ADDITIONAL READING

Bailey, L.H. and E.Z. Bailey. 1976. *Hortus Third.* New York: Macmillan Publishing Co. Inc.

Chase, A.R. 1985. Diseases of foliage plants—Revised list for 1985. *Foliage Digest* 8(6):3-8.

————. 1985. You can prevent foliage diseases. *Greenhouse Grower* 3(12):36-45.

Chase, A.R. and R.T. Poole. 1985. High fertilization increases Myrothecium leaf spot of Dieffenbachia. *Foliage Digest* 8(9):7-8.

Conover, C.A. and R.T. Poole. 1981. Guide for fertilizing foliage plant crops. *ARC-Apopka Research Rpt.* RH-81-1. University of Florida.

————. 1984. Light and fertilizer recommendations for production of acclimatized potted foliage plants. *Foliage Digest* 7(8):1-6.

Conover, C.A., R.T. Poole and T.A. Nell. 1982. Influence of intensity and duration of cool white fluorescent lighting and fertilizer on growth and quality of foliage plants. *J. Amer. Soc. Hort. Sci.* 107:817-822.

Crockett, J.U. 1977. *Foliage House Plants.* Revised. Alexandria, VA: Time-Life Books.

Everett, T.H. 1980. *The New York Botanical Garden Illustrated Encyclopedia of Horticulture.* New York: Garland Publishing Inc.

Florists' Transworld Delivery. 1985. *The Indoor Gardener.* Southfield, MI.

Gaines, R.L. 1977. *Interior Plantscaping: Building Design for Interior Foliage Plants.* New York: Architectural Record Books.

Henny, R.J., C.A. Conover and R.T. Poole. 1986. New hybrid Dieffenbachia released by AREC-Apopka for Florida foliage growers. *Florida Foliage* 12(11):17-20.

Howle, L. 1987. Foliage varieties sharpen your competitive edge. *Greenhouse Manager* 5(9):50-69.

Manaker G.H. 1981. *Interior Plantscapes: Installation, Maintenance and Management.* Englewood Cliffs, NJ: Prentice-Hall.

Marousky F.J. and B.K. Harbaugh. 1978. Deterioration of foliage plants during transit. *Proc. 1978 Natl. Tropical Foliage Short Course,* University of Florida, IFAS Coop. Ext. Serv., Orlando, FL.

McConnell, D.B., R.W. Henley and R.L. Biamonte. 1981. Commercial foliage plants. J.N. Joiner (ed.). *Foliage Plant Production.* Englewood Cliffs, NJ: Prentice-Hall.

Orans, M. 1973. *Houseplants and Indoor Landscaping.* Barrington, IL: A.B. Morse Co.

Peppler, K.Z. 1986. New varieties for 1986. *Greenhouse Manager* 4(1):14-32.

Poole, R.T. and C.A. Conover. 1986. Growth of foliage plants at infrequent low night temperatures. *Foliage Digest* 9(2):7-8.

———. 1987. Foliage variety determines heat. *Greenhouse Grower* 5(1):21-22.

Staby, G.L., J.L. Robertson and D.C. Kiplinger. 1978. *Chain of Life.* Columbus, OH: Ohio Florists' Association.

Sullivan, G.H., J.L. Robertson and G.L. Staby. 1980. Care and handling of foliage plants. *Management for Retail Florists with Applications to Nursery and Garden Centers.* San Francisco: W.H. Freeman and Co.

Wright, M. (ed.). 1979. *The Complete Indoor Gardener.* Rev. ed. New York: Random House.

D

Dizygotheca elegantissima

di-zi-go-*thee*-ka
ay-le-gan-*tis*-i-ma

Family Name: **Araliaceae**
Common Name: **False Aralia**

Originated in New Caledonia and Polynesia. This plant was previously named *Aralia elegantissima.*

D

DIZYGOTHECA ELEGANTISSIMA

Production factors

Light. Use production light levels of 2,000 to 4,000 fc (21.6 to 43.2 klx) for acclimatized plants.

Temperature. Maintain greenhouse temperatures of at least 65°F (18°C) to assure continuous growth.

Nutrition. At recommended production light levels for acclimatized plants, fertilize with 34.5 pounds per 1000 square feet per year (lb/1000 sq.ft/yr) or 168.4 kilograms per 1000 square meters per year (kg/1000 sq. m/yr) of N-P-K. A N-P-K ratio of 3:1:2 is suggested for use with soilless media, while 1:1:1 is recommended for soil-based media. Most media require the addition of micronutrients either by preplant incorporation of a granular source or as part of a liquid fertilization program.

Irrigation. Keep the potting medium uniformly moist but not wet.

Media. Use a potting medium with good drainage characteristics.

Problems.

Diseases: Spot anthracnose—*Sphaceloma araliae;* leaf spot—*Cercospora* sp.; root rot—*Fusarium oxysporum, Rhizoctonia solani.*

Pests: Mealybugs; root mealybugs; scale; spider mites.

Disorders. False aralia is moderately sensitive to airborne fluoride. Mature foliage is not harmed, but leaf tips of new growth are burned.

Postproduction factors

Light. Transport of plants under dark conditions is currently the most common shipping method. If extended holding is necessary before sale or installation, maintain false aralia under at least 150 fc (1.6 klx) of light.

Temperature. Acclimatized plants can be shipped without damage for extended periods when held at 55° to 60°F (13° to 16°C).

Gases. Injury due to ethylene is generally not a problem when plants are shipped within the recommended temperature range. Ethylene may reach damaging levels if plants are shipped with produce or held in

Dizygotheca elegantissima

di-zi-go-*thee*-ka
ay-le-gan-*tis*-i-ma

prolonged storage above the maximum listed temperature.

Lasting qualities. Under appropriate storage conditions acclimatized plants retain good quality when shipped within 4 weeks. Maintain temperatures near the upper end of the recommended range when transport requires only 1 to 7 days.

Care and grooming. Good storage preparation improves quality retention during transit. Moisture content of the potting medium should approximate 50% of soil capacity when plants are packed. Maintain high humidity levels of 80% to 90% during storage to retard desiccation, especially when shipping time exceeds 7 days.

Retail handling

Light. Provide plants with sufficient light upon delivery to recuperate from the stresses of dark storage. A specially designed holding greenhouse or room is ideal. When such a facility is unavailable, maintain false aralia under at least 150 fc (1.6 klx) of light.

Temperature. Average interior temperatures of 65° to 85°F (18° to 29°C) are ideal. Avoid drafty locations and sudden radical temperature changes. When a greenhouse is used to hold plants before installation, maintain 40% to 60% relative humidity for acclimatization to lower interior humidity levels.

Irrigation. Keep the potting medium uniformly moist but not wet.

Disorders. Leaf tips of new growth are burned when exposed to high levels of atmospheric fluoride. Tipburn and loss of older foliage occur when plants are stressed by low soil moisture, low humidity or high soluble salts.

Consumer care

Temperature. Average interior temperatures of 65° to 85°F (18° to 29°C) are ideal. Avoid drafty locations and sudden radical temperature changes.

Location. Areas with bright indirect or curtain-filtered sunlight are excellent for growth and quality maintenance. False aralia prefers medium to high light but maintains good appearance under light levels of 150 to 250 fc (1.6 to 2.7 klx).

Irrigation. Keep the potting medium uniformly moist but not wet.

Grooming. Fertilize every 2 weeks during the growing season (spring to fall) with half-strength houseplant formula. Repot overcrowded plants in early spring. Established specimens may develop mature foliage that is much larger and coarser in texture than the juvenile form. If textural change is not desired, prune that stem back to the pot so new juvenile growth can emerge from the base. Provide humid conditions for best quality retention. False aralia is a graceful interior plant that will retain lasting quality with good care.

Disorders. High concentrations of atmospheric fluoride can burn newly emerging foliage. Tipburn and loss of lower foliage are responses to stressful conditions such as low humidity, low soil moisture and overfertilization.

ADDITIONAL READING

Bailey, L.H. and E.Z. Bailey. 1976. *Hortus Third.* New York: Macmillan Publishing Co. Inc.

Conover C.A. and R.T. Poole. 1981. Guide for fertilizing foliage plant crops. *ARC-Apopka Research Rpt.* RH-81-1. University of Florida.

———. 1983. Handling and overseas transportation of acclimatized foliage plants in reefers. *Foliage Digest* 6(5):3-4.

———. 1984. Light and fertilizer recommendations for production of acclimatized potted foliage plants. *Foliage Digest* 7(8):1-6.

———. 1986. Factors influencing shipping of acclimatized foliage plants. *ARC-Apopka Research Rpt.* RH-86- 11. University of Florida.

———. 1987. Factors influencing shipping of acclimatized foliage plants. *Foliage Digest* 10(4):1-5.

Crockett, J.U. 1977. *Foliage House Plants.* Revised. Alexandria, VA: Time-Life Books.

Everett, T.H. 1980. *The New York Botanical Garden Illustrated Encyclopedia of Horticulture.* New York: Garland Publishing Inc.

Gaines, R.L. 1977. *Interior Plantscaping: Building Design for Interior Foliage Plants.* New York: Architectural Record Books.

McConnell, D.B., R.W. Henley and R.L. Biamonte. 1981. Commercial foliage plants. J.N. Joiner (ed.). *Foliage Plant Production.* Englewood Cliffs, NJ: Prentice-Hall.

Woltz, S.S. and W.E. Waters. 1978. Airborne fluoride effects on some flowering and landscape plants. *HortScience* 13:430-432.

Wright, M. (ed.). 1979. *The Complete Indoor Gardener.* Rev. ed. New York: Random House.

D

Dracaena deremensis 'Janet Craig'

dra-*kie*-na
de-rem-*en*-sis
jah-net krehg

Family Name: **Agavaceae**
Common Name: **Janet Craig Dracaena**

'Janet Craig' is a selection of 'Warneckii.' The species type is native to tropical Africa.

D

DRACAENA DEREMENSIS 'JANET CRAIG'

Production factors

Light. Use production light levels of 2,000 to 3,500 fc (21.6 to 37.8 klx) for acclimatized plants.

Temperature. Maintain root zone temperatures of 75° to 80°F (24° to 27°C) and air temperatures of 70° to 90°F (21° to 32°C) for optimum growth.

Nutrition. At recommended production light levels for acclimatized plants, fertilize with 34.5 pounds per 1000 square feet per year (lb/1000 sq.ft/yr) or 168.4 kilograms per 1000 square meters per year (kg/1000 sq. m/yr) of N-P-K. A N-P-K ratio of 3:1:2 is suggested for use with soilless media, while 1:1:1 is recommended for soil-based media. Avoid fertilizers containing fluoride. Most media require the addition of micronutrients either by preplant incorporation of a granular source or as part of a liquid fertilization program.

Irrigation. Keep the potting medium evenly moist but not wet. Use a water source that is low in fluoride.

Media. Choose a potting medium with good moisture retention and drainage properties. A peat:bark medium (1:1 by volume) provides for these needs well. Maintain pH values within 6.0 to 6.5 to reduce fluoride availability. Amendments should be screened for toxic concentrations of this element before addition to the medium.

Problems.

Diseases that commonly attack Janet Craig dracaena: Leaf spot—*Erwinia carotovora* subsp. *carotovora, Erwinia chrysanthemi;* leaf spot and stem rot—*Fusarium moniliforme.*

Other diseases that attack dracaena, including Janet Craig dracaena: Blight—*Botrytis cinerea, Rhizoctonia microsclerotia, Sclerotium rolfsii;* leaf spot—*Colletotrichum dracaenae, Corynespora cassiicola,*

Dracaena deremensis 'Janet Craig'

dra-*kie*-na
de-rem-*en*-sis
jah-net krehg

Erwinia herbicola, Gloeosporium polymor-phum, Gloeosporium thuemenii, Helm-inthosporium sp., *Phyllosticta dracaenae, Phyllosticta draconis, Phytophthora parasit-ica, Pseudomonas* sp.; stem rot—*Aspergillus niger;* stem and leaf rot—*Phytophthora* sp.

Pests that commonly attack Janet Craig dracaena: Mealybugs; mites; scale; thrips.

Other pests that attack dracaena, includ-ing Janet Craig dracaena: Lesion nema-tode—*Paratylenchus* spp.

Disorders. Temperatures below 70°F (21°C) significantly reduce growth rate. Some exposure to cool conditions is toler-ated depending on temperature and duration. However, damaged tissue develops from chilling injury if Janet Craig dracaena receives 55°F (13°C) for 1 week or 35°F (2°C) for 1 to 2 days.

Janet Craig dracaena is sensitive to fluoride. Symptoms of toxicity include tip chlorosis and necrosis. Very high pH (7.5 to 8.0) values cause iron chlorosis.

Postproduction factors

Light. Transport of plants under dark conditions is currently the most common shipping method. If extended holding is necessary before sale or installation, main-tain Janet Craig dracaena under at least 50 fc (.5 klx) of light. Long-term maintenance under low light produces elongated growth with reduced stem strength. Provide more light if a sprawling growth habit is not desired.

Temperature. Acclimatized plants can be safely shipped when held at 60° to 65°F (16° to 18°C). Avoid exposure to low temperatures during transport.

Gases. Injury due to ethylene is generally not a problem when plants are shipped within the recommended temperature range. Ethylene may reach damaging levels if plants are shipped with produce or held in prolonged storage above the maximum listed temperature.

Lasting qualities. Under appropriate storage conditions acclimatized plants retain good quality when shipped within 2 weeks. Maintain temperatures near the upper end of the recommended range when transport requires only 1 to 7 days.

Care and grooming. Good storage preparation improves quality retention during transit. Moisture content of the potting medium should approximate 50% of soil capacity when plants are packed. Maintain high humidity levels of 80% to 90% during storage to retard desiccation, especially when shipping time exceeds 7 days.

Retail handling

Light. Provide plants with sufficient light upon delivery to recuperate from the stresses of dark storage. A specially designed holding greenhouse or room is ideal. When such a facility is unavailable, maintain Janet Craig dracaena under at least 50 fc (.5 klx) of light. Long-term maintenance under low light produces elongated growth with reduced stem strength. Provide more light if a sprawling growth habit is not desired.

Temperature. Average interior tempera-tures of 65° to 85°F (18° to 29°C) assure good growth and quality maintenance. Occasional brief exposure to cooler tem-peratures of 50° to 60°F (10° to 16°C) is tolerated. When a greenhouse is used to hold plants before installation, maintain 40% to 60% relative humidity for acclimatization to

Dracaena deremensis
'Janet Craig'

dra-*kie*-na
de-rem-*en*-sis
jah-net krehg

lower interior humidity levels.

Irrigation. Keep the potting medium uniformly moist but not wet. Avoid application of water to growth terminals since standing water promotes spread of leaf spot diseases.

Disorders. Janet Craig dracaena develops necrosis of leaf margins when exposed to low humidity and temperatures below 45°F (7°C) during storage. Water stress and fluorinated water cause tipburn and necrosis. Test for soluble salt levels above 1,200 ppm if damage to roots occur.

Consumer care

Temperature. Average interior temperatures of 65° to 85°F (18° to 29°C) assure good growth and quality maintenance. Occasional brief exposure to cooler temperatures of 50° to 60°F (10° to 16°C) is tolerated.

Location. Janet Craig dracaena thrives when installed under bright indirect or curtain-filtered sunlight. This plant also performs quite well under low light, tolerating light levels to 50 fc (.5 klx), but durability and quality retention are improved with 75 to 150 fc (.8 to 1.6 klx).

Irrigation. Keep the potting medium uniformly moist but not wet. Avoid application of water to growth terminals since standing water promotes spread of leaf spot diseases.

Grooming. Fertilize every 6 months or on a schedule that maintains soluble salts below 1,200 ppm. Rootbound plants can be repotted at any season. Rejuvenate old overgrown specimens by pruning stems to any desired height down to 4 to 6 inches (10 to 15 cm). New growth will break from

dormant buds near the cut. Wash foliage periodically with a tepid water shower or damp sponge to remove dust and dirt. Regular cleaning of foliage also aids in control of spider mite populations. Janet Craig dracaena is a durable plant that tolerates interiors well even under low light. Specimens should retain quality indefinitely with good care.

Disorders. Long-term maintenance under low light produces elongated growth with reduced stem strength. Provide more light if a sprawling growth habit is not desired. Water stress and fluorinated water cause tipburn and necrosis. Roots decline in the presence of high soluble salts.

D

ADDITIONAL READING

Bailey, L.H. and E.Z. Bailey. 1976. *Hortus Third.* New York: Macmillan Publishing Co. Inc.

Chase, A.R. 1985. Diseases of foliage plants—Revised list for 1985. *Foliage Digest* 8(6):3-8.

Conover, C.A. and R.T. Poole. 1981. Guide for fertilizing foliage plant crops. *ARC-Apopka Research Rpt.* RH-81-l. University of Florida.

———. 1983. Handling and overseas transportation of acclimatized foliage plants in reefers. *Foliage Digest* 6(5):3-4.

———. 1984. Light and fertilizer recommendations for production of acclimatized potted foliage plants. *Foliage Digest* 7(8):1-6.

———. 1986. Factors influencing shipping of acclimatized foliage plants. *ARC-Apopka Research Rpt.* RH-86-11. University of Florida.

———. 1987. Factors influencing shipping of acclimatized foliage plants. *Foliage Digest* 10(4):1-5.

Crockett, J.U. 1977. *Foliage House Plants.* Revised. Alexandria, VA: Time-Life Books.

Everett, T.H. 1980. *The New York Botanical Garden Illustrated Encyclopedia of Horticulture.* New York: Garland Publishing Inc.

Gaines, R.L. 1977. *Interior Plantscaping: Building Design for Interior Foliage Plants.* New York: Architectural Record Books.

Dracaena deremensis 'Janet Craig'

dra-*kie*-na
de-rem-*en*-sis
jah-net krehg

McConnell, D.B., R.W. Henley and R.L. Biamonte. 1981. Commercial foliage plants. J.N. Joiner (ed.). *Foliage Plant Production.* Englewood Cliffs, NJ: Prentice-Hall.

Poole, R.T., A.R. Chase and L.S. Osborne. 1987. Dracaena 'Warneckii' and 'Janet Craig.' *Foliage Digest* 10(1):1-4.

Staby, G.L., J.L. Robertson and D.C. Kiplinger. 1978. *Chain of Life.* Columbus, OH: Ohio Florists Association.

Sullivan, G.H., J.L. Robertson and G.L. Staby. 1980. Care and handling of foliage plants. *Management for Retail Florists with Applications to Nursery and Garden Centers.* San Francisco: W.H. Freeman and Co.

Wright, M. (ed.). 1979. *The Complete Indoor Gardener.* Rev. ed. New York: Random House.

D

Dracaena deremensis 'Warneckii'

dra-*kie*-na
de-rem-*en*-sis
war-*neck*-ee-eye

Family Name: **Agavaceae**
Common Name: **Warnecki Dracaena, Striped Dracaena**

Originated in tropical Africa.

D

DRACAENA DEREMENSIS 'WARNECKII'

Production factors

Light. Use production light levels of 2,000 to 3,500 fc (21.6 to 37.8 klx) for acclimatized plants.

Temperature. Maintain root zone temperatures of 75° to 80°F (24° to 27°C) and air temperatures of 70° to 90°F (21° to 32°C).

Nutrition. At recommended production light levels for acclimatized plants, fertilize with 34.5 pounds per 1000 square feet per year (lb/1000 sq.ft/yr) or 168.4 kilograms per 1000 square meters per year (kg/1000 sq. m/yr) of N-P-K. A N-P-K ratio of 3:1:2 is suggested for use with soilless media, while 1:1:1 is recommended for soil-based media. Avoid fertilizers containing fluoride. Most media require the addition of micronutrients either by preplant incorporation of a granular source or as part of a liquid fertilization program.

Irrigation. Keep the potting medium evenly moist but not wet. Use a water source that is low in fluoride.

Media. Choose a potting medium with good moisture retention and drainage properties. A peat:bark medium (1:1 by volume) provides for these needs well. Maintain pH values within 6.0 to 6.5 to reduce fluoride availability, and test amendments for toxic concentrations of this element before addition to the medium.

Problems.
Diseases that commonly attack Warnecki dracaena: Leaf spot—*Erwinia carotovora* subsp. *carotovora, Erwinia chrysanthemi;* leaf spot and stem rot—*Fusarium moniliforme.*

Other diseases that attack dracaena, including Warnecki dracaena: Blight—*Botrytis cinerea, Rhizoctonia microsclerotia, Sclerotium rolfsii;* leaf spot—*Colletotrichum dracaenae, Corynespora cassiicola, Erwinia herbicola, Gloeosporium polymor-*

99

Dracaena deremensis 'Warneckii'

dra-*kie*-na
de-rem-*en*-sis
war-*neck*-ee-eye

phum, *Gloeosporium thuemenii, Helminthosporium* sp., *Phyllosticta dracaenae, Phyllosticta draconis, Phytophthora parasitica, Pseudomonas* sp.; stem rot—*Aspergillus niger;* stem and leaf rot—*Phytophthora* sp.

Pests that commonly attack Warnecki dracaena: Mealybugs; mites; scale; thrips.

Other pests that attack dracaena, including Warnecki dracaena: Lesion nematode—*Paratylenchus* spp.

Disorders. Temperatures below 70°F (21°C) significantly reduce growth rate. Some exposure to cool conditions is tolerated depending on temperature and duration. However, tissue destruction from chilling injury appears if Warnecki dracaena receives 55°F (13°C) for 1 week or 35°F (2°C) for 1 to 2 days. Warnecki dracaena develops elongated light to dark brown areas in foliage when exposed to fluoride in water, media and fertilizers. This species is also highly sensitive to airborne fluoride. Dark necrotic blotches appear randomly in white striped areas of the leaf. Very high pH (7.5 to 8.0) values cause iron deficiency. Foliar-applied iron supplement and reduction of pH with acidic fertilizers correct chlorotic appearance. A leaf deformity called notching often occurs when Warnecki dracaena is grown under high light. The base of leaves develop ⅛ to ½ inch-deep serrations perpendicular to the leaf axis.

Postproduction factors

Light. Transport of plants under dark conditions is currently the most common shipping method. Maintain Warnecki dracaena under at least 50 fc (.5 klx) of light if extended holding is necessary before sale or installation.

Temperature. Acclimatized plants can be safely shipped when held at 60° to 65°F (16° to 18°C). Exposure to low temperatures during transport should be avoided.

Gases. Injury due to ethylene is generally not a problem when plants are shipped within the recommended temperature range. Ethylene may reach damaging levels if plants are shipped with produce or held in prolonged storage above the maximum listed temperature.

Lasting qualities. Under appropriate storage conditions acclimatized plants retain good quality when shipped within 2 weeks. Maintain temperatures near the upper end of the recommended range when transport requires only 1 to 7 days.

Care and grooming. Good storage preparation improves quality retention during transit. Moisture content of the potting medium should approximate 50% of soil capacity when plants are packed. Maintain high humidity levels of 80% to 90% during storage to retard desiccation, especially when shipping time exceeds 7 days.

Retail handling

Light. Provide plants with sufficient light upon delivery to recuperate from the stresses of dark storage. A specially designed holding greenhouse or room is ideal. When such a facility is unavailable, maintain Warnecki dracaena under at least 50 fc (.5 klx) of light.

Temperature. Average interior temperatures of 65° to 85°F (18° to 29°C) assure good growth and quality maintenance. Occasional brief exposure to temperatures as low as 45°F (7°C) is tolerated. When a greenhouse is used to hold plants before

D

Dracaena deremensis
'Warneckii'

dra-*kie*-na
de-rem-*en*-sis
war-*neck*-ee-eye

installation, maintain 40% to 60% relative humidity for acclimatization to lower interior humidity levels.

Irrigation. Keep the potting medium uniformly moist but not wet. Avoid application of water to growth terminals since standing water promotes spread of leaf spot diseases.

Disorders. Warnecki dracaena develops necrosis of leaf margins when exposed to low humidity and temperatures below 45°F (7°C) during storage. Water stress and fluorinated water cause tipburn and necrosis. Test for soluble salt levels above 1,200 ppm if damage to roots occurs.

Consumer care

Temperature. Average interior temperatures of 65° to 85°F (18° to 29°C) assure good growth and quality maintenance. Occasional brief exposure to temperatures as low as 45°F (7°C) is tolerated.

Location. Warnecki dracaena thrives when installed under bright indirect or curtain-filtered sunlight. This species also performs quite well under low light, tolerating light levels to 50 fc (.5 klx), but durability and quality retention are improved with 75 to 150 fc (.8 to 1.6 klx).

Irrigation. Keep the potting medium uniformly moist but not wet. Avoid application of water to growth terminals since standing water promotes spread of leaf spot diseases.

Grooming. Fertilize every 6 months or on a schedule that maintains soluble salts below 1,200 ppm. Rootbound plants can be repotted at any season. Rejuvenate old overgrown specimens by pruning stems to

any desired height down to 4 to 6 inches (10 to 15 cm). New growth will break from dormant buds near the cut. Wash foliage periodically with a tepid water shower or damp sponge to remove dust and dirt. Regular cleaning of foliage also aids in control of spider mite populations. Warnecki dracaena is a durable plant that tolerates interiors well even under low light. Specimens should retain quality indefinitely with good care.

Disorders. Warnecki dracaena is highly sensitive to airborne fluoride. Dark necrotic blotches appear randomly in white striped areas of the leaf. Water stress and fluorinated water cause tipburn and necrosis. Roots decline in the presence of high soluble salts.

ADDITIONAL READING
Bailey, L.H. and E.Z. Bailey. 1976. *Hortus Third.* New York: Macmillan Publishing Co. Inc.
Chase, A.R. 1985. Diseases of foliage plants—Revised list for 1985. *Foliage Digest* 8(6):3-8.
Conover, C.A. and R.T. Poole. 1981. Guide for fertilizing foliage plant crops. *ARC-Apopka Research Rpt.* RH-81-1. University of Florida.
———. 1983. Handling and overseas transportation of acclimatized foliage plants in reefers. *Foliage Digest* 6(5):3-4.
———. 1984. Light and fertilizer recommendations for production of acclimatized potted foliage plants. *Foliage Digest* 7(8):1-6.
———. 1986. Factors influencing shipping of acclimatized foliage plants. *ARC-Apopka Research Rpt.* RH-86-11. University of Florida.
———. 1987. Factors influencing shipping of acclimatized foliage plants. *Foliage Digest* 10(4):1-5.
Crockett, J.U. 1977. *Foliage house plants.* Revised. Alexandria, VA: Time-Life Books.
Everett, T.H. 1980. *The New York Botanical Garden Illustrated Encyclopedia of Horticulture.* New York: Garland Publishing Inc.

D

Dracaena deremensis 'Warneckii'

dra-*kie*-na
de-rem-*en*-sis
war-*neck*-ee-eye

Gaines, R.L. 1977. *Interior Plantscaping: building design for interior foliage plants.* New York: Architectural Record Books.

McConnell, D.B., P.W. Henley and R.L. Biamonte. 1981. Commercial foliage plants. J.N. Joiner (ed.). *Foliage plant production.* Englewood Cliffs, NJ: Prentice-Hall.

Poole, R.T., A.R. Chase and L.S. Osborne. 1987. Dracaena 'Warneckii' and 'Janet Craig.' *Foliage Digest* 10(1):1-4.

Staby, G.L., J.L. Robertson and D.C. Kiplinger. 1978. *Chain of Life.* Columbus, OH: Ohio Florists' Association.

Sullivan, G.H., J.L. Robertson and G.L. Staby. 1980. Care and handling of foliage plants. *Management for retail florists with applications to nursery and garden centers.* San Francisco: W.H. Freeman and Co.

Woltz, S.S. and W.E. Waters. 1978. Airborne fluoride effects on some foliage plants. *HortScience* 13:585-586.

Wright, M. (ed.). 1979. *The Complete Indoor Gardener.* Rev. ed. New York: Random House.

D

Dracaena fragrans 'Massangeana'

dra-*kie*-na
frah-granz
mass-ang-ee-*ay*-nuh

D

Family Name: **Agavaceae**
Common Name: **Corn Plant**

Originated in Upper Guinea.

DRACAENA FRAGRANS 'MASSANGEANA'

Production factors

Light. Use production light levels of 3,000 to 3,500 fc (32.4 to 37.8 klx) to provide good interior acclimatization while retaining proper foliage form and color.

Temperature. A temperature range of 65° to 95°F (18° to 35°C) will produce quality growth. Corn plant tolerates some cool weather; however, protect plants from wind if low temperatures cannot be avoided. Maintain temperatures above 55°F (13°C) for best plant health.

Nutrition. At recommended production light levels for acclimatized plants, fertilize with 34.5 pounds per 1000 square feet per year (lb/1000 sq.ft/yr) or 168.4 kilograms per 1000 square meters per year (kg/1000 sq. m/yr) of N-P-K. A N-P-K ratio of 3:1:2 is suggested for use with soilless media, while 1:1:1 is recommended for soil-based media. Plants that receive frequent waterings from rainfall or irrigation systems may need 10% to 20% more fertilizer. However, avoid excessive fertilizer application. Supply a moderate level of micronutrients with 1 pound per cubic yard (.6 kg per cubic m) Micromax or another equivalent source. Check all fertilizers for significant concentrations of fluoride or boron before application.

Irrigation. Keep the medium evenly moist but not wet. Use a water source that is low in fluoride and boron.

Media. The potting medium should support tall, top-heavy canes while retaining good drainage characteristics. Sand is a desirable component to provide necessary weight and support without losing percolation properties. A recommended mixture is 3 peat:1 sand. Maintain pH values within 5.5 to 6.5 to reduce fluoride and boron availability in the medium. Avoid inclusion of any amendment that contains significant amounts of these elements.

Problems.

Diseases that commonly attack corn plant: Leaf spot—*Fusarium moniliforme;* cane and cutting rot—*Erwinia* sp., *Fusarium moniliforme, Fusarium oxysporum.*

Dracaena fragrans 'Massangeana'

dra-*kie*-na
frah-granz
mass-ang-ee-*ay*-nuh

Other diseases that attack dracaena, including corn plant: Blight—*Botrytis cinerea, Rhizoctonia microsclerotia, Sclerotium rolfsii;* leaf spot—*Colletotrichum dracaenae, Corynespora cassiicola, Erwinia carotovora* subsp. *carotovora, Erwinia chrysanthemi, Erwinia herbicola, Gloeosporium polymorphum, Gloeosporium thuemenii, Helminthosporium* sp., *Phyllosticta dracaenae, Phyllosticta draconis, Phytophthora parasitica, Pseudomonas* sp.; soft rot—*Erwinia carotovora* subsp. *carotovora;* stem rot—*Aspergillus niger;* stem and leaf rot—*Phytophthora* sp.

Pests that commonly attack corn plant: Ambrosia beetles; mealybugs; scales; thrips.

Other pests that attack dracaena, including corn plant: Mites; lesion nematode—*Paratylenchus* spp.

Disorders. Plants grown under high light develop pale green, undesirable foliage. Reduced variegation and thin, elongated leaf blades are characteristic of plants produced under low light. Chilling injury can develop if plants are exposed to 35° to 50°F (2° to 10°C) in the presence of wind. Symptoms of damage include light gray to brown leaf margins on mature leaves. New growth may also be affected. A distinct band of injured tissue remains at the point of exposure as developing leaves expand from the whorled terminal. Consistently cool nights, especially in fall and early winter, stimulate the flowering response of corn plant. This natural phenomenon destroys terminal growing points, delays growth production, and significantly alters plant growth habit from the commercially marketed form. Tipburn from high soluble salts reduces plant quality. Corn plant is sensitive to both boron and fluoride. Leaf tips turn a tan color with boron toxicity. Mottling of green leaf

areas progresses to chlorosis and necrosis in the presence of fluoride. Yellow borders separate necrotic and healthy areas. Leaf margins are damaged in the most severe cases. Chlorosis due to iron deficiency occurs when pH values exceed 6.5.

Postproduction factors

Light. Transport of plants under dark conditions is currently the most common shipping method. If extended holding is necessary before sale or installation, maintain corn plant under at least 50 fc (.5 klx) of light. Long-term maintenance under low light reduces foliage variegation and causes leaf elongation. Increase storage light levels to 75 to 150 fc (.8 to 1.6 klx) if change in the growth habit is not desired.

Temperature. Acclimatized plants can be shipped for extended periods when held at 60° to 65°F (16° to 18°C).

Gases. Injury due to ethylene is generally not a problem when plants are shipped within the recommended temperature range. Ethylene may reach damaging levels if plants are shipped with produce or held in prolonged storage above the maximum listed temperature.

Lasting qualities. Under appropriate storage conditions acclimatized plants retain good quality when shipped within 4 weeks. Maintain temperatures near the upper end of the recommended range when transport requires only 1 to 7 days.

Care and grooming. Good storage preparation improves quality retention during transit. Corn plant sometimes suffers from leaf breakdown that is not attributed to ethylene. Leaves become chlorotic or necrotic several days after removal from

Dracaena fragrans 'Massangeana'

dra-*kie*-na
frah-granz
mass-ang-ee-*ay*-nuh

storage. Plants are most affected when produced under high light and fertilizer conditions and when shipped with excessively moist media. Follow recommended production guidelines and ship with moderately moist potting medium. Moisture content of the potting medium should approximate 50% of soil capacity when plants are packed. Corn plant can receive the last watering up to a week before packing so long as the medium is not dry during shipment. Maintain high humidity levels of 80% to 90% during storage to retard desiccation, especially when shipping time exceeds 7 days. Physical damage to cane-form plants can also occur during transit. Avoid leaning canes by using a stable potting medium, developing good roots over all the potted cane portion and using packing spacers to immobilize the plants during shipment.

Retail handling

Light. Provide plants with sufficient light upon delivery to recuperate from the stresses of dark storage. A specially designed holding greenhouse or room is ideal. When such a facility is unavailable, maintain corn plant under at least 50 fc (.5 klx) of light. Increase storage light levels to 75 to 150 fc (.8 to 1.6 klx) if change in the growth habit is not desired during long-term holding.

Temperature. Average interior temperatures of 65° to 85°F (18° to 29°C) assure good growth and quality maintenance. When a greenhouse is used to hold plants before installation, maintain 40% to 60% relative humidity for acclimatization to lower interior humidity levels.

Irrigation. Keep the potting medium

uniformly moist but not wet.

Disorders. Marginal necrosis and terminal growth damage develop with exposure to chilling temperatures. Plants produced under high light and fertilizer conditions and shipped with excessively moist media develop chlorotic or necrotic leaves several days after removal from storage. High concentrations of fluoride or boron cause foliage damage. Loose canes occur when plants are produced in very light media, have poorly developed roots or are not supported during transit. Soluble salt levels above 1,200 ppm promote tipburn. Long-term maintenance under low light reduces foliage variegation and causes leaf elongation.

Consumer care

Temperature. Average interior temperatures of 65° to 85°F (18° to 29°C) assure good growth and quality maintenance.

Location. Corn plant thrives when placed under bright indirect or curtain-filtered sunlight. This plant also performs quite well under low light, tolerating lighting as low as 50 fc (.5 klx); but durability and quality retention are improved with 75 to 150 fc (.8 to 1.6 klx).

Irrigation. Keep the potting medium uniformly moist but not wet.

Grooming. Fertilize every 6 months or on a schedule that maintains soluble salts below 1,200 ppm. Rootbound plants can be repotted at any season. Rejuvenate old overgrown specimens by pruning stems to any desired height down to 4 to 6 inches (10 to 15 cm). New growth will break from dormant buds near the cut. Wash foliage periodically with a tepid water shower or

D

Dracaena fragrans 'Massangeana'

dra-*kie*-na
frah-granz
mass-ang-ee-*ay*-nuh

damp sponge to remove dust and dirt. Regular cleaning of foliage also aids in control of spider mite populations. Corn plant is a durable plant that tolerates interiors well even under low light. Specimens should retain quality indefinitely with good care.

Disorders. Long-term maintenance under low light reduces foliage variegation and causes leaf elongation. High soluble salts and fluorinated water cause foliage damage.

ADDITIONAL READING

Arthurs, Kathryn (ed.). 1974. *How to Grow House Plants*. Menlo Park, CA: Lane Publishing Co.

Bailey, L.H. and E.Z. Bailey. 1976. *Hortus Third*. New York: Macmillan Publishing Co. Inc.

Chase, A.R. 1985. Diseases of foliage plants— Revised list for 1985. *Foliage Digest* 8(6):3-8.

Chase, A.R. and R.T. Poole. 1986. Troubleshooting guide to foliage. *Greenhouse Grower* 4(3):76-77.

Conover, C.A., A.R. Chase and L.S. Osborne. 1986. Corn plant. *Foliage Digest* 9(1):4-6.

Conover, C.A. and R.T. Poole. 1981. Guide for fertilizing foliage plant crops. *ARC-Apopka Research Rpt*. RH-81-1. University of Florida.

———. 1983. Handling and overseas transportation of acclimatized foliage plants in reefers. *Foliage Digest* 6(5):3-4.

———. 1984. Light and fertilizer recommendations for production of acclimatized potted foliage plants. *Foliage Digest* 7(8):1-6.

———. 1986. Factors influencing shipping of acclimatized foliage plants. *ARC-Apopka Research Rpt*. RH-86-11. University of Florida.

———. 1987. Factors influencing shipping of acclimatized foliage plants. *Foliage Digest* 10(4)1-5.

Crockett, J.U. 1977. *Foliage House Plants*. Revised. Alexandria, VA: Time-Life Books.

Everett, T.H. 1980. *The New York Botanical Garden Illustrated Encyclopedia of Horticulture*. New York: Garland Publishing Inc.

Gaines, R.L. 1977. *Interior Plantscaping: Building Design for Interior Foliage Plants*. New York: Architectural Record Books.

McConnell, D.B., R.W. Henley and R.L. Biamonte. 1981. Commercial foliage plants. J.N. Joiner (ed.). *Foliage Plant Production*. Englewood Cliffs, NJ: Prentice-Hall.

Staby, G.L., J.L. Robertson and D.C. Kiplinger. 1978. *Chain of Life*. Columbus, OH: Ohio Florists' Association.

Sullivan, G.H., J.L. Robertson and G.L. Staby. 1980. Care and handling of foliage plants. *Management for Retail Florists with Applications to Nursery and Garden Centers*. San Francisco: W.H. Freeman and Co.

Dracaena marginata

dra-*kie*-na
mar-gi-*nah*-ta

Family Name: **Agavaceae**
Common Name: **Madagascar Dragon Tree, Red-edged Dracaena**

Originated in Madagascar.

D

DRACAENA MARGINATA

Production factors

Light. Use production light levels of 3,000 to 6,000 fc (32.4 to 64.8 klx) to provide interior acclimatization while retaining proper foliage form and color.

Temperature. Provide a minimum greenhouse temperature of 60°F (16°C) for steady growth production at an acceptable level of energy consumption. Loss of quality can be avoided by keeping temperatures above 45°F (7°C).

Nutrition. At recommended production light levels for acclimatized plants, fertilize with 48.3 pounds per 1000 square feet per year (lb/1000 sq.ft/yr) or 235.8 kilograms per 1000 square meters per year (kg/1000 sq. m/yr) of N-P-K. A N-P-K ratio of 3:1:2 is suggested for use with soilless media, while 1:1:1 is recommended for soil-based media. Most media require the addition of micronutrients either by preplant incorporation of a granular source or as part of a liquid fertilization program. Avoid fertilizers containing boron.

Irrigation. Allow the potting medium to dry slightly between thorough waterings. Use a water source that is low in boron.

Media. Choose a potting medium with good drainage properties. Madagascar dragon tree appears to have some tolerance to fluoride compared to other species of dracaena. However, amendments should be screened for significant concentrations of boron before addition to the medium.

Problems.

Diseases that commonly attack Madagascar dragon tree: Leaf spot—*Fusarium moniliforme*.

Other diseases that attack dracaena, including Madagascar dragon tree: Blight—*Botrytis cinerea, Rhizoctonia microsclerotia, Sclerotium rolfsi*; leaf spot—*Colletotrichum dracaenae, Corynespora cassiicola, Erwinia*

Dracaena marginata

dra-*kie*-na
mar-gi-*nah*-ta

carotovora subsp. *carotovora, Erwinia chrysanthemi, Erwinia herbicola, Gloeosporium polymorphum, Gloeosporium thuemenii, Helminthosporium* sp., *Phyllosticta dracaenae, Phyllosticta draconis, Phytophthora parasitica, Pseudomonas* sp.; soft rot—*Erwinia carotovora* subsp. *carotovora;* stem rot—*Aspergillus niger;* stem and leaf rot—*Phytophthora* sp.

Pests that commonly attack Madagascar dragon tree: Florida red scale; mealybugs; mites.

Other pests that attack dracaena, including Madagascar dragon tree: Lesion nematodes—*Paratylenchus* spp.; thrips.

Disorders. Plants grown under high light develop pale green, undesirable foliage. Thin, elongated leaf blades and loss of red coloration occur under low light. Temperatures of 30° to 35°F (-1° to 2°C) produce chlorotic or necrotic banding across leaf blades. Chilling injury becomes apparent only as damaged new growth emerges from the whorled terminal. Flecking sometimes occurs on tips of new growth. These white to yellow spots should green and fade out as growth matures except in severe cases. Low temperature combined with high light produces the most severe symptoms. The best current recommendation to prevent flecking is to avoid stress during growth. Toxic levels of boron cause tan leaf tips. Madagascar dragon tree is sensitive to the fungicide vinclozolin.

Postproduction factors

Light. Transport of plants under dark conditions is currently the most common shipping method. If extended holding is necessary before sale or installation, main-tain Madagascar dragon tree under at least 75 to 100 fc (.8 to 1.1 klx) of light.

Temperature. Acclimatized plants can be shipped without damage for 1 to 14 days when held at 55° to 65°F (13° to 18°C). For longer shipping durations of 15 to 28 days, provide temperatures of 60° to 65°F (16° to 18°C).

Gases. Injury due to ethylene is generally not a problem when plants are shipped within the recommended temperature range. Ethylene may reach damaging levels if plants are shipped with produce or held in prolonged storage above the maximum listed temperature.

Lasting qualities. Under appropriate storage conditions acclimatized plants retain good quality when shipped within 2 weeks. Maintain temperatures near the upper end of the recommended range when transport requires only 1 to 7 days. Quality loss of 25% per week is expected when Madagascar dragon tree is stored for more than 2 weeks.

Care and grooming. Good storage preparation improves quality retention during transit. Moisture content of the potting medium should approximate 50% of soil capacity when plants are packed. Maintain high humidity levels of 80% to 90% during storage to retard desiccation, especially when shipping time exceeds 7 days.

Retail handling

Light. Provide plants with sufficient light upon delivery to recuperate from the stresses of dark storage. A specially designed holding greenhouse or room is ideal. When such a facility is unavailable, maintain Madagascar dragon tree under at least 75 to 100 fc (.8 to 1.1 klx) of light.

Dracaena marginata

dra-*kie*-na
mar-gi-*nah*-ta

Temperature. Maintain average interior temperatures of 65° to 80°F (18° to 27°C) to assure good growth and quality maintenance. When a greenhouse is used to hold plants before installation, maintain 40% to 60% relative humidity for acclimatization to lower interior humidity levels.

Irrigation. Allow the potting medium to dry slightly between thorough waterings.

Disorders. Chilling injury appears as chlorotic or necrotic banding across leaf blades. Damage becomes apparent only as new growth emerges from the whorled terminal. Tipburn may indicate toxic levels of boron in water, media or fertilizers.

Consumer care

Temperature. Average interior temperatures of 65° to 80°F (18° to 27°C) assure good growth and quality maintenance.

Location. Areas that provide bright indirect or curtain-filtered sunlight are ideal for growth, form and color. Madagascar dragon tree can support enough new growth to replace loss of older foliage with 75 to 100 fc (.8 to 1.1 klx) of light. Increase lighting to 200 fc (2.2 klx) for best quality retention.

Irrigation. Allow the potting medium to dry slightly between thorough waterings.

Grooming. Wash foliage periodically with a tepid water shower or damp sponge to remove dust and dirt. Regular cleaning of foliage also aids in control of spider mite populations. Fertilize every 2 months or on a schedule that maintains soluble salt levels below 1,200 ppm. Repot in early spring only when the plant becomes quite rootbound. Large specimens grow very slowly and can tolerate several years in the same pot if some of the surface medium is replaced with a fresh supply each spring. Rejuvenate old overgrown specimens by pruning stems to any desired height down to 4 to 6 inches (10 to 15 cm). New growth will break from dormant buds near the cut. Madagascar dragon tree is a slow growing, enduring plant that tolerates interiors well even under hostile conditions. Specimens should retain quality indefinitely with good care.

Disorders. Tipburn may indicate toxic levels of boron in water, media or fertilizers.

Cultivars. Dracaena marginata 'Tricolor' (rainbow tree) is similar to the species type in growth habit and has foliage with colorful stripes of green, cream and rose pink. Rainbow tree tolerates interiors well but requires good light conditions for best results.

ADDITIONAL READING

Bailey, L.H. and E.Z. Bailey. 1976. *Hortus Third.* New York: Macmillan Publishing Co. Inc.

Chase, A.R. 1985. Diseases of foliage plants—Revised list for 1985. *Foliage Digest* 8(6):3-8.

Chase, A.R. and R.T. Poole. 1986. Troubleshooting guide to foliage. *Greenhouse Grower* 4(7):104-105.

Conover, C.A. and R.T. Poole. 1981. Guide for fertilizing foliage plant crops. *ARC-Apopka Research Rpt.* RH-81-1. University of Florida.

———. 1983. Handling and overseas transportation of acclimatized foliage plants in reefers. *Foliage Digest* 6(5):3-4.

———. 1984. Light and fertilizer recommendations for production of acclimatized potted foliage plants. *Foliage Digest* 7(8):1-6.

———. 1986. Factors influencing shipping of acclimatized foliage plants. *ARC-Apopka Research Rpt.* RH-86-11. University of Florida.

———. 1987. Factors influencing shipping of acclimatized foliage plants. *Foliage Digest* 10(4):1-5.

Crockett, J.U. 1977. *Foliage House Plants.* Revised. Alexandria, VA: Time-Life Books.

D

D

Everett, T.H. 1980. *The New York Botanical Garden Illustrated Encyclopedia of Horticulture*. New York: Garland Publishing Inc.

Florists' Transworld Delivery. 1985. *The Indoor Gardener*. Southfield, MI.

Gaines, R.L. 1977. *Interior Plantscaping: Building Design for Interior Foliage Plants*. New York: Architectural Record Books.

McConnell, D.B., R.W. Henley and R.L. Biamonte. 1981. Commercial foliage plants. J.N. Joiner (ed.). *Foliage Plant Production*. Englewood Cliffs, NJ: Prentice-Hall.

Poole, R.T. and C.A. Conover. 1986. Boron and fluoride toxicity of foliage plants. *Foliage Digest* 9(3):3-6.

————. 1987. Foliage variety determines heat. *Greenhouse Grower* 5(1):21-22.

Staby, G.L., J.L. Robertson and D.C. Kiplinger. 1978. *Chain of Life*. Columbus, OH: Ohio Florists' Association.

Sullivan, G.H., J.L. Robertson and G.L. Staby. 1980. Care and handling of foliage plants. *Management for Retail Florists with Applications to Nursery and Garden Centers*. San Francisco: W.H. Freeman and Co.

Wright, M. (ed.). 1979. *The Complete Indoor Gardener*. Rev. ed. New York: Random House.

Dracaena sanderana

dra-*kie*-na
san-der-*ay*-nah

Family Name: **Agavaceae**
Common Name: **Ribbon Plant, Belgian Evergreen**

Originated in Cameroons.

D

DRACAENA SANDERANA

Production factors

Light. Use production light levels of 1,500 to 3,500 fc (16.2 to 37.8 klx) for acclimatized plants.

Nutrition. At recommended production light levels for acclimatized plants, fertilize with 34.5 pounds per 1000 square feet per year (lb/1000 sq.ft/yr) or 168.4 kilograms per 1000 square meters per year (kg/1000 sq. m/yr) of N-P-K. A N-P-K ratio of 3:1:2 is suggested for use with soilless media, while 1:1:1 is recommended for soil-based media. Most media require the addition of micronutrients either by preplant incorporation of a granular source or as part of a liquid fertilization program.

Irrigation. Keep the potting medium evenly moist but not wet.

Media. Choose a potting medium with good drainage characteristics.

Problems.

Diseases that attack dracaena, including ribbon plant: Blight—*Botrytis cinerea, Rhizoctonia microsclerotia, Sclerotium rolfsii;* leaf spot—*Colletotrichum dracaenae, Corynespora cassiicola, Erwinia carotovora* subsp. *carotovora, Erwinia chrysanthemi, Erwinia herbicola, Gloeosporium polymorphum, Gloeosporium thuemenii, Helminthosporium* sp., *Phyllosticta dracaenae, Phyllosticta draconis, Phytophthora parasitica, Pseudomonas* sp.; leaf spot and stem rot—*Fusarium moniliforme;* soft rot—*Erwinia carotovora* subsp. *carotovora;* stem rot—*Aspergillus niger;* stem and leaf rot—*Phytophthora* sp.

Pests that commonly attack ribbon plant: Mealybugs; mites.

Other pests that attack dracaena, including ribbon plant: Lesion nematodes—*Paratylenchus* spp.; thrips.

Postproduction factors

Light. Transport of plants under dark conditions is currently the most common shipping method. Maintain ribbon plant under 75 to 150 fc (.8 to 1.6 klx) of light if extended holding is necessary before sale or installation.

Temperature. Plants can be shipped safely at temperatures of 60° to 70°F (16° to 21°C).

111

Gases. Tipburn and yellow or necrotic leaf spots indicate exposure to fluoride during transit.

Lasting qualities. Under appropriate storage conditions acclimatized plants retain good quality without yellowing of lower leaves when shipped within a week.

Care and grooming. Provide relative humidity levels of 65% to 85% during storage.

Retail handling

Light. Provide plants with sufficient light upon delivery to recuperate from the stresses of dark storage. If extended holding is necessary before sale or installation, maintain ribbon plant under 75 to 150 fc (.8 to 1.6 klx) of light.

Temperature. Maintain average interior temperatures of 65° to 85°F (18° to 29°C) to assure good growth and quality maintenance. Occasional brief exposure to temperatures as low as 50°F (10°C) is tolerated.

Irrigation. Keep the potting medium uniformly moist but not wet.

Disorders. Chilling injury can occur under the combination of low temperature (below 45°F; 7°C) and low humidity. Damage appears as leaf margin necrosis. Tipburn and yellow or necrotic leaf spots indicate exposure to fluoride during transit. Interior quality is reduced when soluble salt levels exceed 1,200 ppm in the medium.

Consumer care

Temperature. Maintain average interior temperatures of 65° to 85°F (18° to 29°C) to assure good growth and quality maintenance. Occasional brief exposure to temperatures as low as 50°F (10°C) is tolerated.

Location. Ribbon plant thrives in areas with bright indirect or curtain-filtered sunlight. However, plants retain good quality with low light levels of 75 to 150 fc (.8 to 1.6 klx).

Irrigation. Keep the potting medium uniformly moist but not wet.

Grooming. Fertilize every 6 months or on a schedule that maintains soluble salts below 1,200 ppm. Rootbound plants can be repotted at any season. Plant several stems per pot if a massed effect is desired. Old overgrown specimens can be rejuvenated by pruning stems close to the soil surface and encouraging new growth from buds near the cut. Wash foliage periodically with a tepid water shower or damp sponge to remove dust and dirt. Regular cleaning of foliage also aids in control of spider mite populations. Ribbon plant is a durable plant that tolerates interiors well even under low light. Although specimens eventually become leggy and require rejuvenation or replacement, they provide interesting form and color for a long time with low maintenance demands.

Disorders. Water stress and fluorinated water cause tipburn. Interior quality is reduced by high soluble salts in the medium.

Dracaena sanderana

dra-*kie*-na
san-der-*ay*-nah

ADDITIONAL READING

Bailey, L.H. and E.Z. Bailey. 1976. *Hortus Third.* New York: Macmillan Publishing Co. Inc.

Chase, A.R. 1985. Diseases of foliage plants— Revised list for 1985. *Foliage Digest* 8(6):3-8.

Conover, C.A. and R.T. Poole. 1981. Guide for fertilizing foliage plant crops. *ARC-Apopka Research Rpt.* RH-81-1. University of Florida.

———. 1984. Light and fertilizer recommendations for production of acclimatized potted foliage plants. *Foliage Digest* 7(8):1-6.

Crockett, J.U. 1977. *Foliage House Plants.* Revised. Alexandria, VA: Time-Life Books.

Everett, T.H. 1980. *The New York Botanical Garden Illustrated Encyclopedia of Horticulture.* New York: Garland Publishing Inc.

Holstead, C.L. 1985. *Care and Handling of Flowers and Plants.* Floralife Inc. Society of American Florists. Alexandria, VA.

McConnell, D.B., R.W. Henley and R.L. Biamonte. 1981. Commercial foliage plants. J.N. Joiner (ed.). *Foliage Plant Production.* Englewood Cliffs, NJ: Prentice Hall Inc.

Staby, G.L., J.L. Robertson and D.C. Kiplinger. 1978. *Chain of Life.* Columbus, OH: Ohio Florists' Association.

Sullivan, G.H., J.L. Robertson and G.L. Staby. 1980. Care and handling of foliage plants. *Management for Retail Florists with Applications to Nursery and Garden Centers.* San Francisco: W.H. Freeman and Co.

Wright, M. (ed.). 1979. *The Complete Indoor Gardener.* Rev. ed. New York: Random House.

Epipremnum aureum

e-pi-*prem*-num
ow-ree-um

Family Name: **Araceae**
Common Name: **Pothos, Golden Pothos**

Originated in Solomon Islands. Previous names were *Pothos aureus*; *Raphidophora aurea*; *Scindapsus aureus*.

EPIPREMNUM AUREUM

Production factors

Light. Use production light levels of 1,500 to 3,000 fc (16.2 to 32.4 klx) for acclimatized plants.

Temperature. Provide greenhouse temperatures of at least 65° to 70°F (18° to 21°C) to promote good growth. Occasional cool conditions are tolerated, but temperatures above 50° (10°C) are preferred to avoid quality loss.

Nutrition. At recommended production light levels for acclimatized plants, fertilize with 34.5 pounds per 1000 square feet per year (lb/1000 sq.ft/yr) or 168.4 kilograms per 1000 square meters per year (kg/1000 sq. m/yr) of N-P-K. A N-P-K ratio of 3:1:2 is suggested for use with soilless media, while 1:1:1 is recommended for soil-based media. Most media require the addition of micronutrients either by preplant incorporation of a granular source or as part of a liquid fertilization program.

Irrigation. Allow the medium to dry slightly between waterings. Avoid extremely wet or dry soil conditions.

Media. Provide a potting medium with good drainage characteristics to avoid root rot.

Problems.

Diseases: Anthracnose—*Glomerella cingulata;* blight—*Botrytis cinerea, Sclerotium rolfsii;* leaf spot—*Cercospora richardiaecola, Erwinia* spp., *Phyllosticta* sp., *Pseudomonas cichorii, Rhizoctonia solani;* leaf rot—*Colletotrichum* sp.; root rot—*Phytophthora* sp., *Pythium splendens;* soft rot—*Erwinia aroideae, Erwinia carotovora* subsp. *carotovora*; stem rot—*Rhizoctonia solani.*

Pests: Mealybugs; mites; root knot nematodes—*Meloidogyne* spp.; root mealybugs; scale; thrips.

Disorders. Chilling injury can occur if temperatures fall below 50°F (10°C) for 12 hours or more.

Epipremnum aureum

e-pi-*prem*-num
ow-ree-um

Postproduction factors

Light. Transport of plants under dark conditions is currently the most common method of shipping. If immediate delivery is not possible, maintain pothos under at least 50 fc (.5 klx) of light. Increase light levels to 150 to 250 fc (1.6 to 2.7 klx) if change in growth habit is not desired during long-term holding.

Temperature. Recommended temperatures for shipping are 55° to 60°F (13° to 16°C).

Gases. Foliage discoloration develops when ethylene levels exceed 2 ppm. Avoid exposure to fruits and vegetables during storage and to shipping temperatures above recommended levels.

Lasting qualities. Under appropriate storage conditions acclimatized plants retain good quality when shipping time does not exceed 2 weeks. Maintain temperatures near the upper end of the recommended range when transport requires only 1 to 7 days. Severe quality loss is expected when plants require more than 2 weeks to reach their destination.

Care and grooming. Good storage preparation improves quality retention during transit. Moisture content of the potting medium should approximate 50% of soil capacity when plants are packed. Pothos is highly susceptible to waterborne diseases. Control of these organisms during transit is improved if foliage remains dry when packed. Maintain high humidity levels of 80% to 90% during storage to retard desiccation, especially when shipping time exceeds 7 days.

Retail handling

Light. Provide plants with sufficient light upon delivery to recuperate from the stresses of dark storage. A specially designed holding greenhouse or room is ideal. When such a facility is unavailable, light levels of 150 to 250 fc (1.6 to 2.7 klx) are recommended for quality retention in interior locations. However, pothos can survive under 50 fc (.5 klx) of light.

Temperature. Normal interior temperatures of 65° to 80°F (18° to 27°C) support growth and quality retention. When a greenhouse is used to hold plants before installation, maintain 40% to 60% relative humidity for acclimatization to lower interior humidity levels.

Irrigation. Allow the potting medium to dry slightly between waterings to avoid development of root rot diseases. Tests indicate that pothos responds well to weekly irrigations during winter. More frequent waterings may become necessary during warm seasons.

Disorders. Long-term maintenance under marginal lighting reduces foliage variegation and causes stem elongation and leaf size reduction. Foliage becomes discolored when exposed to toxic concentrations of ethylene during storage. Water stress stimulates leaf drop primarily of older foliage.

Consumer care

Temperature. Normal interior temperatures of 65° to 80°F (18° to 27°C) support growth and quality retention.

Location. Plants flourish when installed under bright indirect or curtain-filtered

E

sunlight. Pothos tolerates low light levels to 50 fc (.5 klx), but compact growth habit and variegation are better maintained under 150 to 250 fc (1.6 to 2.7 klx).

Irrigation. Allow the potting medium to dry slightly between waterings to avoid development of root rot diseases. Tests indicate that pothos responds well to weekly irrigations during winter. More frequent waterings may become necessary during warm seasons.

Grooming. Pinch stems back whenever they become too long for a given space. Stem cuttings can be rooted at any time of the year. Fertilize every 4 months. Avoid buildup of high soluble salts by leaching or repotting in fresh media if necessary. Pothos is tolerant to a wide range of interior conditions and will maintain quality indefinitely with good care.

Disorders. Long-term maintenance under marginal lighting reduces foliage variegation and causes stem elongation and leaf size reduction. Water stress stimulates leaf drop primarily of older foliage.

Cultivars. *Epipremnum aureum* 'Marble Queen' (Marble Queen pothos) foliage is white to cream with flecks and blotches of green to gray-green. Petioles are ivory-colored and stems are striped with green.

ADDITIONAL READING

Bailey, L.H. and E.Z. Bailey. 1976. *Hortus Third.* New York: Macmillan Publishing Co. Inc.

Chase, A.R. 1985. Diseases of foliage plants— Revised list for 1985. *Foliage Digest* 8(6):3-8.

Conover, C.A. and R.T. Poole. 1981. Guide for fertilizing foliage plant crops. *ARC-Apopka Research Rpt.* RH-81-1. University of Florida.

———. 1984. Light and fertilizer recommendations for production of acclimatized potted foliage plants. *Foliage Digest* 7(8):1-6.

———. 1987. Factors influencing shipping of acclimatized foliage plants. *Foliage Digest* 10(4):1-5.

Crockett, J.U. 1977. *Foliage House Plants.* Revised. Alexandria, VA: Time-Life Books.

Florists' Transworld Delivery. 1985. *The Indoor Gardener.* Southfield, MI.

Gaines, R.L. 1977. *Interior Plantscaping: Building Design for Interior Foliage Plants.* New York: Architectural Record Books.

McConnell, D.B., R.W. Henley and R.L. Biamonte. 1981. Commercial foliage plants. J.N. Joiner (ed.). *Foliage Plant Production.* Englewood Cliffs, NJ: Prentice-Hall.

Poole, R.T. and A.R. Chase. 1987. Response of foliage plants in an interior environment to irrigation frequencies. *Foliage Digest* 10(6):1-3.

Poole, R.T. and C.A. Conover. 1986. Growth of foliage plants at infrequent low night temperatures. *Foliage Digest* 9(2):7-8.

———. 1987. Foliage variety determines heat. *Greenhouse Grower* 5(1):21-22.

Sullivan, G.H., J.L. Robertson and G.L. Staby. 1980. Care and handling of foliage plants. *Management for Retail Florists with Applications to Nursery and Garden Centers.* San Francisco: W.H. Freeman and Co.

Fatsia japonica

fats-ee-a
ja-*pon*-i-ka

Family Name: **Araliaceae**
Common Name: **Japanese Fatsia**

Originated in Japan. Previous names were *Aralia japonica* and *Aralia siboldii* .

FATSIA JAPONICA

Production factors

Light. Commercial production light levels of 4,000 to 6,000 fc (43.2 to 64.8 klx) are reported for Japanese fatsia, which is more commonly used as a landscape ornamental in mild temperate climates. Recent studies indicate that shade-grown plants (47% to 64% shade) can maintain satisfactory quality under interior conditions. Alternaria leaf spot disease is also less severe when plants are grown under moderately heavy shade of 73% (1,000 fc; 10.8 klx) compared to 47% shade (3,000 fc; 32.4 klx). These results suggest that production of Japanese fatsia for interior use has good potential.

Temperature. Japanese fatsia tolerates cool conditions well. Provide greenhouse temperatures of 50°F (10°C) or more for good growth.

Nutrition. At recommended production light levels, fertilize with 34.5 pounds per 1000 square feet per year (lb/1000 sq.ft/yr) or 168.4 kilograms per 1000 square meters per year (kg/1000 sq. m/yr) of N-P-K.

Irrigation. Allow the medium to dry slightly between waterings.

Media. Provide a potting medium with good drainage characteristics to avoid root rot.

Problems.

Diseases: Anthracnose—*Colletotrichum* sp.; blight—*Rhizoctonia solani, Sclerotium rolfsii;* leaf spot—*Alternaria panax, Cercospora* sp., *Phyllosticta* sp., *Pseudomonas cichorii, Xanthomonas campestris* pv. *hederae;* root rot—*Pythium splendens;* stem rot—*Phytophthora parasitica.*

Pests: Aphids; mealybugs; mites; scale; thrips.

F

Fatsia japonica

Postproduction factors

Light. Transport of plants under dark conditions is currently the most common method of shipping. If immediate delivery is not possible, provide at least 100 fc (1.1 klx) of light. Increase storage light to 150 to 250 fc (1.6 to 2.7 klx) if change in growth habit is not desired during long-term holding.

Retail handling

Light. Provide plants with sufficient light upon delivery to recuperate from the stresses of dark storage. Where extended holding is necessary before sale or installation, maintain light levels of 150 to 250 fc (1.6 to 2.7 klx) to preserve quality. Japanese fatsia survives under 100 fc (1.1 klx) of light, but higher light levels improve durability and form.

Temperature. Japanese fatsia prefers somewhat cooler temperatures than tropical species. Maintain good quality with interior temperatures of 62° to 70°F (17° to 21°C). Plants perform well even when night temperatures fall as low as 45° to 50°F (7° to 10°C).

Irrigation. Allow the potting medium to dry slightly between waterings to avoid development of root rot diseases.

Disorders. Long-term holding under low light produces weak, elongated growth. Overwatering promotes lower leaf abscission.

Consumer care

Temperature. Japanese fatsia prefers somewhat cooler temperatures than tropical species. Maintain good quality with interior temperatures of 62° to 70°F (17° to 21°C). Plants perform well even when night temperatures fall as low as 45° to 50°F (7° to 10°C).

Location. Interior locations with bright indirect light or some direct sunlight are ideal for growth and quality retention. Japanese fatsia tolerates low light to 100 fc (1.1 klx), but a more typical growth habit is retained under 150 to 250 fc (1.6 to 2.7 klx).

Irrigation. Allow the potting medium to dry slightly between waterings to avoid development of root rot diseases.

Grooming. The flowers are not especially ornamental, so floral buds can be removed to encourage larger foliage. Early spring is the best time to groom this temperate climate plant. Repot overcrowded plants and prune before new growth begins. Basal suckers can be removed at this time for propagation purposes. Fertilize in early spring and early summer.

Disorders. Long-term holding under low light produces weak, elongated growth. Overwatering promotes lower leaf abscission.

Cultivars. *Fatsia japonica* 'Variegata' (variegated Japanese fatsia) leaves are green with cream white margins.

x *Fatshedera lizei* (aralia ivy) is a hybrid of fatsia and hedera that can reach 8 feet (2.4 m) or more on weak-stemmed growth. The glossy, leathery leaves are approximately 8 inches (20 cm) long and 12 inches (30 cm) wide.

F

Fatsia japonica

x *Fatshedera lizei* 'Variegata' (variegated fatshedera) is similar to the monochrome hybrid but has leaves edged in white.

ADDITIONAL READING

Bailey, L.H. and E.Z. Bailey. 1976. *Hortus Third.* New York: Macmillan Publishing Co. Inc.

Chase, A.R. 1985. Diseases of foliage plants— Revised list for 1985. *Foliage Digest* 8(6):3-8.

Chase, A.R. and R.T. Poole. 1987. Factors affecting growth of Fatsia. *Foliage Digest* 10(1):8.

Crockett, J.U. 1977. *Foliage House Plants.* Revised. Alexandria, VA: Time-Life Books.

Gaines, R.L. 1977. *Interior Plantscaping: Building Design for Interior Foliage Plants.* New York: Architectural Record Books.

Keever, G.J. and G.S. Cobb. 1986. Temperate zone woody plants for interior environments. *J. Environ. Hort.* 4(1):16-18.

McConnell, D.B., R.W. Henley and R.L. Biamonte. 1981. Commercial foliage plants. J.N. Joiner (ed.). *Foliage Plant Production.* Englewood Cliffs, NJ: Prentice-Hall.

F

Ficus benjamina

fee-kus
ben-ja-*meen*-a

Family Name: **Moraceae**
Common Name: **Weeping Fig, Benjamin Tree, Weeping Laurel**

Originated in India, Southeast Asia, Malay Archipelago, northern tropical Australia.

FICUS BENJAMINA

Production factors

Light. Use production light levels of 4,000 to 6,000 fc (43.2 to 64.8 klx) for acclimatized plants. Regulation of production light is especially important to the finished appearance and potential interior quality retention of weeping fig. Plants grown under shade have a loose growth habit and large, thin, dark green leaves held out in a horizontal manner to efficiently capture light. Sun-grown plants have stout trunks and bushy canopies of thick, light green leaves that hang vertically

to protect the leaf surface from intense light. Shade-grown plants demonstrate less leaf loss and maintain quality better than sun-grown plants when placed indoors under marginal light situations. Weeping fig can be produced under full sun and then held under shaded conditions until the foliage is fully acclimatized where planting designs call for large, tree-form specimens with considerable trunk caliper. This process can take more than six months with large trees, and full conditioning requires total replacement of foliage with shade-grown leaves. With careful attention these converted plants maintain good quality except under marginal light situations. Lasting quality is preserved best when production light decisions are based on the interior light conditions that specimens will encounter.

Nutrition. At recommended production light levels for acclimatized plants, fertilize with 48.3 pounds per 1000 square feet per year (lb/1000 sq.ft/yr) or 235.8 kilograms per 1000 square meters per year (kg/1000 sq. m/yr) of N-P-K. A N-P-K ratio of 3:1:2 is suggested for use with soilless media, while 1:1:1 is recommended for soil-based media. Most media require the addition of micronutrients either by preplant incorporation of a granular source or as part of a liquid fertilization program. Current recommendations for boron are .5 pounds per acre per year (lb/A/yr) or 1.84 ounces per 1000

F

square feet per year (oz/1000 sq. ft/yr) or 56.1 grams per 1000 square meters per year (g/1000 sq. m/yr). Adjust application concentrations where this element is naturally abundant.

Irrigation. The medium should be allowed to dry slightly between waterings. Avoid extremely wet or dry soil conditions. Use irrigation water with less than 0.5 ppm boron concentration.

Media. Choose a potting medium with good drainage characteristics. Regulate pH values within 6.0 to 6.5 to reduce availability of boron in the medium.

Problems.

Diseases: Blight—*Sclerotium rolfsii;* dieback—*Diplodia* sp., *Phomopsis* sp.; crown gall—*Agrobacterium tumefaciens;* leaf spot—*Corynespora cassiicola;* wilt—*Verticillium albo-atrum.*

Pests: Aphids; chewing insects; mealybugs; mites; lesion nematodes—*Paratylenchus* spp.; scale; thrips; whitefly.

Disorders. Plants grown in constantly wet media are not prepared for drier conditions found in interiors. Conversely, severe water stress stimulates leaf abscission and reduces plant growth. Weeping fig reacts to excessive amounts of boron. Symptoms of toxicity progress from leaf chlorosis to necrosis as the concentration increases.

Postproduction factors

Light. Transport of plants under dark conditions is currently the most common method of shipping. If immediate delivery is not possible, place weeping fig in a holding greenhouse or room with at least 150 to 250 fc (1.6 to 2.7 klx). Weeping fig tolerates low light levels of 75 to 100 fc (.8 to 1.1 klx),

but long-term maintenance at this level is stressful, particularly after extended storage. Leaf abscission can be significant even in acclimatized plants. Increase light duration to 24 hours and use a combination of cool white fluorescent and incandescent lamps if light intensity must remain low. Light from incandescent lamps penetrates the foliage canopy better than fluorescent light, while light from fluorescent lamps maintains a higher chlorophyll content in the leaves.

Temperature. Acclimatized plants can be shipped without damage for extended periods when held at 55° to 60°F (13° to 16°C).

Gases. Injury due to ethylene is generally not a problem when plants are shipped within the recommended temperature range. Ethylene may reach damaging levels if plants are shipped with produce or held in prolonged storage above the maximum listed temperature.

Lasting qualities. Under appropriate storage conditions acclimatized plants retain good quality when shipped within 4 weeks. Maintain temperatures near the upper end of the recommended range when transport requires only 1 to 7 days.

Care and grooming. Good storage preparation improves quality retention during transit. Moisture content of the potting medium should approximate 50% of soil capacity when plants are packed. Maintain high humidity levels of 80% to 90% during storage to retard desiccation, especially when shipping time exceeds 7 days.

Retail handling

Light. Provide plants with sufficient light upon delivery to recuperate from the stresses of dark storage. A specially designed

Ficus benjamina

fee-kus
ben-ja-*meen*-a

holding greenhouse or room is ideal. When such a facility is unavailable, light levels of 150 to 250 fc (1.6 to 2.7 klx) are recommended for quality retention. Weeping fig survives under 75 to 100 fc (.8 to 1.1 klx) of light, but leaf loss occurs over time. Increase light duration to 24 hours and use a combination of cool white fluorescent and incandescent lamps if light intensity must remain low. Light from incandescent lamps penetrates the foliage canopy better than fluorescent light, while light from fluorescent lamps maintains a higher chlorophyll content in the leaves.

Temperature. Normal interior temperatures of 65° to 80°F (18° to 27°C) support growth and quality retention. Occasional brief exposure to cool temperatures (to 50°F; 10°C) is tolerated. When a greenhouse is used to hold plants before installation, maintain 40% to 60% relative humidity for acclimatization to lower interior humidity levels.

Irrigation. Keep the potting medium moist but not wet. Allow the surface to dry slightly between waterings.

Disorders. Prolonged exposure to temperature extremes during storage can significantly reduce plant quality by chilling injury or desiccation. Leaf loss is the most common problem encountered after shipping and may be caused by protracted storage in the dark, exposure to temperature extremes, low humidity, water stress or inadequate acclimatization conditioning. Quality loss also occurs if retailers hold plants under insufficient light after delivery. Response to low light may require 6 weeks or more to become noticeable, but leaf abscission can be significant even in acclimatized plants.

Consumer care

Temperature. Provide normal interior temperatures of 65° to 80°F (18° to 27°C) to support growth and quality retention. Occasional brief exposure to cool temperatures (to 50°F; 10°C) is tolerated.

Location. Weeping fig thrives when installed under bright indirect or curtain-filtered sunlight but also performs well under interior lighting when properly acclimatized. Good quality is preserved under 150 to 250 fc (1.6 to 2.7 klx) of light. Low light levels of 75 to 100 fc (.8 to 1.1 klx) are tolerated, but quality maintenance becomes more difficult.

Irrigation. Keep the potting medium moist but not wet. Allow the surface to dry slightly between waterings.

Grooming. Repot only when growth becomes stunted from overcrowded roots. Early spring is a good time to repot and prune vigorous plants. Prune to keep the size and shape appropriate for the location and container. Fertilize every 2 to 6 months depending on the size and health of the specimen. Intense maintenance is required to keep a healthy appearance under low light. The canopy becomes loose and open. This change in growth habit can be enhanced with removal of dead branches to keep a neat appearance. Prune long branches back to force new growth to the center of the plant canopy if a more bushy habit is desired. Overwatering is a serious problem under low light because the roots are less active. Strict monitoring of water use controls excess moisture. Methods that speed media drying include repotting into porous containers and gradual reduction of the soil ball as roots recede. Weeping fig can maintain quality indoors for a very long time if good care is provided.

Disorders. Leaf abscission increases and growth habit becomes more loose and open when plants are placed under low light. *Phomopsis* spp. are weak pathogens that cause little damage under normal production conditions but attack plants under stress especially in low interior light situations. Symptoms include progressive dieback of twigs and defoliation. Leaf drop occurs after installation occasionally for no apparent cultural reason. Mercury vapor from interior paints can be the culprit.

ADDITIONAL READING

Bailey, L.H. and E.Z. Bailey. 1976. *Hortus Third.* New York: Macmillan Publishing Co. Inc.

Benschop, K., J.P Tewari and E.W. Toop. 1985. Phomopsis twig die-back of some woody interior ornamentals in Alberta. *Foliage Digest* 8(9):2-3

Chase, A.R. 1985. Diseases of foliage plants—Revised list for 1985. *Foliage Digest* 8(6):3-8.

Collins, P.C. and T.M. Blessington. 1982. Postharvest effects of dark storage, light duration, and source on keeping quality of *Ficus benjamina* L. *HortScience* 17:906-908.

———. 1982. Postharvest effects of various light sources and duration on keeping quality of *Ficus benjamina* L. *HortScience* 17:908-909.

———. 1983. Postharvest effects of shipping temperatures and subsequent interior keeping quality of *Ficus benjamina. HortScience* 18:757-758.

———. 1985. Keeping quality of *Ficus benjamina* as affected by production light levels and postproduction light quality and level. *HortScience* 20:390-391.

Conover, C.A. and R.T. Poole. 1977. Effects of cultural practices on acclimatization of *Ficus benjamina* L. *J. Amer. Soc. Hort. Sci.* 102:529-531.

———. 1981. Guide for fertilizing foliage plant crops. *ARC-Apopka Research Rpt.* RH-81-1. University of Florida.

———. 1984. Light and fertilizer recommendations for production of acclimatized potted foliage plants. *Foliage Digest* 7(8):1-6.

———. 1987. Factors influencing shipping of acclimatized foliage plants. *Foliage Digest* 10(4):1-5.

Crockett, J.U. 1977. Foliage House Plants. Revised. Alexandria, VA: Time-Life Books.

Fails, B.S., A.J. Lewis and J.A. Barden. 1982. Anatomy and morphology of sun- and shade-grown *Ficus benjamina. J. Amer. Soc. Hort. Sci.* 107:754-757.

Florists' Transworld Delivery Association. 1985. The Indoor Gardener. Southfield, MI.

Gaines, R.L. 1977. *Interior Plantscaping: Building Design for Interior Foliage Plants.* New York: Architectural Record Books.

Hamilton, David L. 1985. Low light care. *Interiorscape* 4(6):10.

Holstead, C.L. 1985. *Care and handling of flowers and plants.* Floralife Inc. Society of American Florists. Alexandria, VA.

Johnson, C.R., D.L. Ingram and J.E. Barrett. 1981. Effects of irrigation frequency on growth, transpiration, and acclimatization of *Ficus benjamina. HortScience* 16:80-81.

McConnell, D.B., R.W. Henley and R.L. Biamonte. 1981. Commercial foliage plants. J.N. Joiner (ed.). *Foliage Plant Production.* Englewood Cliffs, NJ: Prentice-Hall Inc.

Peterson, J.C., J.N. Sacalis and D.J. Durkin. 1980. Promotion of leaf abscission in intact *Ficus benjamina* by exposure to water stress. *J. Amer. Soc. Hort. Sci.* 105:788-793.

Peterson, N.C. and T.M. Blessington. 1981. Postharvest effects of dark storage and light source on keeping quality of *Ficus benjamina* L. *HortScience* 16:681-682.

Poole, R.T. and C.A. Conover. 1986. Boron and fluoride toxicity of foliage plants. *Foliage Digest* 9(3):3-6.

———. 1987. Response of foliage plants to commercial interior paints. *Foliage Digest* 10(1):4-5.

F

Ficus elastica 'Decora'

fee-kus
e-*las*-ti-ka
de-*kor*-uh

Family Name: **Moraceae**
Common Name: **India Rubber Tree, Rubber Plant**

Originated in Nepal to Assam and Burma.

FICUS ELASTICA 'DECORA'

Production factors

Light. Use production light levels of 5,000 to 8,000 fc (54 to 86.4 klx) for acclimatized plants.

Nutrition. At recommended production light levels for acclimatized plants, fertilize with 48.3 pounds per 1000 square feet per year (lb/1000 sq.ft/yr) or 235.8 kilograms per 1000 square meters per year (kg/1000 sq. m/yr) of N-P-K. A N-P-K ratio of 3:1:2 is suggested for use with soilless media,

while 1:1:1 is recommended for soil-based media. Most media require the addition of micronutrients either by preplant incorporation of a granular source or as part of a liquid fertilization program.

Irrigation. Keep the potting medium uniformly moist but not wet.

Media. Use a potting medium with good drainage characteristics.

Problems.

Diseases: Blight—*Botrytis cinerea, Sclerotium rolfsii;* crown gall—*Agrobacterium tumefaciens;* leaf spot—*Cercospora* sp., *Glomerella cingulata (Colletotrichum gloeosporioides);* virus—fig mosaic virus.

Pests: Chewing insects; mealybugs; mites; foliar nematodes—*Aphelenchoides besseyi*; lesion nematodes—*Paratylenchus* spp.; scale; thrips; whitefly.

Postproduction factors

Light. Transport of plants under dark conditions is currently the most common method of shipping. If immediate delivery is not possible, place Indian rubber tree in a holding greenhouse or room with more than 200 fc (2.2 klx) of light. Indian rubber tree can tolerate low light of 75 to 100 fc (.8 to 1.1 klx), but typical upright growth habit and lower canopy leaves are lost with time.

Temperature. Acclimatized plants of similar cultivars can be shipped without

Ficus elastica 'Decora'

fee-kus
e-*las*-ti-ka
de-*kor*-uh

damage for extended periods. The cultivar 'Robusta' ships well at 50° to 60°F (10° to 16°C). Store 'Burgundy' at 50° to 60°F (10° to 16°C) for transit times of 1 to 14 days. If transit of 'Burgundy' requires additional time to 28 days, maintain temperatures within 50° to 55°F (10° to 13°C).

Gases. Injury due to ethylene is generally not a problem when plants are shipped within the recommended temperature range. Ethylene may reach damaging levels if plants are shipped with produce or held in prolonged storage above the maximum listed temperature.

Lasting qualities. Under appropriate storage conditions acclimatized plants retain good quality when shipped within 4 weeks. Maintain temperatures near the upper end of the recommended range when transport requires only 1 to 7 days.

Care and grooming. Good storage preparation improves quality retention during transit. Moisture content of the potting medium should approximate 50% of soil capacity when plants are packed. Maintain high humidity levels of 80% to 90% during storage to retard desiccation, especially when shipping time exceeds 7 days.

Retail handling

Light. Provide plants with sufficient light upon delivery to recuperate from the stresses of dark storage. A specially designed holding greenhouse or room is ideal. When such a facility is unavailable, light levels above 200 fc (2.2 klx) are recommended to preserve a premium appearance. Indian rubber tree tolerates low light of 75 to 100 fc (.8 to 1.1 klx), but plant form is affected.

Temperature. Normal interior tempera-tures of 65° to 85°F (18° to 29°C) support growth and quality retention. When a greenhouse is used to hold plants before installation, maintain 40% to 60% relative humidity for acclimatization to lower interior humidity levels.

Irrigation. Keep the potting medium uniformly moist but not wet.

Disorders. Typical upright growth habit and lower canopy leaves are lost with long-term holding under low light.

Consumer care

Temperature. Keep normal interior temperatures of 65° to 85°F (18° to 29°C) to support growth and quality retention.

Location. Indian rubber tree thrives in areas with bright indirect or curtain-filtered sunlight. Normal growth habit and foliage are more easily retained with light levels above 200 fc (2.2 klx), although Indian rubber tree tolerates low light of 75 to 100 fc (.8 to 1.1 klx).

Irrigation. Keep the potting medium uniformly moist but not wet.

Grooming. Repot only when growth becomes stunted from overcrowded roots. Early spring is a good time to repot and prune vigorous plants. Prune to keep size and shape appropriate for the location and container. Plants can be cut back almost to the soil level in early spring if desired, and new foliage will emerge from the stump. Fertilize established plants every 6 months. Indian rubber tree will maintain quality indoors indefinitely with good care.

Disorders. Typical upright growth habit and lower canopy leaves are lost when plants are located under low light.

Cultivars. *Ficus elastica* 'Doescheri'

F

125

Ficus elastica 'Decora'

fee-kus
e-*las*-ti-ka
de-*kor*-uh

(Doescher rubber plant) foliage is variegated with green margins and gray-green marbling. Midribs are cream-yellow and petioles are pink.

Ficus elastica 'Variegata' (variegated rubber plant) foliage is variegated with light green blades edged in white or yellow.

Ficus lyrata (fiddle-leaf fig), from tropical Africa, has large, fiddle-shaped leaves. The 1¼-inch fruit is round, dotted with white, and formed close to the stem in paired or single fashion.

ADDITIONAL READING

Bailey, L.H. and E.Z. Bailey. 1976. Hor*tus Third*. New York: Macmillan Publishing Co. Inc.

Chase, A.R. 1985. Diseases of foliage plants— Revised list for 1985. *Foliage Digest* 8(6):3-8.

Conover, C.A. and R.T. Poole. 1981. Guide for fertilizing foliage plant crops. *ARC-Apopka Research Rpt*. RH-81-1. University of Florida.

———. 1984. Light and fertilizer recommendations for production of acclimatized potted foliage plants. *Foliage Digest* 7(8):1-6.

———. 1987. Factors influencing shipping of acclimatized foliage plants. *Foliage Digest* 10(4):1-5.

Crockett, J.U. 1977. *Foliage House Plants*. Revised. Alexandria, VA: Time-Life Books.

Everett, T.H. 1980. *The New York Botanical Garden Illustrated Encyclopedia of Horticulture*. New York: Garland Publishing Inc.

Gaines, R.L. 1977. *Interior Plantscaping: Building Design for Interior Foliage Plants*. New York: Architectural Record Books.

McConnell, D.B., R.W. Henley and R.L. Biamonte. 1981. Commercial foliage plants. J.N. Joiner (ed.). *Foliage Plant Production*. Englewood Cliffs, NJ: Prentice-Hall Inc.

F

Fittonia verschaffeltii

fi-*ton*-ee-a
vair-sha-*felt*-ee-ee

Family Name: **Acanthaceae**
Common Name: **Nerve Plant, Mosaic Plant**

Originated in Andean South America.

FITTONIA VERSCHAFFELTII

Production factors

Light. Use production light levels of 1,000 to 2,500 fc (10.8 to 27 klx) for acclimatized plants.

Temperature. Keep greenhouse temperatures above 60°F (16°C) to promote steady growth.

Nutrition. At recommended production light levels for acclimatized plants, fertilize with 27.6 pounds per 1000 square feet per year (lb/1000 sq.ft/yr) or 134.8 kilograms per 1000 square meters per year (kg/1000 sq. m/yr) of N-P-K. A N-P-K ratio of 3:1:2 is suggested for use with soilless media, while 1:1:1 is recommended for soil-based media. Most media require the addition of micronutrients either by preplant incorporation of a granular source or as part of a liquid fertilization program.

Irrigation. Keep the potting medium evenly moist.

Media. Use a potting medium with good drainage characteristics.

Problems.

Diseases: Blight—*Rhizoctonia solani, Sclerotium rolfsii;* leaf spot—*Xanthomonas campestris;* virus—Biden's mottle virus.

Pests: Mealybugs; mites; scale; slugs.

Postproduction factors

Light. Transport of plants under dark conditions is currently the most common method of shipping. Hold nerve plant under at least 150 fc (1.6 klx) of light if immediate delivery is not possible.

Temperature. Nerve plant is very susceptible to chilling injury. Some damage has been recorded at 55°F (13°C) with exposures of only 3 days. Reduce production fertilizer and irrigation rates to control injury-prone, succulent growth when short exposure to chilling temperatures during transit is expected.

Gases. Exposure to ethylene levels of 5 ppm for 3 days causes leaf abscission.

F

Fittonia verschaffeltii

fi-*ton*-ee-a
vair-sha-*felt*-ee-ee

Retail handling

Light. Provide plants with sufficient light upon delivery to recuperate from the stresses of dark storage. Use light levels of 150 fc (1.6 klx) or more to preserve quality.

Temperature. Keep normal interior temperatures of 65° to 85°F (18° to 29°C) to support growth and quality retention. Avoid drafts and provide humidity levels of at least 50% for best plant health.

Irrigation. Keep the potting medium evenly moist.

Disorders. Quality loss during transit can be caused by exposure to low temperatures or to toxic levels of ethylene.

Consumer care

Temperature. Keep normal interior temperatures of 65° to 85°F (18° to 29°C) to support growth and quality retention. Avoid drafts and provide humidity levels of at least 50% for best plant health.

Location. Plants flourish when placed under shadowless light from a north window. Provide at least 150 fc (1.6 klx) of light. Locate nerve plant where high humidity can be maintained such as in a terrarium or on a moist, pebbled tray.

Irrigation. Keep the potting medium evenly moist.

Grooming. Nerve plant requires consistent maintenance and proper environmental conditions for best quality retention. Growth habit becomes unkept with age. Repot overcrowded plants at any season, and replace old plants with freshly rooted cuttings if rejuvenation is desired. Fertilize every 2 to 3 months.

Cultivars. *Fittonia verschaffeltii argyroneura* (silver-net plant, silver nerve, silver-threads) has light green leaves marked with white midribs and veins.

ADDITIONAL READING

Bailey, L.H. and E.Z. Bailey. 1976. *Hortus Third.* New York: Macmillan Publishing Co. Inc.

Chase, A.R. 1985. Diseases of foliage plants—Revised list for 1985. *Foliage Digest* 8(6):3-8.

———. 1988. Diseases of foliage plants—1988 updated listing. *Foliage Digest* 11(6):5-8.

Conover C.A. and R.T. Poole. 1981. Guide for fertilizing foliage plant crops. *ARC-Apopka Research Rpt.* RH-81-1. University of Florida.

———. 1984. Light and fertilizer recommendations for production of acclimatized potted foliage plants. *Foliage Digest* 7(8):1-6.

Crockett, J.U. 1977. *Foliage House Plants.* Revised. Alexandria, VA: Time-Life Books.

Everett, T.H. 1980. *The New York Botanical Garden Illustrated Encyclopedia of Horticulture.* New York: Garland Publishing Inc.

Florists' Transworld Delivery Association. 1985. The Indoor Gardener. Southfield, MI.

Marousky, F.J. and B.K. Harbaugh. 1978. Deterioration of foliage plants during transit. *Proc. 1978 Natl. Tropical Foliage Short Course,* University of Florida, IFAS Coop. Ext. Serv., Orlando, FL.

McConnell, D.B., R.W. Henley and R.L. Biamonte. 1981. Commercial foliage plants. J.N. Joiner (ed.). *Foliage plant production.* Englewood Cliffs, NJ: Prentice-Hall Inc.

Poole, R.T. and C.A. Conover. 1983. Factors influencing chilling damage of foliage plants. *Foliage Digest* 6(8):3-4.

F

Foliage Plants *Fittonia verschaffeltii*

Gynura aurantiaca

gin-*ew*-ra
ow-ran-tee-*ah*-ka

Family Name: **Compositae**
Common Name: **Velvet Plant**

Originated in Old World tropics from Africa to Malay Archipelago.

GYNURA AURANTIACA

Production factors

Light. Use production light levels of 1,500 to 3,000 fc (16.2 to 32.4 klx) for acclimatized plants.

Temperature. Maintain greenhouse temperatures above 55°F (13°C) to promote continuous growth.

Nutrition. At recommended production light levels for acclimatized plants, fertilize with 34.5 pounds per 1000 square feet per year (lb/1000 sq.ft/yr) or 168.4 kilograms per 1000 square meters per year (kg/1000 sq. m/yr) of N-P-K. A N-P-K ratio of 3:1:2 is suggested for use with soilless media, while 1:1:1 is recommended for soil-based media. Most media require the addition of micronutrients either by preplant incorporation of a granular source or as part of a liquid fertilization program.

Irrigation. Keep the potting medium uniformly moist but not wet.

Media. Use a potting medium with good drainage characteristics.

Problems.

Diseases: Anthracnose—*Glomerella cingulata (Colletotrichum gloeosporioides)*; blight—*Botrytis cinerea*; white mold—*Sclerotinia* sp.; leaf rot—*Phytophthora* sp.; root rot—*Pythium* sp.; root and stem rot—*Fusarium oxysporum, Rhizoctonia solani*.

Pests: Aphids; mealybugs; scale; whitefly.

Postproduction factors

Light. Transport of plants under dark conditions is currently the most common method of shipping. If immediate delivery is not possible hold velvet plant under at least 300 fc (3.2 klx) of light.

Retail handling

Light. Provide plants with sufficient light upon delivery to recuperate from the stresses of dark storage. Light levels of 300 fc (3.2 klx) or more are recommended to retain good plant appearance.

Temperature. Maintain normal interior temperatures of 65° to 85°F (18° to 29°C) to support growth and quality retention.

G

Gynura aurantiaca

gin-*ew*-ra
ow-ran-tee-*ah*-ka

Irrigation. Keep the potting medium uniformly moist but not wet.

Disorders. Water stress causes yellowing of foliage and loss of older leaves. Conversely, root rot develops if the potting medium is not sufficiently porous to drain well between frequent waterings.

Consumer care

Temperature. Maintain normal interior temperatures of 65° to 85°F (18° to 29°C) to support growth and quality retention.

Location. Velvet plant prefers high light locations with several hours of direct sunlight daily, but will grow under bright indirect light. Minimum light levels of 300 to 500 fc (3.2 to 5.4 klx) are recommended to maintain a healthy appearance.

Irrigation. Keep the potting medium uniformly moist but not wet.

Grooming. Velvet plant provides unique foliage color and texture in interior plantings. However, a high level of maintenance is required to preserve good form and vigor. Pinch long branches to promote a bushy growth habit and to force production of fresh, brightly colored new growth. The flowers produce an unpleasant odor and may be removed where the odor is objectionable. Overcrowded plants can be repotted in spring or early summer. Provide half-strength houseplant fertilizer monthly.

Disorders. Water stress causes yellowing of foliage and loss of older leaves. Conversely, root rot develops if the potting medium is not sufficiently porous to drain well between frequent waterings.

ADDITIONAL READING

Bailey, L.H. and E.Z. Bailey. 1976. *Hortus Third.* New York: Macmillan Publishing Co. Inc.

Chase, A.R. 1985. Diseases of foliage plants— Revised list for 1985. *Foliage Digest* 8(6):3-8.

Chase, A.R. 1988. Diseases of foliage plants—1988 updated listing. *Foliage Digest* 11(6):5-8.

Conover C.A. and R.T. Poole. 1981. Guide for fertilizing foliage plant crops. *ARC-Apopka Research Rpt.* RH-81-1. University of Florida.

————. 1984. Light and fertilizer recommendations for production of acclimatized potted foliage plants. *Foliage Digest* 7(8):1-6.

Crockett, J.U. 1977. *Foliage House Plants.* Revised. Alexandria, VA: Time-Life Books.

Everett, T.H. 1980. *The New York Botanical Garden Illustrated Encyclopedia of Horticulture.* New York: Garland Publishing Inc.

McConnell, D.B., R.W. Henley and R.L. Biamonte. 1981. Commercial foliage plants. J.N. Joiner (ed.). *Foliage Plant Production.* Englewood Cliffs, NJ: Prentice-Hall Inc.

G

Hedera helix

he-de-ra *he*-liks

Family Name: **Araliaceae**
Common Name: **English Ivy**

Originated in Europe, West Asia and North Africa.

HEDERA HELIX

Production factors

Light. Use production light levels of 1,500 to 2,500 fc (16.2 to 27 klx) for acclimatized plants.

Temperature. Maintain greenhouse temperatures of 65° to 80°F (18° to 27°C) for continuous growth. However, if winter fuel costs or supplies are a problem, English ivy can produce good growth with a minimum temperature of 60°F (16°C). Keep plants below 90°F (32°C) to sustain growth and rooting development.

Nutrition. At recommended production light levels for acclimatized plants, fertilize with 34.5 pounds per 1000 square feet per year (lb/1000 sq.ft/yr) or 168.4 kilograms per 1000 square meters per year (kg/1000 sq. m/yr) of N-P-K. A ratio of 3:1:2 is suggested for use with soilless media.

Provide micronutrients either by premixing with the medium or as part of a liquid fertilization program.

Irrigation. Allow the medium to dry slightly between waterings. Avoid extremely wet or dry soil conditions. Minimize overhead irrigation to control Xanthomonas leaf spot disease.

Media. Use a potting medium that has good water holding capacity and drainage characteristics. Adjust pH to 6.0 with dolomite.

Problems.

Diseases: Anthracnose—*Colletotrichum* sp., *Gloeosporium* sp.; blight—*Botrytis cinerea, Rhizoctonia solani, Sclerotium rolfsii;* stem gall—*Nectria* sp., *Volutella* sp.; leaf spot—*Cephaleuros virescens, Cercospora hederae, Colletotrichum trichellum, Coniothyrium* sp., *Corynespora* sp., *Phytophthora palmivora, Phyllosticta concentrica;* leaf spot and stem canker—*Xanthomonas campestris pv. hederae;* root rot—*Pythium* sp., *Phythophthora* spp.

Pests: Aphids; mealybugs; mites (broad, cyclamen, two-spotted spider); moths (worms); scale; thrips.

Disorders. Chemical treatment for Xanthomonas leaf spot is difficult because Streptomycin sulfate is toxic to many cultivars of English ivy. A white marginal chlorosis develops with a single treatment of 100 ppm. Sensitive cultivars include 'Brokamp,' 'California' and 'Manda Crested.' Combina-

H

tions of copper compounds cannot be used due to undesirable foliage residues. Because chemical use is limited, control depends on choosing disease-free stock, limiting overhead irrigation and rouging infected plants. Variegated cultivars experience decreased foliage display for several reasons. New growth is less variegated when produced under low light. Patterns are restored when light is increased. Some plants lose variegation as leaves age; therefore, select cultivars that retain color throughout leaf maturation. New shoots can arbitrarily develop with no variegation. Prune out atypical growth to retain true coloration. Some cultivars revert to species type growth more readily than others. Growth rate and rooting can slow significantly during summer heat.

Postproduction factors

Light. Transport of plants under dark conditions is currently the most common method of shipping. If immediate delivery is not possible, place English ivy in a holding greenhouse or room with at least 150 to 250 fc (1.6 to 2.7 klx). Some cultivars tolerate low light to 50 fc (.5 klx) if carefully acclimatized for marginal situations; however, higher light is preferred to retain a quality appearance.

Temperature. Acclimatized plants maintain quality during transit, but tolerance to shipping conditions varies among cultivars. For example, temperatures of 50° to 60°F (10° to 16°C) are recommended for the cultivar 'Eva' when transit requires 1 to 14 days. Longer durations to 28 days require more specific temperatures of 50° to 55°F (10° to 13°C). The cultivar 'Sweetheart'

ships best when held at 50° to 55°F (10° to 13°C). Quality loss of approximately 25% per week is expected with 'Sweetheart' if transit requires more than 2 weeks.

Gases. Injury due to ethylene is generally not a problem when plants are shipped within the recommended temperature range. Ethylene may reach damaging levels if plants are shipped with produce or held in prolonged storage above the maximum listed temperature.

Lasting qualities. Under appropriate storage conditions acclimatized plants retain good quality for at least 2 weeks. Ability to retain marketable quality with longer storage times depends on cultivar hardiness and maintenance of specific storage temperatures. Hold storage temperatures near the upper end of the recommended range when transport requires only 1 to 7 days.

Care and grooming. Good storage preparation improves quality retention during transit. Moisture content of the potting medium should approximate 50% of soil capacity when plants are packed. Maintain high humidity levels of 80% to 90% during storage to retard desiccation, especially when shipping time exceeds 7 days.

Retail handling

Light. Provide plants with sufficient light upon delivery to recuperate from the stresses of dark storage. A specially designed holding greenhouse or room is ideal. When such a facility is unavailable, provide at least 150 to 250 fc (1.6 to 2.7 klx) to maintain quality. Some cultivars of English ivy can survive low light of 50 to 75 fc (.5 to .8 klx) with careful acclimatization during production. Higher light levels are preferred for best quality retention.

Temperature. Maintain interior temperatures of 60°F to 75°F (16° to 24°C) for good growth and quality. Some cultivars survive low temperatures of 35°F (2°C) or less; however, avoid exposing less hardy indoor ivy selections to temperatures below 45°F (7°C). When a greenhouse is used to hold plants before installation, maintain 40% to 60% relative humidity for acclimatization to lower interior humidity levels.

Irrigation. Allow the medium to dry slightly between waterings. Avoid extremely wet or dry soil conditions.

Disorders. Water stress promotes yellowing of leaves and loss of older foliage. Latent pest or disease problems can develop rapidly during storage. English ivy cultivars are variously susceptible to Xanthomonas leaf spot and spider mites. The cultivars 'Sweetheart,' 'Gold Dust' and 'Eva' are resistant to both problems. Cultivars susceptible to Xanthomonas leaf spot include 'Green Feather,' 'Ivalace,' 'Hahn Variegated' and 'Brokamp.' Examples of cultivars susceptible to spider mite infestations are 'Green Feather,' 'Ivalace,' 'Perfection,' 'Hahn Variegated,' 'Brokamp,' 'California,' 'Manda Crested' and 'Gold Heart.' Immediate attention to any outbreak is recommended to prevent further quality loss or movement to adjacent plants.

Consumer care

Temperature. Interior temperatures of 60° to 75°F (16° to 24°C) maintain good growth and quality. Some cultivars survive low temperatures of 35°F (2°C) or less; however, avoid exposing less hardy indoor ivy selections to temperatures below 45°F (7°C).

Location. English ivy thrives in areas with some daily sunlight or bright indirect light. Many cultivars maintain good quality with less light especially when produced under acclimatizing conditions. Light levels of at least 150 to 250 fc (1.6 to 2.7 klx) are recommended to maintain a high quality appearance. Shade tolerant cultivars produced under acclimatizing conditions can adapt to low light of 50 to 75 fc (.5 to .8 klx), but higher light levels are preferred for best quality retention.

Irrigation. Allow the medium to dry slightly between waterings. Avoid extremely wet or dry soil conditions.

Grooming. Pinch long stems to promote a bushy growth habit. Overcrowded plants can be repotted at any time of the year. Fertilize every 3 to 4 months.

Disorders. Water stress stimulates yellowing of leaves and loss of older foliage. Variegated cultivars experience decreased foliage display because of low light, leaf maturity or reversion to species type growth.

Cultivars. English ivies are highly variable and many cultivars exist with a wide range of distinguishing characteristics. The American Ivy Society separates cultivars into classes, and a few examples are listed below that are in commercial production.

Hedera helix 'Brokamp,' 'Green Feather,' 'Needlepoint,' 'Perfection'—bird's foot class—leaves have narrow lobes.

Hedera helix 'Big Deal,' 'Manda Crested,' 'Telecurl'—curlies class—leaves have ruffles, ripples or pleats.

Hedera helix 'California Fan'—fans class—all leaves are of equal length, and are broad and fan-shaped.

Hedera helix 'Deltoidea' ('Sweetheart')—heart shape class—leaves are heart-shaped or valentine-shaped.

Hedera helix 'Hahn,' 'Pittsburg'—ivy ivies class—leaves possess the typical species shape.

Hedera helix 'Ivalace'—miniatures class—leaves are less than ½-inch long.

Hedera helix 'Glacier,' 'Gold Dust,' 'Gold Heart,' 'Hahn Variegated'—variegateds class—leaves are variegated.

ADDITIONAL READING

Bailey, L.H. and E.Z. Bailey. 1976. *Hortus Third.* New York: Macmillan Publishing Co. Inc.

Chase, A.R. 1985. Diseases of foliage plants—Revised list for 1985. *Foliage Digest* 8(6):3-8.

Conover, C.A. and R.T. Poole. 1981. Guide for fertilizing foliage plant crops. *ARC-Apopka Research Rpt.* RH-81-1. University of Florida.

———. 1984. Light and fertilizer recommendations for production of acclimatized potted foliage plants. *Foliage Digest* 7(8):1-6.

———. 1987. Factors influencing shipping of acclimatized foliage plants. *Foliage Digest* 10(4):1-5.

Crockett, J.U. 1977. *Foliage House Plants.* Revised. Alexandria, VA: Time-Life Books.

Florists' Transworld Delivery Association. 1985. The Indoor Gardener. Southfield, MI.

McConnell, D.B., R.W. Henley and R.L. Biamonte. 1981. Commercial foliage plants. J.N. Joiner (ed.). *Foliage Plant Production.* Englewood Cliffs, NJ: Prentice-Hall Inc.

Osborne, L.S. and A.R. Chase. 1986. Susceptibility of English Ivy cultivars to two-spotted spider mite and Xanthomonas leaf spot. *Foliage Digest* 9(3):1-3.

Osborne, L.S., A.R. Chase and R.W. Henley. 1985. English Ivy. *Foliage Digest* 8(7):2-6.

Poole, R.T. and C.A. Conover. 1987. Foliage variety determines heat. *Greenhouse Grower.* 5(1):21-22.

H

Howea forsterana

how-ee-a for-sta-*rah*-na

Family Name: **Palmae**
Common Name: **Kentia Palm, Sentry Palm**

Originated on Lord Howe Island (Australia).

HOWEA FORSTERANA

Production factors

Light. Use production light levels of 2,500 to 6,000 fc (27 to 64.8 klx) for acclimatized plants.

Temperature. Maintain greenhouse temperatures of 60°F (16°C) or more to sustain continuous growth.

Nutrition. At recommended production light levels for acclimatized plants, fertilize with 27.5 to 34.4 pounds per 1000 square feet per year (lb/1000 sq.ft/yr) or 134.5 to 168.1 kilograms per 1000 square meters per year (kg/1000 sq. m/yr) of N-P-K. Soluble

salt concentrations below 1,000 ppm are desired prior to sale to prevent root damage under interior conditions.

Irrigation. Keep the medium moist but not wet.

Media. Use a potting medium with good drainage characteristics.

Problems.

Diseases: Anthracnose—*Gloeosporium* sp., *Glomerella cingulata (Colletotrichum gloeosporioides);* black spot—*Catacauma palmicola;* leaf spot—*Alternaria* sp., *Cercospora* sp., *Curvularia lunata, Cylindrocladium scoparium, Cytospora* sp., *Didymella phacidiomorpha, Didymopleella* sp., *Diplodia* sp., *Exosporium palmivorum, Gloeosporium* sp., *Helminthosporium* sp., *Leptothyrium* sp., *Monilochaetes* sp., *Pestalotia palmarum, Phomopsis* sp., *Phyllachora* sp., *Phyllosticta* sp., *Physalospora rhodina, Stigmina palmivora;* microplasma—lethal yellowing; bud rot—*Cytospora palmarum, Fusarium* sp., *Phytophthora palmivora;* root rot—*Ceratocystis paradoxa, Clitocybe tabescens, Endoconidiophora paradoxa, Ganoderma sulcatum, Pythium* sp., *Rhizoctonia solani;* wood rot—*Ganoderma* spp.; false smut—*Graphiola phoenicis.*

Pests: Saddleback caterpillars; chewing beetles; leaf skeletonizer; mealybugs; mites; nematodes; scale; seed weevils; thrips.

Disorders. Kentia palm is sensitive to atmospheric fluoride. Symptoms of toxicity

H

progress from interveinal chlorosis to general chlorosis of newly mature leaves as concentrations increase. Brown necrotic splotches, marginal necrosis and tipburn also occur with exposure to fluoride. Avoid high levels of soluble salts in the potting medium. Weakened roots are more likely to suffer from root rot.

Postproduction factors

Light. Transport of plants under dark conditions is currently the most common method of shipping. If immediate delivery is not possible, place plants in a holding greenhouse or room with at least 75 to 100 fc (.8 to 1.1 klx). Kentia palm tolerates light levels to 50 fc (.5 klx), but more light is preferred for best quality retention.

Temperature. Acclimatized plants can be shipped without damage for extended periods when held at 50° to 65°F (10° to 18°C).

Gases. Injury due to ethylene is generally not a problem when plants are shipped within the recommended temperature range. Ethylene may reach damaging levels if plants are shipped with produce or held in prolonged storage above the maximum listed temperature.

Lasting qualities. Under appropriate storage conditions acclimatized plants retain good quality when shipped within 4 weeks. Maintain temperatures near the upper end of the recommended range when transport requires only 1 to 7 days.

Care and grooming. Good storage preparation improves quality retention during transit. Moisture content of the potting medium should approximate 50% of soil capacity when plants are packed.

Maintain high humidity levels of 80% to 90% during storage to retard desiccation, especially when shipping time exceeds 7 days. Avoid extreme drying of the potting medium during shipping. Roots are susceptible to injury, especially when soluble salts are above recommended levels.

Retail handling

Light. Provide plants with sufficient light upon delivery to recuperate from the stresses of dark storage. A specially designed holding greenhouse or room is ideal. When such a facility is unavailable, minimum light levels of 75 to 100 fc (.8 to 1.1 klx) are recommended to preserve quality. Kentia palm tolerates marginal lighting better than many foliage plants and can survive under 50 fc (.5 klx). However, higher light levels are preferred for best appearance.

Temperature. Keep interior temperatures of 60° to 85°F (16° to 29°C) for best plant health, although Kentia palm tolerates occasional exposure to cool temperatures (to 50°F; 10°C). When a greenhouse is used to hold plants before installation, maintain 40% to 60% relative humidity for acclimatization to lower interior humidity levels.

Irrigation. Keep the potting medium moist but not wet.

Disorders. Chlorosis and necrosis are symptoms of fluoride toxicity. Check for high soluble salts in the medium if roots are damaged. Latent pest or disease problems develop rapidly under favorable conditions during storage. Examine plants especially for damaged roots or for infestations of scale or spider mites. Immediate attention to any problem prevents further quality loss or movement to adjacent plants.

Howea forsterana

how-ee-a
for-sta-*rah*-na

Consumer care

Temperature. Keep interior temperatures of 60° to 85°F (16° to 29°C) for best plant health, although occasional exposure to cool temperatures (to 50°F; 10°C) is tolerated.

Location. Plants flourish when installed under bright indirect or curtain-filtered sunlight. Minimum light levels of 75 to 100 fc (.8 to 1.1 klx) are recommended to preserve quality. Kentia palm tolerates marginal lighting better than many foliage plants and can survive under 50 fc (.5 klx). However, higher light levels are preferred for best appearance.

Irrigation. Keep the potting medium moist but not wet.

Grooming. Kentia palm is a durable plant for interiors and will maintain quality indefinitely with good care. Wash foliage periodically with a tepid water shower or damp sponge to remove dust and dirt. Regular cleaning of foliage also aids in control of spider mite populations. Fertilize monthly during the growing season or on a schedule that maintains soluble salts below 1,000 ppm. Repot in early spring only when the plant becomes quite rootbound.

Disorders. Air pollutants containing toxic levels of fluoride cause chlorosis and necrosis of foliage. Check soluble salts content of the medium if roots weaken.

ADDITIONAL READING
Bailey, L.H. and E.Z. Bailey. 1976. *Hortus Third.* New York: Macmillan Publishing Co. Inc.

Conover C.A. and R.T. Poole. 1987.Factors influencing shipping of acclimatized foliage plants. *Foliage Digest* 10(4):15.

Crockett, J.U. 1977. *Foliage Houseplants.* Revised. Alexandria, VA: Time-Life Books.

Everett, T.H. 1980. *The New York Botanical Garden Illustrated Encyclopedia of Horticulture.* New York: Garland Publishing Inc.

Gaines, R.L. 1977. *Interior Plantscaping: Building Design for Interior Foliage Plants.* New York: Architectural Record Books.

Holstead, C.L. 1985. *Care and Handling of Flowers and Plants.* Floralife Inc. Society of American Florists. Alexandria, VA.

McConnell, D.B., R.W. Henley and R.L. Biamonte. 1981. Commercial foliage plants. J.N. Joiner (ed.). *Foliage Plant Production.* Englewood Cliffs, NJ: Prentice-Hall Inc.

Sullivan, G.H., J.L. Robertson and G.L. Staby. 1980. Care and handling of foliage plants. *Management for Retail Florists with Applications to Nursery and Garden Centers.* San Francisco: W.H. Freeman and Co.

Woltz, S.S. and W.E. Waters. 1978. Airborne fluoride effects on some flowering and landscape plants. *HortScience* 13:430-432.

H

Hoya carnosa 'Variegata'

hoy-a
kar-*no*-sa
vare-ee-gay-tuh

Family Name: **Aslepiadaceae**
Common Name: **Variegated Wax Plant**

Originated in South China to Australia.

HOYA CARNOSA 'VARIEGATA'

Production factors

Light. Use production light levels of 1,500 to 2,500 fc (16.2 to 27 klx) for acclimatized plants.

Temperature. Maintain temperatures of 68° to 75°F (20° to 24°C) for best growth. Avoid temperature extremes.

Nutrition. At recommended production light levels for acclimatized plants, fertilize with 34.5 pounds per 1000 square feet per year (lb/1000 sq.ft/yr) or 168.4 kilograms per 1000 square meters per year (kg/1000 sq. m/yr) of N-P-K. Variegated wax plant grows slowly; therefore, a liquid fertilizer program using ratios of 2:1:2 or 3:1:2 with addition of micronutrients is suggested to allow for adjustment of fertility levels in the growing medium whenever irrigation frequencies require seasonal change.

Irrigation. Allow the potting medium to dry moderately between waterings after roots are well developed.

Media. Use a highly organic potting medium with good drainage characteristics.

Problems.

Diseases: Anthracnose—*Colletotrichum gloeosporioides;* blight—*Botrytis cinerea, Rhizoctonia solani;* leaf spot—*Cercospora* sp., *Corynespora sp., Gleosporium* sp.; stem and root rot—*Phytophthora* sp., *Pythium* sp.; virus—ring spot virus.

Pests: Aphids; fungus gnats; mealybugs; broad mites; scale; thrips.

Disorders. Temperatures above 90°F (32°C) reduce root development and growth, and cool winter temperatures force plants into dormancy.

Postproduction factors

Light. Transport of plants under dark conditions is currently the most common method of shipping. If immediate plant delivery is not possible, place variegated wax plant in a holding greenhouse or room with at least 125 fc (1.4 klx). Provide approximately 10 hours of light per day for optimum quality maintenance.

Temperature. Acclimatized plants can be shipped without damage for extended periods when held at 55° to 65°F (13° to 18°C).

Gases. Injury due to ethylene is generally

H

138

Foliage Plants   *Hoya carnosa* 'Variegata'

Hoya carnosa 'Variegata'

hoy-a
kar-*no*-sa
vare-ee-gay-tuh

not a problem when plants are shipped within the recommended temperature range. Ethylene may reach damaging levels if plants are shipped with produce or held in prolonged storage above the maximum listed temperature.

Lasting qualities. Under appropriate storage conditions acclimatized plants retain good quality when shipped within 4 weeks. Maintain temperatures near the upper end of the recommended range when transport requires only 1 to 7 days.

Care and grooming. Good storage preparation improves quality retention during transit. Moisture content of the potting medium should approximate 50% of soil capacity when plants are packed. Maintain high humidity levels of 80% to 90% during storage to retard desiccation, especially when shipping time exceeds 7 days.

Retail handling

Light. Provide plants with sufficient light upon delivery to recuperate from the stresses of dark storage. A specially designed holding greenhouse or room is ideal. When such a facility is unavailable, provide light levels of 125 fc (1.4 klx) or more for 10 hours a day to maintain quality.

Temperature. Interior temperatures of 65° to 80°F (18° to 27°C) are best for growth and quality. When a greenhouse is used to hold plants before installation, maintain 40% to 60% relative humidity for acclimatization to lower interior humidity levels.

Irrigation. Keep the potting medium moist but not wet. Allow the medium to dry moderately between waterings during winter months.

Disorders. Epinasty occurs with exposure to high levels of ethylene during transit. The effect is temporary if ethylene concentration does not exceed 5 ppm for 3 days.

Consumer care

Temperature. Keep interior temperatures of 65° to 80°F (18° to 27°C) for best growth and quality.

Location. Variegated wax plant prefers locations with bright, filtered light but also maintains good quality under less light (to 125 fc; 1.4 klx). Provide light for approximately 10 hours a day.

Irrigation. Keep the potting medium moist but not wet. Allow the medium to dry moderately between waterings during winter months.

Grooming. Variegated wax plant produces attractive clusters of flowers periodically. Remove faded blooms carefully without damaging the floral spur since new bloom clusters develop from these structures throughout the life of the plant. Keep specimens potbound for best flowering response. Plants become partially dormant during winter months and require less light, water and fertilizer. Fertilize every 2 months during the growing season.

Cultivars. *Hoya carnosa* 'Krinkle Curl' ('Green Curls') (Hindu-rope) leaves are contorted and crowded onto the stem producing a thickened, ropey appearance.

H

Hoya carnosa 'Variegata'

hoy-a
kar-*no*-sa
vare-ee-gay-tuh

ADDITIONAL READING

Arthurs, Kathryn (ed.). 1974. *How to Grow House Plants.* Menlo Park, CA: Lane Publishing Co.

Bailey, L.H. and E.Z. Bailey. 1976. *Hortus Third.* New York: Macmillan Publishing Co. Inc.

Chase, A.R. 1985. Diseases of foliage plants— Revised list for 1985. *Foliage Digest* 8(6):3-8.

Conover C.A. and R.T. Poole. 1981. Guide for fertilizing foliage plant crops. *ARC-Apopka Research Rpt.* RH-81-1. University of Florida.

———. 1984. Light and fertilizer recommendations for production of acclimatized potted foliage plants. *Foliage Digest* 7(8):1-6.

———. 1987. Factors influencing shipping of acclimatized foliage plants. *Foliage Digest* 10(4):1-5.

Everett, T.H. 1980. *The New York Botanical Garden Illustrated Encyclopedia of Horticulture.* New York: Garland Publishing Inc.

Florists' Transworld Delivery Association. 1985. The Indoor Gardener. Southfield, MI.

Marousky, F.J. and B.K. Harbaugh. 1978. Deterioration of foliage plants during transit. *Proc. 1978 Natl. Tropical Foliage Short Course,* University of Florida, IFAS Coop. Ext. Serv., Orlando, FL.

McConnell, D.B., R.W. Henley and R.L. Biamonte. 1981. Commercial foliage plants. J.N. Joiner (ed.). *Foliage Plant Production.* Englewood Cliffs, NJ: Prentice-Hall Inc.

Osborne, L.S., R.W. Henley and A.R. Chase. 1986. Wax plant. *Foliage Digest* 9(8):1-4.

H

Maranta leuconeura kerchoviana

ma-*ran*-ta
loo-ko-*newr*-ra
ker-chov-ee-*ah*-nuh

Family Name: **Marantaceae**
Common Name: **Prayer Plant, Rabbit's Tracks**

Originated in Brazil.

MARANTA LEUCONEURA KERCHOVIANA

Production factors

Light. Use production light levels of 1,000 to 2,500 fc (10.8 to 27 klx) for acclimatized plants.

Temperature. Maintain greenhouse temperatures of 70° to 80°F (21° to 27°C) for the best root development and growth. However, if winter fuel costs or supplies are a problem, prayer plant can be produced with a minimum temperature of 60°F (16°C). Avoid temperatures above 90°F (32°C) or below 50°F (10°C).

Nutrition. At recommended production light levels, fertilize with 27.6 pounds per 1000 square feet per year (lb/1000 sq.ft/yr) or 134.8 kilograms per 1000 square meters per year (kg/1000 sq. m/yr) of N-P-K. A ratio of 3:1:2 is suggested for use with soilless potting medium. Incorporate 1 pound per cubic yard (.6 kg per cubic m) of Micromax or another equivalent micronutrient source to the potting medium prior to planting. Fertilizer sources containing ammoniacal nitrogen are recommended. Do not use superphosphate or any other fertilizer containing fluoride.

Irrigation. Keep the potting medium moist but not wet. Either eliminate use of overhead sprinklers or irrigate early in the day to allow quick drying of foliage. Constantly wet foliage is more susceptible to disease development.

Media. Use a moisture-retentive organic medium with good drainage characteristics. Adjust the pH with dolomite to 5.5 to 6.0. Where fluoride concentrations are a problem, maintain pH values near 6.5 to reduce availability. Amendments should be screened for significant concentrations of this element before inclusion in the medium.

Problems.

Diseases: Leaf spot—*Alternaria* sp., *Bipolaris setariae, Drechslera setariae (Helminthosporium setariae);* root rot—*Pythium* sp., *Rhizoctonia solani;* soft rot—*Erwinia carotovora;* stem rot—*Rhizoctonia solani;* rust—*Puccinia cannae;* virus—cucumber mosaic virus.

Pests: Caterpillars; mealybugs; two-spotted spider mite—*Steneotarsonemus furcatus;* burrowing nematodes—*Radopho-*

M

Maranta leuconeura kerchoviana

ma-*ran*-ta
loo-ko-*newr*-ra
ker-chov-ee-*ah*-nuh

lus similis; root knot nematodes—*Meloidogyne javanica*; scale; slugs; snails.

Disorders. Temperatures above 90°F (32°C) reduce rate of growth. Reddened or necrotic foliage develops after exposure to chilling temperatures of 45°F (7°C) or less. Damage appears on mature leaves approximately 2 days after exposure. High production light levels and temperatures cause marginal necrosis and tipburn. Excessive soluble salts in the medium increase plant injury. Chlorosis from iron deficiency develops when the pH rises above 6.0 or when fertilizer sources high in nitrate nitrogen are used. Foliage color can be restored by reducing pH levels, using an ammoniacal nitrogen or treating with iron chelate. Prayer plant is sensitive to fluoride in either potting media or the atmosphere. Symptoms include marginal necrosis and tipburn. *Maranta leuconeura erythroneura* develops scattered, irregular necrotic splotches and fading of typical leaf markings from atmospheric exposure.

Postproduction factors

Light. Transport of plants under dark conditions is currently the most common method of shipping. If immediate plant delivery is not possible, place prayer plant in a holding greenhouse or room with at least 75 to 150 fc (.8 to 1.6 klx) of light. Light levels to 50 fc (.5 klx) are tolerated, but more light is preferred for best appearance. Avoid bright light or full sun exposures that can burn the foliage.

Temperature. Recommended temperatures for shipping are 50° to 55°F (10° to 13°C).

Gases. Injury due to ethylene is generally not a problem when plants are shipped within the recommended temperature range. Ethylene may reach damaging levels if plants are shipped with produce or held in prolonged storage above the maximum listed temperature.

Lasting qualities. Under appropriate storage conditions acclimatized plants retain good quality when shipping time does not exceed 2 weeks. Maintain storage temperatures near the upper end of the recommended range when transport requires only 1 to 7 days. Severe quality loss is expected when plants require more than 2 weeks to reach their destination.

Care and grooming. Good storage preparation improves quality retention during transit. Moisture content of the potting medium should approximate 50% of soil capacity when plants are packed. Maintain high humidity levels of 80% to 90% during storage to retard desiccation, especially when shipping time exceeds 7 days.

Retail handling

Light. Provide plants with sufficient light upon delivery to recuperate from the stresses of dark storage. A specially designed holding greenhouse or room is ideal. When such a facility is unavailable, maintain plants under at least 75 to 150 fc (.8 to 1.6 klx) of light. Light levels to 50 fc (.5 klx) are tolerated, but more light is preferred to retain prime appearance. Avoid bright light or full sun exposures that can burn the foliage.

Temperature. Keep interior temperatures of 65° to 85°F (18° to 29°C) to protect growth and quality. When a greenhouse is used to hold plants before installation, maintain 40% to 60% relative humidity for

M

Maranta leuconeura kerchoviana

ma-*ran*-ta
loo-ko-*newr*-ra
ker-chov-ee-*ah*-nuh

acclimatization to lower interior humidity levels.

Irrigation. Keep the potting medium moist but not wet. Use high-quality, unfluoridated water.

Disorders. Foliage necrosis can develop from exposure to fluoride or from high soluble salts in the medium. Chilling injury occurs with exposure to temperatures of 45°F (7°C) or less during storage.

Consumer care

Temperature. Keep interior temperatures of 65° to 85°F (18° to 29°C) to protect growth and quality.

Location. Plants flourish when placed under bright indirect or curtain-filtered sunlight, but also maintain quality under interior lighting of 75 to 150 fc (.8 to 1.6 klx). Light levels to 50 fc (.5 klx) are tolerated, but more light is preferred to retain prime appearance. Avoid bright light or full sun exposures that can burn the foliage. Moderate to high humidity levels enhance plant performance.

Irrigation. Keep the potting medium moist but not wet. Use high-quality, unfluoridated water.

Grooming. Repot in early spring when needed. Fertilize every 4 to 6 months.

Disorders. Foliage necrosis can develop from exposure to fluoride or from high soluble salts in the medium. Chilling injury occurs with exposure to temperatures of 45°F (7°C) or less.

Cultivars. *Maranta leuconeura erythroneura* foliage is highly colored with rose red lateral veins, dark green blotches extending almost to the margins and a red purple lower surface.

Bailey, L.H. and E.Z. Bailey. 1976. *Hortus Third.* New York: Macmillan Publishing Co. Inc.

Chase, A.R. 1985. Diseases of foliage plants—Revised list for 1985. *Foliage Digest* 8 (6):3-8.

Chase, A.R., R.W. Henley and L.S. Osborne. 1985. Maranta. *Foliage Digest* 8(12):6-8.

Chase, A.R. and R.T. Poole. 1986. Troubleshooting guide to foliage. *Greenhouse Grower* 4(9):30-31.

Conover C.A. and R.T. Poole. 1981. Guide for fertilizing foliage plant crops. *ARC-Apopka Research Rpt.* RH-81-1. University of Florida.

———. 1984. Light and fertilizer recommendations for production of acclimatized potted foliage plants. *Foliage Digest* 7(8):1-6.

———. 1987. Factors influencing shipping of acclimatized foliage plants. *Foliage Digest* 10(4):1-5.

Crockett, J.U. 1977. *Foliage House Plants.* Revised. Alexandria, VA: Time-Life Books.

Everett, T.H. 1980. *The New York Botanical Garden Illustrated Encyclopedia of Horticulture.* New York: Garland Publishing Inc.

Florists' Transworld Delivery Association. 1985. *The Indoor Gardener.* Southfield, MI.

Gaines, R.L. 1977. *Interior Plantscaping: Building Design for Interior Foliage Plants.* New York: Architectural Record Books.

McConnell, D.B., R.W. Henley and R.L. Biamonte. 1981. Commercial foliage plants. J.N. Joiner (ed.). *Foliage Plant Production.* Englewood Cliffs, NJ: Prentice-Hall Inc.

Poole, R.T. and C.A. Conover. 1987. Foliage variety determines heat. *Greenhouse Grower* 5(1):21-22.

Woltz, S.S. and W.E. Waters. 1978. Airborne fluoride effects on some foliage plants. *HortScience* 13:585-586.

M

143

Foliage Plants *Maranta leuconeura kerchoviana*

Monstera deliciosa

mon-*ste*-ra
day-li-kee-*o*-sa

Family Name: **Araceae**
Common Name: **Ceriman, Swiss-Cheese Plant, Mexican Breadfruit, Split-Leaf Philodendron**

Originated in Mexico and Central America. This plant was previously named *Philodendron pertusum*.

MONSTERA DELICIOSA

Production factors

Light. Use production light levels of 2,000 to 4,000 fc (21.6 to 43.2 klx) for acclimatized plants.

Nutrition. At recommended production light levels, fertilize with 41.4 pounds per 1000 square feet per year (lb/1000 sq.ft/yr) or 202.1 kilograms per 1000 square meters per year (kg/1000 sq. m/yr) of N-P-K. A N-P-K ratio of 3:1:2 is suggested for use with soilless media, while 1:1:1 is recommended for soil-based media. Most media require the addition of micronutrients either by preplant incorporation of a granular source or as part of a liquid fertilization program.

Irrigation. Keep the potting medium moist but not wet.

Media. Use a moisture-retentive organic medium with good drainage characteristics.

Problems.

Diseases: Anthracnose—*Glomerella cingulata;* blight—*Rhizoctonia solani, Sclerotium rolfsii;* leaf spot—*Colletotrichum* sp., *Leptosphaeria* sp., *Macrophoma philodendri, Phyllosticta* sp., *Phytophthora* sp., *Pseudomonas cichorii;* root rot—*Pythium splendens;* soft rot—*Erwinia carotovora* subsp. *carotovora.*

Pests: Mealybugs; mites; scale; thrips.

Postproduction factors

Light. Transport of plants under dark conditions is currently the most common method of shipping. If immediate delivery is not possible, hold under at least 150 to 250 fc (1.6 to 2.7 klx) of light. Light levels of 500 fc (5.4 klx) or more are recommended to maintain typical leaf size and split-leaf form on emerging foliage.

M

Monstera deliciosa

Retail handling

Light. Provide plants with sufficient light upon delivery to recuperate from the stresses of dark storage. Place ceriman under at least 150 to 250 fc (1.6 to 2.7 klx) of light. Light levels of 500 fc (5.4 klx) or more are recommended to maintain typical leaf size and split-leaf form on emerging foliage.

Temperature. Keep interior temperatures of 65° to 85°F (18° to 29°C) to sustain growth and quality. Ceriman prefers humid conditions; therefore, maintain temperatures near the lower end of the recommended range if humidity levels are low. Avoid exposure to temperatures below 55°F (13°C).

Irrigation. Keep the potting medium moist but not wet.

Disorders. Plants are subject to chilling injury at temperatures below 55°F (13°C).

Consumer care

Temperature. Keep interior temperatures of 65° to 85°F (18° to 29°C) to sustain growth and quality. Ceriman prefers humid conditions; therefore, maintain temperatures near the lower end of the recommended range if humidity levels are low. Avoid exposure to temperatures below 55° (13°C).

Location. Ceriman thrives in areas with bright indirect or curtain-filtered sunlight, but also maintains quality under interior lighting of 150 to 250 fc (1.6 to 2.7 klx). Light levels of 500 fc (5.4 klx) or more are recommended to maintain typical leaf size and split-leaf form on emerging foliage.

Irrigation. Keep the potting medium moist but not wet.

Grooming. Overcrowded plants can be repotted at any time of the year. Fertilize established specimens in early spring and early summer.

Disorders. Plants are subject to chilling injury at temperatures below 55°F (13°C).

ADDITIONAL READING
Bailey, L.H. and E.Z. Bailey. 1976. *Hortus Third.* New York: Macmillan Publishing Co. Inc.
Chase, A.R. 1985. Diseases of foliage plants—Revised list for 1985. *Foliage Digest* 8(6):3-8.
Conover C.A. and R.T. Poole. 1981. Guide for fertilizing foliage plant crops. *ARC-Apopka Research Rpt.* RH-81-1. University of Florida.
———. 1984. Light and fertilizer recommendations for production of acclimatized potted foliage plants. *Foliage Digest* 7(8):1-6.
Crockett, J.U. 1977. *Foliage House Plants.* Revised. Alexandria, VA: Time-Life Books.
Everett, T.H. 1980. *The New York Botanical Garden Illustrated Encyclopedia of Horticulture.* New York: Garland Publishing Inc.
McConnell, D.B., R.W. Henley and R.L. Biamonte. 1981. Commercial foliage plants. J.N. Joiner (ed.). *Foliage plant production.* Englewood Cliffs, NJ: Prentice-Hall Inc.
Orans, M. 1973. *Houseplants and Indoor Landscaping.* Barrington, IL: A.B. Morse Co.

M

Nephrolepis exaltata 'Bostoniensis'

nef-ro-*lep*-is
eks-al-*tah*-ta
bos-ton-ee-*en*-sis

Family Name: **Polypodiaceae**
Common Name: **Boston Fern**

Originated in tropics.

NEPHROLEPIS EXALTATA 'BOSTONIENSIS'

Production factors

Light. Use production light levels of 1,500 to 3,000 fc (16.2 to 32.4 klx) for acclimatized plants. Best quality is obtained with light levels near 2,000 fc (21.6 klx).

Temperature. Maintain greenhouse temperatures of 65° to 95°F (18° to 35°C) to assure quality growth, although slightly more extreme temperatures are tolerated without injury.

Nutrition. At recommended production light levels for acclimatized plants, fertilize with 34.5 pounds per 1000 square feet per year (lb/1000 sq. ft/yr) or 168.4 kilograms per 1000 square meters per year (kg/1000 sq. m/yr) of N-P-K. A ratio of 3:1:2 is suggested for use with soilless media. Most media require the addition of micronutrients. Incorporation of 1 pound per cubic yard (.6 kg per cubic m) Micromax or another equivalent source into the medium prior to potting is advised for Boston fern.

Irrigation. Keep the potting medium evenly moist but not wet.

Media. Choose a potting medium that has good aeration and drainage properties, and yet holds water well without drying too quickly. Adjust the medium to pH 5.0 to 5.5 with dolomite.

Problems.

Diseases: Blight—*Botrytis cinerea, Rhizoctonia solani;* leaf spot—*Cercospora phyllitidis, Cylindrocladium pteridis, Phyllosticta* sp., *Pseudomonas gladioli;* root rot—*Pythium* spp.

Pests: Caterpillars, mealybugs; foliar nematodes—*Aphelenchoides fragariae*; lesion nemotodes—*Paratylenchus* spp.; scale; thrips.

Disorders. Frond number is reduced and fronds become dark green, long and weak when Boston fern is grown under extreme shade. Foliage becomes light green under high light levels. Water stress causes graying of foliage and growth rate reduction. Tipburn and death of runners are caused by high soluble salts or poor water quality. High pH values reduce growth rate. Boston fern displays phytotoxic responses to a wide range of chemicals. Test each chemical on a small number of plants before general use.

N

Nephrolepis exaltata 'Bostoniensis'

nef-ro-*lep*-is
eks-al-*tah*-ta
bos-ton-ee-*en*-sis

Postproduction factors

Light. Transport of plants under dark conditions is currently the most common method of shipping. If immediate delivery is not possible, place Boston fern in a holding greenhouse or room with 75 to 200 fc (.8 to 2.2 klx) of light to maintain typical appearance.

Temperature. Recommended temperatures for shipping are 55° to 60°F (13° to 16°C).

Gases. Leaflet loss is a serious problem when ethylene concentration exceeds 1 ppm. Avoid exposure to fruits and vegetables during storage and to shipping temperatures above recommended levels.

Lasting qualities. Under appropriate storage conditions acclimatized plants retain good quality when shipped within 2 weeks. Maintain storage temperatures near the upper end of the recommended range when transport requires only 1 to 7 days. Severe quality loss is expected when plants require more than 2 weeks to reach their destination.

Care and grooming. Good storage preparation improves quality retention during transit. Moisture content of the potting medium should approximate 50% of soil capacity when plants are packed. Maintain high humidity levels of 80% to 90% during storage to retard desiccation, especially when shipping time exceeds 7 days.

Retail handling

Light. Provide plants with sufficient light upon delivery to recuperate from the stresses of dark storage. A specially designed holding greenhouse or room is ideal. When such a facility is unavailable, light levels of 75 to 200 fc (.8 to 2.2 klx) are recommended for quality retention.

Temperature. Interior temperatures of 60° to 75°F (16° to 24°C) are preferred to sustain growth and quality, but cool night temperatures to 50°F (10°C) are tolerated without injury. Maintain temperatures near the lower end of the recommended range if low humidity and water stress are encountered. When a greenhouse is used to hold plants before installation, maintain 40% to 60% relative humidity for acclimatization to lower interior humidity levels.

Irrigation. Keep the potting medium evenly moist but not wet.

Disorders. Plants exposed to more than 1 ppm ethylene during storage suffer serious leaflet loss. Growth becomes weak, elongated and pale if plants are held under less than the recommended minimum light level. Boston fern develops marginal browning of leaflets in response to low humidity, water stress, saturated media or high soluble salts.

Consumer care

Temperature. Interior temperatures of 60° to 75°F (16° to 24°C) are preferred to sustain growth and quality, but cool night temperatures to 50°F (10°C) are tolerated without injury. Maintain temperatures near the lower end of the recommended range if low humidity and water stress are encountered.

Location. Plants flourish when installed under bright indirect or curtain-filtered sunlight, but also maintain quality under interior lighting of 75 to 200 fc (.8 to 2.2 klx).

Irrigation. Keep the potting medium evenly moist but not wet.

N

Nephrolepis exaltata 'Bostoniensis'

nef-ro-*lep*-is
eks-al-*tah*-ta
bos-ton-ee-*en*-sis

Grooming. Overcrowded plants can be repotted and divided if desired in early spring. Older growth naturally dies as new growth emerges from the crown and should be removed to maintain an attractive appearance. Fertilize every 3 months.

Disorders. Growth becomes weak, elongated and pale if plants are located in areas with less than the recommended minimum light level. Boston fern develops marginal browning of leaflets in response to low humidity, water stress, saturated media, or high soluble salts.

Cultivars. There are numerous variants of Boston fern with differences in leaflet shape and leaf divisions.

ADDITIONAL READING

Bailey, L.H. and E.Z. Bailey. 1976. *Hortus Third.* New York: Macmillan Publishing Co. Inc.

Chase, A.R. 1985. Diseases of foliage plants— Revised list for 1985. *Foliage Digest.* 8(6):3-8.

Conover, C.A., L.S. Osborne and A.R. Chase. 1987. Boston Ferns. *Foliage Digest* 10(3):1-4.

Conover C.A. and R.T. Poole. 1981. Guide for fertilizing foliage plant crops. *ARC-Apopka Research Rpt.* RH-81-1. University of Florida.

————. 1984. Light and fertilizer recommendations for production of acclimatized potted foliage plants. *Foliage Digest* 7(8):1-6.

————. 1987. Factors influencing shipping of acclimatized foliage plants. *Foliage Digest* 10(4):1-5.

Crockett, J.U. 1977. *Foliage House Plants.* Revised. Alexandria, VA: Time-Life Books.

Florists' Transworld Delivery Association. 1985. *The Indoor Gardener.* Southfield, MI.

Gaines, R.L. 1977. *Interior Plantscaping: Building Design for Interior Foliage Plants.* New York: Architectural Record Books.

Holstead, C.L. 1985. *Care and Handling of Flowers and Plants.* Floralife Inc.

McConnell, D.B., R.W. Henley and R.L. Biamonte. 1981. Commercial foliage plants. J.N. Joiner (ed.). *Foliage plant production.* Englewood Cliffs, NJ: Prentice-Hall Inc.

Sullivan, G.H., J.L. Robertson and G.L. Staby. 1980. Care and handling of foliage plants. *Management for Retail Florists with Applications to Nursery and Garden Centers.* San Francisco: W.H. Freeman and Co.

N

Peperomia caperata

pe-pe-*rom*-ee-a
ka-pe-*rah*-ta

Family Name: **Piperaceae**
Common Name: **Emerald-Ripple Peperomia**

Originated in Brazil.

PEPEROMIA CAPERATA

Production factors

Light. Use production light levels of 1,500 to 3,000 fc (10.8 to 27 klx) for acclimatized plants.

Temperature. Maintain greenhouse temperatures of at least 65°F (18°C) to promote good growth.

Nutrition. At recommended production light levels, fertilize with 27.6 pounds per 1000 square feet per year (lb/1000 sq. ft/yr) or 134.8 kilograms per 1000 square meters per year (kg/1000 sq. m/yr) of N-P-K. A N-P-K ratio of 3:1:2 is suggested for use with soilless media, while 1:1:1 is recommended for soil-based media. Most media require the addition of micronutrients either by preplant incorporation of a granular source or as part of a liquid fertilization program.

Irrigation. Allow the potting medium to dry slightly between waterings. Avoid extremely wet or dry conditions.

Media. Use a potting medium that has water-holding capacity and good drainage characteristics.

Problems.

Diseases: Blight—*Botrytis cinerea, Sclerotium rolfsii;* edema—*Cercospora* sp.; leaf spot—*Cephaleuros virescens, Cercospora* spp., *Colletrotrichum* spp., *Corynespora* sp., *Myrothecium roridum; Phyllosticta* sp., *Rhizoctonia* sp.; root rot—*Pythium splendens,* root and stem rot—*Phytophthora parasitica;* wilt—*Verticillium dahliae;* virus—cucumber mosaic virus, necrotic ring spot virus.

Pests: Aphids; mealybugs; broad mites; cyclamen mites; scale; thrips.

Disorders. Root rot is a serious problem in saturated media. Conversely, water stress causes weak stems that sprawl instead of grow upright. The leaves eventually turn yellow and abscise.

Postproduction factors

Light. Transport of plants under dark conditions is currently the most common method of shipping. If immediate plant delivery is not possible, provide emerald-ripple peperomia with at least 100 to 250 fc (1.1 to 2.7 klx) of light. Low light levels of

P

149

Peperomia caperata

50 to 75 fc (.5 to .8 klx) are tolerated, but more light is advised to preserve a high quality condition. Avoid light levels above 2,000 fc (21.6 klx).

Temperature. Recommended temperatures for shipping are 60° to 68°F (16° to 20°C).

Gases. Leaf abscission occurs when ethylene concentration exceeds 1 ppm.

Lasting qualities. Peperomias generally tolerate 7 days of dark storage. Expect quality loss if transit requires more than 10 days.

Care and grooming. Pack plants when the potting medium is moist but not saturated and ship with the foliage dry. These precautions decrease the possibility of root rot. Relative humidity levels of 65% to 85% are recommended for quality retention when shipped within the above guidelines.

Retail handling

Light. Provide plants with sufficient light upon delivery to recuperate from the stresses of dark storage. Maintain emerald-ripple peperomia under 100 to 250 fc (1.2 to 2.7 klx) of light. Low light levels of 50 to 75 fc (.5 to .8 klx) are tolerated, but more light is advised to preserve a high quality condition. Avoid light levels above 2,000 fc (21.6 klx).

Temperature. Interior temperatures of 65° to 85°F (18° to 29°C) sustain growth and quality. Protect plants from temperatures below 50°F (10°C). Provide moderate to high levels of humidity, especially if temperatures are near the upper end of the recommended range.

Irrigation. Allow the potting medium to dry slightly between waterings. Avoid extremely wet or dry conditions.

Disorders. Leaf abscission occurs when ethylene concentration exceeds 1 ppm. Light levels above 2,000 fc (21.6 klx) cause plant damage particularly when combined with high temperatures and low humidity. Chilling injury can occur when temperatures fall below 50°F (10°C). Root rot is a serious problem in saturated media. Conversely, water stress causes weak stems that sprawl instead of grow upright. The leaves eventually turn yellow and abscise.

Consumer care

Temperature. Keep interior temperatures of 65° to 85°F (18° to 29°C) to sustain growth and quality. Protect plants from exposure to temperatures below 50°F (10°C). Provide moderate to high levels of humidity, especially if temperatures are near the upper end of the recommended range.

Location. Emerald-ripple peperomia thrives when placed under bright indirect or curtain-filtered sunlight, but also retains quality under interior lighting of 100 to 250 fc (1.1 to 2.7 klx). Low light levels of 50 to 75 fc (.5 to .8 klx) are tolerated, but more light is advised to preserve a healthy appearance. Avoid light levels above 2,000 fc (21.6 klx).

Irrigation. Allow the potting medium to dry slightly between waterings. Avoid extremely wet or dry conditions.

Grooming. Repotting is rarely needed with Emerald-Ripple peperomia. If overcrowding occurs, early spring prior to new growth emergence is the best time for repotting. Propagation by leaf cuttings or division of crowns in early spring are recommended methods of rejuvenating old plants. Fertilize every 3 to 4 months with half-strength houseplant formula.

P

Peperomia caperata

pe-pe-*rom*-ee-a
ka-pe-*rah*-ta

Disorders. Light levels above 2,000 fc (21.6 klx) cause plant damage particularly when combined with high temperatures and low humidity. Chilling injury can occur when temperatures fall below 50°F (10°C). Root rot is a serious problem in saturated media. Conversely, water stress causes weak stems that sprawl instead of grow upright. The leaves eventually turn yellow and abscise.

ADDITIONAL READING

Bailey, L.H. and E.Z. Bailey. 1976. *Hortus Third*.New York: Macmillan Publishing Co. Inc.

Chase, A.R. 1985. Diseases of foliage plants— Revised list for 1985. *Foliage Digest*. 8(6):3-8.

Conover, C.A. and R.T. Poole. 1981. Guide for fertilizing foliage plant crops. *ARC-Apopka Research Rpt*. RH-81-1. University of Florida.

———. 1984. Light and fertilizer recommendations for production of acclimatized potted foliage plants. *Foliage Digest* 7(8):1-6.

Crockett, J.U. 1977. *Foliage House Plants*. Revised. Alexandria, VA: Time-Life Books.

Everett, T.H. 1980. *The New York Botanical Garden Illustrated Encyclopedia of Horticulture*. New York: Garland Publishing Inc.

McConnell, D.B., R.W. Henley and R.L. Biamonte. 1981. Commercial foliage plants. J.N. Joiner (ed.). *Foliage Plant Production*. Englewood Cliffs, NJ: Prentice-Hall Inc.

Poole, R.T. and C.A. Conover. 1987. Foliage variety determines heat. *Greenhouse Grower* 5(1):21-22.

Sullivan, G.H., J.L. Robertson and G.L. Staby. 1980. Care and handling of foliage plants. *Management for Retail Florists with Applications to Nursery and Garden Centers*. San Francisco: W.H. Freeman and Co.

P

Peperomia obtusifolia

pe-pe-*rom*-ee-a
ob-tew-si-*fo*-lee-a

Family Name: **Piperaceae**
Common Name: **Baby Rubber Plant, Pepper-Face**

Originated in tropical America and south Florida.

PEPEROMIA OBTUSIFOLIA

Production factors

Light. Use production light levels of 1,500 to 3,000 fc (10.8 to 27 klx) for acclimatized plants. Variegated cultivars show more color as production light is reduced, but growth is also reduced. Choose cultivars that are naturally more variegated rather than decrease production light if highly patterned foliage is desired.

Temperature. Maintain greenhouse temperatures of at least 65°F (18°C) to promote continuous growth.

Nutrition. At recommended production light levels, fertilize with 27.6 pounds per 1000 square feet per year (lb/1000 sq. ft/yr)

or 134.8 kilograms per 1000 square meters per year (kg/1000 sq. m/yr) of N-P-K. A N-P-K ratio of 3:1:2 is suggested for use with soilless media, while 1:1:1 is recommended for soil-based media. Most media require the addition of micronutrients either by preplant incorporation of a granular source or as part of a liquid fertilization program.

Irrigation. Allow the potting medium to dry slightly between waterings. Avoid extremely wet or dry conditions.

Media. Use a potting medium that has water-holding capacity and good drainage characteristics.

Problems

Diseases: Blight—*Botrytis cinerea, Sclerotium rolfsii;* edema—*Cercospora* sp.; leaf spot—*Cephaleuros virescens, Cercospora* spp., *Colletrotrichum* spp., *Corynespora* sp., *Myrothecium roridum; Phyllosticta* sp., *Rhizoctonia* sp.; root rot—*Pythium splendens;* root and stem rot—*Phytophthora parasitica;* wilt—*Verticillium dahliae;* virus—cucumber mosaic virus, necrotic ring spot virus.

Pests: Aphids; mealybugs; broad mites; cyclamen mites; scale; thrips.

Disorders. Root rot is a serious problem in saturated media. Conversely, water stress causes weak stems that sprawl instead of grow upright. The leaves eventually turn yellow and abscise.

P

Postproduction factors

Light. Transport of plants under dark conditions is currently the most common method of shipping. If immediate plant delivery is not possible, provide baby rubber plant with at least 100 to 250 fc (1.1 to 2.7 klx) of light. Low light levels of 50 to 75 fc (.5 to .8 klx) are tolerated, but more light is advised to preserve a quality appearance. Avoid light exposures above 2,000 fc (21.6 klx).

Temperature. Recommended temperatures for shipping are 60° to 68°F (16° to 20°C).

Gases. Leaf abscission occurs when ethylene concentration exceeds 1 ppm.

Lasting qualities. Peperomias generally tolerate 7 days of dark storage. Expect quality loss if transit requires more than 10 days.

Care and grooming. Pack plants when the potting medium is moist but not saturated and ship with dry foliage. These precautions decrease the possibility of root rot. Relative humidity levels of 65% to 85% are recommended for quality retention when shipped within the above guidelines.

Retail handling

Light. Provide plants with sufficient light upon delivery to recuperate from the stresses of dark storage. Maintain baby rubber plant under 100 to 250 fc (1.1 to 2.7 klx) of light. Low light levels of 50 to 75 fc (.5 to .8 klx) are tolerated, but more light is advised to preserve a quality appearance. Avoid light exposures above 2,000 fc (21.6 klx).

Temperature. Maintain interior temperatures of 65° to 85°F (18° to 29°C) to sustain growth and quality. Avoid temperatures below 50°F (10°C). Most peperomias prefer moderate to high levels of humidity, especially if temperatures are near the upper end of the recommended range. However, the thick, succulent stems and leaves of baby rubber plant are less sensitive to normal interior humidity.

Irrigation. Allow the potting medium to dry slightly between waterings. Avoid extremely wet or dry conditions. Carefully monitor indoor watering needs since baby rubber plant requires less frequent waterings during winter.

Disorders. Leaf abscission occurs when ethylene concentration exceeds 1 ppm. Light levels above 2,000 fc (21.6 klx) cause plant damage particularly when combined with high temperatures and low humidity. Chilling injury can occur when temperatures fall below 50°F (10°C). Root rot is a serious problem in saturated media. Conversely, water stress causes weak stems that sprawl instead of grow upright. The leaves eventually turn yellow and abscise.

P

Consumer care

Temperature. Maintain interior temperatures of 65° to 85°F (18° to 29°C) to sustain growth and quality. Protect plants from exposure to temperatures below 50°F (10°C). Most peperomias prefer moderate to high levels of humidity, especially if temperatures are near the upper end of the recommended range. However, the thick, succulent stems and leaves of baby rubber plant are less sensitive to normal interior humidity.

Location. Baby rubber plant thrives when

Peperomia obtusifolia

pe-pe-*rom*-ee-a
ob-tew-si-*fo*-lee-a

placed under bright indirect or curtain-filtered sunlight, but also retains quality under interior lighting of 100 to 250 fc (1.1 to 2.7 klx). Low light levels of 50 to 75 fc (.5 to .8 klx) are tolerated, but more light is advised to preserve high quality. Avoid light levels above 2,000 fc (21.6 klx).

Irrigation. Allow the potting medium to dry slightly between waterings. Avoid extremely wet or dry conditions. Carefully monitor indoor watering needs since baby rubber plant requires less frequent waterings during winter.

Grooming. Repotting is rarely needed with baby rubber plant. Early spring prior to new growth emergence is the best time for repotting if overcrowding occurs. Propagation by leaf cuttings, stem cuttings or division of crowns in early spring are recommended methods of rejuvenating old plants. Fertilize every 3 to 4 months with half-strength houseplant formula.

Disorders. Chilling injury can occur when temperatures fall below 50°F (10°C). Light levels above 2,000 fc (21.6 klx) cause plant damage particularly when combined with high temperatures and low humidity. Root rot is a serious problem in saturated media. Conversely, water stress causes weak stems that sprawl instead of grow upright. The leaves eventually turn yellow and abscise.

Cultivars. *Peperomia obtusifolia* 'Albo-marginata' (Silver-Edge) leaves are gray-green with a silver border.

Peperomia obtusifolia 'Variegata' leaves have a green center marked with gray-green, and the margins are broadly and irregularly edged with cream-white.

ADDITIONAL READING

Bailey, L.H. and E.Z. Bailey. 1976. *Hortus Third*.New York: Macmillan Publishing Co. Inc.

Chase, A.R. 1985. Diseases of foliage plants—Revised list for 1985. *Foliage Digest* 8(6):3-8.

Conover, C.A. and R.T. Poole. 1981. Guide for fertilizing foliage plant crops. *ARC-Apopka Research Rpt.* RH-81-1. University of Florida.

———. 1984. Light and fertilizer recommendations for production of acclimatized potted foliage plants. *Foliage Digest* 7(8):1-6.

Crockett, J.U. 1977. *Foliage House Plants*. Revised. Alexandria, VA: Time-Life Books.

Everett, T.H. 1980. *The New York Botanical Garden Illustrated Encyclopedia of Horticulture*. New York: Garland Publishing Inc.

McConnell, D.B., R.W. Henley and R.L. Biamonte. 1981. Commercial foliage plants. J.N. Joiner (ed.). *Foliage Plant Production*. Englewood Cliffs, NJ: Prentice-Hall Inc.

Poole, R.T. and A.R. Chase. 1987. Response of foliage plants in an interior environment to irrigation frequencies. *Foliage Digest* 10(6):1-3.

———. 1987. Foliage variety determines heat. *Greenhouse Grower* 5(1):21-22.

Shen, G.W. and J.G. Seeley. 1983. The effect of shading and nutrient supply on variegation and nutrient content of variegated cultivars of *Peperomia obtusifolia*. *J. Amer. Soc. Hort. Sci.* 108:429-433.

Sullivan, G.H., J.L. Robertson and G.L. Staby. 1980. Care and handling of foliage plants. *Management for Retail Florists with Applications to Nursery and Garden Centers*. San Francisco: W.H. Freeman and Co.

P

Philodendron scandens oxycardium

fi-lo-*den*-dron
skan-denz
oks-ee-*kar*-dee-um

Family Name: **Araceae**
Common Name: **Common Philodendron, Parlor Ivy**

Originated in East Mexico. This plant was previously named *Philodendron cordatum* and *Philodendron oxycardium*.

PHILODENDRON SCANDENS OXYCARDIUM

Production factors

Light. Use production light levels of 1,500 to 3,000 fc (16.2 to 32.4 klx) for acclimatized plants.

Temperature. Keep greenhouse temperatures of at least 65°F (18°C) to maintain good growth.

Nutrition. At recommended production light levels for acclimatized plants, fertilize with 34.5 pounds per 1000 square feet per year (lb/1000 sq. ft/yr) or 168.4 kilograms per 1000 square meters per year (kg/1000

sq. m/yr) of N-P-K. A N-P-K ratio of 3:1:2 is suggested for use with soilless media, while 1:1:1 is recommended for soil-based media. Most media require the addition of micronutrients either by preplant incorporation of a granular source or as part of a liquid fertilization program.

Irrigation. Keep the potting medium moist but not wet. Protect plants from rainfall and avoid overhead irrigation to reduce quality loss from disease.

Media. Use an organic potting medium with good aeration and drainage characteristics.

Problems.

Diseases: Anthracnose—*Colletotrichum philodendri;* blight—*Botrytis cinerea, Erwinia chrysanthemi, Rhizoctonia solani, Sclerotium rolfsii;* leaf spot—*Cephalosporium cinnamomeum, Cercospora* sp., *Colletotrichum* sp., *Dactylaria humicola, Erwinia aroidea, Gloeosporium* sp., *Glomerella cingulata, Myrothecium roridum, Phyllosticta* sp., *Phytophthora parasitica var. nicotianae, Pseudomonas cichorii;* red edge—*Xanthomonas campestris* pv. *dieffenbachiae;* root rot—*Pythium* spp.; soft rot—*Erwinia carotovora* subsp. *carotovora;* virus, cucumber mosaic virus, Dasheen mosaic virus.

Pests: Mealybugs; mites; root knot nematodes—*Meloidogyne* spp.; scale; thrips.

Disorders. Common philodendron is moderately sensitive to atmospheric fluo-

P

Philodendron scandens oxycardium

fi-lo-*den*-dron
skan-denz
oks-ee-*kar*-dee-um

ride. Symptoms first appear as marginal and tip chlorosis on young leaves and as marginal and interveinal chlorosis on mature leaves. The chlorotic areas progress from water-soaked to necrotic and finally to dry, tan lesions.

Postproduction factors

Light. Transport of plants under dark conditions is currently the most common method of shipping. If immediate delivery is not possible, maintain plants under at least 50 fc (.5 klx) of light. Common philodendron tolerates low light better than many other foliage plants, but minimum lighting of 75 to 150 fc (.8 to 1.6 klx) is recommended to preserve typical growth habit.

Temperature. Recommended temperatures for shipping are 55° to 60°F (13° to 16°C).

Gases. Common philodendron develops chlorosis and leaf abscission when exposed to ethylene for several days. Damage increases with time, ethylene concentration and temperatures of 75°F (24°C) or more. Injury due to ethylene is generally not a problem when plants are shipped within the recommended temperature range. Ethylene may reach damaging levels if plants are shipped with produce or held in prolonged storage above the maximum listed temperature.

Lasting qualities. Under appropriate storage conditions acclimatized plants retain good quality when shipped within 2 weeks. Maintain storage temperatures near the upper end of the recommended range when transport requires only 1 to 7 days. Severe quality loss is expected when plants take more than 2 weeks to reach their destination.

Care and grooming. Good storage preparation improves quality retention during transit. Moisture content of the potting medium should approximate 50% of soil capacity when plants are packed. Common philodendron is highly susceptible to waterborne diseases. Control of these organisms is improved if foliage remains dry when packed. Maintain high humidity levels of 80% to 90% during storage to retard desiccation, especially when shipping time exceeds 7 days.

Retail handling

Light. Provide plants with sufficient light upon delivery to recuperate from the stresses of dark storage. A specially designed holding greenhouse or room is ideal. When such a facility is unavailable, minimum light levels of 75 to 150 fc (.8 to 1.6 klx) are recommended for quality retention.

Temperature. Keep interior temperatures of 65° to 85°F (18° to 29°C) to sustain growth and quality. Avoid temperatures below 50°F (10°C). When a greenhouse is used to hold plants before installation, maintain 40% to 60% relative humidity for acclimatization to lower interior humidity levels.

Irrigation. Keep the potting medium moist but not wet.

Disorders. Foliage can be damaged during shipping by ethylene exposure. Long-term holding under marginal light causes stem elongation and leaf size reduction. Chilling injury occurs when plants are exposed to temperatures below 50°F (10°C).

P

Philodendron scandens oxycardium

fi-lo-*den*-dron
skan-denz
oks-ee-*kar*-dee-um

Consumer care

Temperature. Maintain interior temperatures of 65° to 85°F (18° to 29°C) to sustain growth and quality. Avoid exposure to temperatures below 50°F (10°C).

Location. Plants flourish when installed under bright indirect or curtain-filtered sunlight, but also maintain quality under interior lighting of 75 to 150 fc (.8 to 1.6 klx). Common philodendron tolerates marginal lighting to 50 fc (.5 klx), but higher light preserves typical growth habit.

Irrigation. Keep the potting medium moist but not wet.

Grooming. Overcrowded plants can be repotted at any time of the year. Fertilize every 3 to 4 months.

Disorders. Chilling injury occurs when plants are exposed to temperatures below 50°F (10°C). Long-term holding under marginal light causes stem elongation and leaf size reduction. Common philodendron is moderately sensitive to atmospheric fluoride.

ADDITIONAL READING

Bailey, L.H. and E.Z. Bailey. 1976. *Hortus Third.* New York: New York: Macmillan Publishing Co. Inc.

Chase, A.R. 1985a. Diseases of foliage plants—Revised list for 1985. *Foliage Digest* 8(6):3-8.

———. 1985b. You can prevent foliage diseases. *Greenhouse Grower* 3(12):36-45.

Conover C.A. and R.T. Poole. 1981. Guide for fertilizing foliage plant crops. *ARC-Apopka Research Rpt.* RH-81-1. University of Florida.

———. 1984. Light and fertilizer recommendations for production of acclimatized potted foliage plants. *Foliage Digest* 7(8):1-6.

———. 1987. Factors influencing shipping of acclimatized foliage plants. *Foliage Digest* 10(4):1-5.

Crockett, J.U. 1977. *Foliage House Plants.* Revised. Alexandria, VA: Time-Life Books.

Everett, T.H. 1980. *The New York Botanical Garden Illustrated Encyclopedia of Horticulture.* New York: Garland Publishing Inc.

Gaines, R.L. 1977. *Interior Plantscaping: Building Design for Interior Foliage Plants.* New York: Architectural Record Books.

Marousky, F.J. and B.K. Harbaugh. 1978. Deterioration of foliage plants during transit. *Proc. 1978 Natl. Tropical Foliage Short Course,* University of Florida, IFAS Coop. Ext. Serv., Orlando, FL.

McConnell, D.B., R.W. Henley and R.L. Biamonte. 1981. Commercial foliage plants. J.N. Joiner (ed.). *Foliage Plant Production.* Englewood Cliffs, NJ: Prentice-Hall Inc.

Poole, R.T. and C.A. Conover. 1987. Foliage variety determines heat. *Greenhouse Grower* 5(1):21-22.

Sullivan, G.H., J.L. Robertson and G.L. Staby. 1980. Care and handling of foliage plants. *Management for Retail Florists with Applications to Nursery and Garden Centers.* San Francisco: W.H. Freeman and Co.

Woltz, S.S. and W.E. Waters. 1978. Airborne fluoride effects on some foliage plants. *HortScience* 13:585-586.

P

Philodendron selloum

fi-lo-*den*-dron
se-*lo*-um

Family Name: **Araceae**
Common Name: **Lacy-Tree Philodendron, Tree Philodendron, Saddle-Leaf Philodendron**

Originated in South Brazil.

PHILODENDRON SELLOUM

Production factors

Light. Lacy-tree philodendron is produced by seed which require 300 to 600 fc (3.2 to 6.5 klx) for germination. Seedlings develop healthy, compact growth habits under 1,500 to 2,500 fc (16.2 to 27 klx). Maintain light levels of 3,000 to 6,000 fc (32.4 to 64.8 klx) to produce finished, acclimatized plants.

Temperature. This species is more tolerant of cold than other philodendron, and dormant, mature outdoor specimens survive temperatures to 22°F (-6°C). However, young plants are tender and should be protected from cold weather.

Nutrition. At recommended production light levels, fertilize with 41.4 pounds per 1000 square feet per year (lb/1000 sq. ft/yr) or 202.1 kilograms per 1000 square meters per year (kg/1000 sq. m/yr) of N-P-K. A ratio of 3:1:2 or 2:1:2 is suggested for production of lacy-tree philodendron. Micronutrients can be mixed with the medium prior to potting or applied in solution as part of a liquid fertilizer program. Plants receiving fertilizer rates higher or lower than the recommended amount are more susceptible to attack by *Erwinia*.

Irrigation. Keep the potting medium moist but not wet. Protect plants from rainfall and avoid overhead irrigation to reduce quality loss from disease. Disease control is further improved if plants are spaced adequately to speed drying after irrigation.

Media. Use an organic potting medium with high water-holding capacity, and good aeration and drainage characteristics. Incorporate dolomite into the medium to provide a pH of 6.0.

P

Philodendron selloum

fi-lo-*den*-dron
se-*lo*-um

Problems.

Diseases: Anthracnose—*Colletrotrichum philodendri*; blight—*Botrytis cinerea, Erwinia chrysanthemi, Rhizoctonia solani, Sclerotium rolfsii*; leaf spot—*Cephalosporium cinnamomeum, Cercospora* sp., *Colletrotrichum* sp., *Dactylaria humicola, Erwinia aroidea, Gloeosporium* sp., *Glomerella cingulata, Myrothecium roridum, Phyllosticta* sp., *Phytophthora parasitica* var. *nicotianae, Pseudomonas cichorii;* red edge—*Xanthomonas campestris* pv. *dieffenbachiae;* root rot—*Pythium* spp.; soft rot—*Erwinia carotovora* subsp. *carotovora;* virus—cucumber mosaic virus, Dasheen mosaic virus.

Pests: Aphids; caterpillars; mealybugs; mites; root knot nematodes—*Meloidogyne* spp.; scale; thrips.

Disorders. Lower leaves develop poor color when exposed to winter chilling temperatures. Production light below recommended levels causes plants to develop abnormally long petioles and leaf blades with reduced lobe count. Lacy-tree philodendron is moderately sensitive to atmospheric fluoride. Symptoms include marginal and interveinal chlorosis. Older leaves develop watersoaked areas that eventually dry to a crisp, white texture.

Temperature. Acclimatized plants can be shipped without damage for extended periods when held at 55° to 60°F (13° to 16°C).

Gases. Injury due to ethylene is generally not a problem when plants are shipped within the recommended temperature range. Ethylene may reach damaging levels if plants are shipped with produce or held in prolonged storage above the maximum listed temperature.

Lasting qualities. Under appropriate storage conditions acclimatized plants retain good quality when shipped within 4 weeks. Maintain temperatures near the upper end of the recommended range when transport requires only 1 to 7 days.

Care and grooming. Good storage preparation improves quality retention during transit. Moisture content of the potting medium should approximate 50% of soil capacity when plants are packed. Lacy-tree philodendron is highly susceptible to waterborne diseases. Control of these organisms is improved if foliage remains dry when packed. Maintain high relative humidities of 80% to 90% during storage to retard desiccation, especially when shipping time exceeds 7 days.

Postproduction factors

Light. Transport of plants under dark conditions is currently the most common method of shipping. If immediate delivery is not possible, maintain plants under at least 75 to 250 fc (.8 to 2.7 klx) of light. The growth habit changes with protracted holding under low light; therefore, increase light levels to 250 fc (2.7 klx) or more if retention of typical form is desired.

Retail handling

Light. Upon delivery provide plants with sufficient light to recuperate from the stresses of dark storage. A specially designed holding greenhouse or room is ideal for this purpose. When such a facility is unavailable, maintain plants under at least 75 to 250 fc (.8 to 2.7 klx) of light. Increase light levels to 250 fc (2.7 klx) or more for best retention of typical growth.

P

159

Foliage Plants *Philodendron selloum*

Temperature. Keep interior temperatures of 65° to 85°F (18° to 29°C) to sustain growth and quality. This durable philodendron tolerates brief exposure to cool temperatures (to 40°F; 4°C) without injury. When a greenhouse is used to hold plants before installation, maintain 40% to 60% relative humidity for acclimatization to lower interior humidity levels.

Irrigation. Keep the potting medium moist but not wet.

Disorders. Long-term maintenance under marginal light causes elongation of petioles and reduction in the number of lobes on leaf blades.

Consumer care

Temperature. Keep interior temperatures of 65° to 85°F (18° to 29°C) to sustain growth and quality. Occasional brief exposure to cool temperatures (to 40°F; 4°C) is tolerated.

Location. Lacy-tree philodendron thrives in areas with bright indirect or curtain-filtered sunlight. Typical growth habit is preserved with light levels above 250 fc (2.7 klx); however, plants retain sufficient quality under 75 to 250 fc (.8 to 2.7 klx) of light.

Irrigation. Keep the potting medium moist but not wet.

Grooming. Overcrowded plants can be repotted at any time of the year. Fertilize every 3 to 4 months.

Disorders. Long-term maintenance under marginal light causes elongation of petioles and reduction in the number of lobes on leaf blades. Lacy-tree philodendron is moderately sensitive to atmospheric fluoride.

ADDITIONAL READING

Bailey, L.H. and E.Z. Bailey. 1976. *Hortus Third.* New York: Macmillan Publishing Co. Inc.

Chase, A.R. 1985a. Diseases of foliage plants—Revised list for 1985. *Foliage Digest* 8(6):3-8.

———. 1985b. You can prevent foliage diseases. *Greenhouse Grower* 3(12):36-45.

Conover, C.A. and R.T. Poole. 1981. Guide for fertilizing foliage plant crops. *ARC-Apopka Research Rpt.* RH-81-1. University of Florida.

———. 1984. Light and fertilizer recommendations for production of acclimatized potted foliage plants. *Foliage Digest* 7(8):1-6.

———. 1987. Factors influencing shipping of acclimatized foliage plants. *Foliage Digest* 10(4):1-5.

Crockett, J.U. 1977. *Foliage House Plants.* Revised. Alexandria, VA: Time-Life Books.

Everett, T.H. 1980. *The New York Botanical Garden Illustrated Encyclopedia of Horticulture.* New York: Publishing Inc.

Henley, R.W., L.S. Osborne and A.R. Chase. 1986. Lacy-tree Philodendron. *Foliage Digest* 12(4):6-8.

Holstead, C.L. 1985. *Care and Handling of Flowers and Plants.* Floralife Inc., Society of American Florists. Alexandria, VA.

Manaker, G.H. 1981. *Interior Plantscapes: Installation, Maintenance, and Management.* Englewood Cliffs, NJ: Prentice-Hall Inc.

McConnell, D.B., R.W. Henley and R.L. Biamonte. 1981. Commercial foliage plants. J.N. Joiner (ed.). *Foliage Plant Production.* Englewood Cliffs, NJ: Prentice-Hall Inc.

Woltz, S.S. and W.E. Waters. 1978. Airborne fluoride effects on some foliage plants. *HortScience* 13:585-586.

P

Pilea cadierei

pee-lee-a
ka-dee-*e*-ree-ee

Family Name: **Urticaceae**
Common Name: **Aluminum Plant**

Originated in Vietnam.

PILEA CADIEREI

Production factors

Light. Use production light levels of
1,000 to 2,000 fc (10.8 to 21.6 klx) for
acclimatized plants.

Temperature. Maintain greenhouse
temperatures of 65° to 85°F (18° to 29°C) to
promote rooting and rapid growth.

Nutrition. At recommended production
light levels, fertilize with 20.7 pounds per
1000 square feet per year (lb/1000 sq. ft/yr)
or 101.1 kilograms per 1000 square meters
per year (kg/1000 sq. m/yr) of N-P-K. A
liquid or soluble form of 2:1:2 or 3:1:2 ratio
is suggested for the rapidly growing aluminum plant. Micronutrients can be mixed with
the medium prior to potting or applied in
solution as part of a liquid fertilizer program.

Irrigation. Keep the potting medium
moist but not wet. Quality loss from disease
is reduced when constant wetting of foliage
from rainfall and overhead irrigation is
eliminated. Disease control is further improved if plants are spaced adequately to
speed drying after irrigation.

Media. Use a moisture-retentive organic
potting medium with good aeration and
drainage characteristics. Incorporate dolomite to provide a pH of 5.0 to 6.0. Do not
compress the soil mass when potting.

Problems.

Diseases: Anthracnose—*Colletotrichum
capisci;* blight—*Botrytis cinerea, Phytophthora parasitica, Rhizoctonia solani, Sclerotium rolfsii;* leaf spot—*Cercospora pileae,
Myrothecium roridum, Xanthomonas
campestris;* powdery mildew—*Erysiphe
cichoracearum;* root rot—*Pythium* spp.

Pests: Aphids; mealybugs; mites; scale;
slugs; snails; whitefly.

Disorders. Foliage color intensity is lost
when plants are produced under light levels
exceeding recommendations. A poor quality
medium inhibits root development and stunts
growth.

Postproduction factors

Light. Transport of plants under dark
conditions is currently the most common
method of shipping. If immediate delivery is

P

not possible, maintain plants under at least 150 to 250 fc (1.6 to 2.7 klx) of light to preserve typical growth habit.

Temperature. Specific recommendations for shipping aluminum plant are unavailable. However, guidelines for shipping two hybrids with similar upright growth habits are provided. Response to shipping conditions is different for each hybrid and reflects the variable nature of this genus. Moon Valley Pilea can be shipped at 55° to 65°F (13° to 18°C) for extended periods without damage. Silver Tree Pilea should be maintained within 55° to 60°F (13° to 16°C) during transit.

Gases. Epinasty develops when foliage is exposed to ethylene during shipping. Storage at cool but not chilling temperatures during transit limits the response. Ethylene may reach damaging levels if plants are shipped with produce or held in prolonged storage above the maximum listed temperature.

Lasting qualities. Again, information on shipping tolerance is not available for aluminum plant. Under appropriate storage conditions Moon Valley Pilea retains good quality when shipped within 4 weeks. Silver Tree Pilea requires a shorter shipping duration for best quality maintenance. Severe loss is expected when Silver Tree Pilea requires more than 2 weeks to reach its destination. Maintain temperatures near the upper end of the recommended range when transport requires only 1 to 7 days.

Care and grooming. Good storage preparation improves quality retention during transit. Moisture content of the potting medium should approximate 50% of soil capacity when plants are packed. Aluminum plant is highly susceptible to waterborne diseases. Control of these organisms is improved if foliage remains dry when packed. Maintain high relative humidities of 80% to 90% during storage to retard desiccation, especially when shipping time exceeds 7 days.

Retail handling

Light. Provide plants with sufficient light upon delivery to recuperate from the stresses of dark storage. Maintain plants under at least 150 to 250 fc (1.6 to 2.7 klx) of light.

Temperature. Keep interior temperatures of 65° to 85°F (18° to 29°C) to sustain growth and quality. Avoid exposure to temperatures below 55°F (13°C). Aluminum plant prefers locations with moderate to high humidity levels; therefore, maintain interior temperatures near the lower end of the recommended range if humidity is low.

Irrigation. Keep the potting medium moist but not wet.

Disorders. Epinasty develops if foliage is exposed to ethylene during transit. The effect is temporary if ethylene concentration does not exceed 5 ppm for 3 days. Extended holding under marginal light causes stem elongation. Chilling injury occurs at temperatures below 55°F (13°C). Water stress stimulates lower canopy leaf abscission.

Consumer care

Temperature. Keep interior temperatures of 65° to 85°F (18° to 29°C) to sustain growth and quality. Aluminum plant prefers areas with moderate to high humidity levels; therefore, maintain interior temperatures near the lower end of the recommended

P

Pilea cadierei

pee-lee-a ka-dee-*e*-ree-ee

range if humidity is low.

Location. Aluminum plant thrives in areas with bright indirect or curtain-filtered sunlight, but also retains quality under interior lighting of 150 to 250 fc (1.6 to 2.7 klx).

Irrigation. Keep the potting medium moist but not wet.

Grooming. Under good growing conditions aluminum plant increases rapidly and requires frequent pinching to keep a tidy appearance. Plants tolerate occasional severe pruning to rejuvenate old specimens, but replacement with new plants from easily rooted cuttings may be desired for best appearance. Early spring is a good time for repotting and propagation. Small 3- to 4-inch (8- to 10-cm) pots, dish gardens and terrariums are recommended settings for this small scale plant. Fertilize every 2 months with half-strength solution.

Disorders. Chilling injury occurs if plants are exposed to temperatures below 55°F (13°C). Long-term maintenance under marginal light causes stem elongation. Water stress stimulates lower canopy leaf abscission.

Cultivars. *Pilea* 'Moon Valley' has an upright growth habit. Quilted leaves are brown around the veins and bright green along margins. Pink flower clusters form in stem terminals.

Pilea 'Silvertree' also has an upright growth habit. Quilted leaves are bronze with a silver band down the leaf center and silver spots along the margin.

ADDITIONAL READING

Arthurs, Kathryn (ed.). 1974. *How to Grow House Plants*. Menlo Park, CA: Lane Publishing Co.

Bailey, L.H. and E.Z. Bailey. 1976. *Hortus Third*. New York: Macmillan Publishing Co. Inc.

Chase, A.R. 1985. Diseases of foliage plants— Revised list for 1985. *Foliage Digest* 8(6):3-8.

Conover C.A. and R.T. Poole. 1981. Guide for fertilizing foliage plant crops. *ARC-Apopka Research Rpt*. RH-81-1. University of Florida.

————. 1984. Light and fertilizer recommendations for production of acclimatized potted foliage plants. *Foliage Digest* 7(8):1-6.

————. 1987. Factors influencing shipping of acclimatized foliage plants. *Foliage Digest* 10(4):1-5.

Crockett, J.U. 1977. *Foliage House Plants*. Revised. Alexandria, VA: Time-Life Books.

Everett, T.H. 1980. *The New York Botanical Garden Illustrated Encyclopedia of Horticulture*. New York: Publishing Inc.

Marousky, F.J. and B.K. Harbaugh. 1978. Deterioration of foliage plants during transit. *Proc. 1978 Natl. Tropical Foliage Short Course*, University of Florida, IFAS Coop. Ext. Serv., Orlando, FL.

McConnell, D.B., R.W. Henley and R.L. Biamonte. 1981. Commercial foliage plants. J.N. Joiner (ed.). *Foliage plant production*. Englewood Cliffs, NJ: Prentice-Hall Inc.

Osborne, L.S., A.R. Chase and R.W. Henley. 1986. Pilea. *Foliage Digest* 9(11):3-6.

Wright, M. (ed.). 1979. *The Complete Indoor Gardener*. Rev. ed. New York: Random House.

P

163

Foliage Plants *Pilea cadierei*

Pilea microphylla

pee-lee-a
mik-ro-*fil*-la

Family Name: **Urticaceae**
Common Name: **Artillery Plant**

Originated in American tropics.

PILEA MICROPHYLLA

Production factors

Light. Use production light levels of 1,000 to 2,000 fc (10.8 to 21.6 klx) for acclimatized plants.

Temperature. Provide greenhouse temperatures of 65° to 85°F (18° to 29°C) to promote rooting and rapid growth.

Nutrition. At recommended production light levels, fertilize with 20.7 pounds per 1000 square feet per year (lb/1000 sq. ft/yr) or 101.1 kilograms per 1000 square meters per year (kg/1000 sq. m/yr) of N-P-K. A liquid or soluble form of 2:1:2 or 3:1:2 ratio is suggested for the rapidly growing artillery plant. Micronutrients can be mixed with the medium prior to potting or applied in solution as part of a liquid fertilizer program.

Irrigation. Keep the potting medium moist but not wet. Quality loss from disease is reduced when constant wetting of foliage from rainfall and overhead irrigation is eliminated. Disease control is farther improved if plants are spaced adequately to speed drying after irrigation.

Media. Use a moisture-retentive organic potting medium with good aeration and drainage characteristics. Incorporate dolomite to provide a pH of 5.0 to 6.0. Do not compress the soil mass when potting.

Problems.

Diseases: Anthracnose—*Colletotrichum capisci;* blight—*Botrytis cinerea, Phytophthora parasitica, Rhizoctonia solani, Sclerotium rolfsii;* leaf spot—*Cercospora pileae, Myrothecium roridum, Xanthomonas campestris;* powdery mildew—*Erysiphe cichorocearum;* root rot—*Pythium* spp.

Pests: Aphids; mealybugs; mites; scale; slugs; snails; whitefly.

Disorders. Foliage is a pale green when plants are produced under light levels exceeding recommendations. A poor quality medium inhibits root development and stunts growth.

Postproduction factors

Light. Transport of plants under dark conditions is currently the most common method of shipping. If immediate delivery is

P

164

Foliage Plants *Pilea microphylla*

Pilea microphylla

pee-lee-a
mik-ro-fil-la

not possible, maintain plants under at least 150 to 250 fc (1.6 to 2.7 klx) of light to preserve typical growth habit.

Retail handling

Light. Provide plants with sufficient light upon delivery to recuperate from the stresses of dark storage. Maintain plants under at least 150 to 250 fc (1.6 to 2.7 klx) of light.

Temperature. Maintain interior temperatures of 65° to 85°F (18° to 29°C) to sustain growth and quality. Avoid exposure to temperatures below 55°F (13°C). Artillery plant is more tolerant of average interior humidity levels than most pileas.

Irrigation. Keep the potting medium moist but not wet.

Disorders. Extended holding under marginal light causes stem elongation. Chilling injury occurs at temperatures below 55°F (13°C). Water stress stimulates lower canopy leaf abscission.

Consumer care

Temperature. Maintain interior temperatures of 65° to 85°F (18° to 29°C) to sustain growth and quality. Avoid exposure to temperatures below 55°F (13°C). Artillery plant is more tolerant of average interior humidity levels than most pileas.

Location. Artillery plant thrives in areas with bright indirect or curtain-filtered sunlight, but also retains quality under interior lighting of 150 to 250 fc (1.6 to 2.7 klx).

Irrigation. Keep the potting medium moist but not wet.

Grooming. Prune regularly to keep

growth compact. Replace old, untidy plants in early spring with easily rooted cuttings to maintain an attractive appearance. Appropriate containers for display of this small scale plant include 3- to 4-inch (7- to 10-cm) pots, hanging baskets, dish gardens and terrariums. Fertilize every 2 months with half-strength solution.

Disorders. Plants are sensitive to temperatures below 55°F (13°C). Long-term maintenance under marginal light causes stem elongation. Water stress stimulates lower canopy leaf abscission.

Cultivars. *Pilea depressa* (baby's tears) has a creeping, trailing growth habit with stems that root freely at leaf nodes. Tiny bright green leaves are clustered along herbaceous stems.

Pilea involucrata (panamiga, friendship plant) growth habit is trailing to erect, and the 1½-inch (4 cm) long puckered leaves are bronze green with a purplish lower surface.

Pilea nummulariifolia (creeping Charlie) has a creeping, trailing growth habit, and the herbaceous stems root freely at leaf nodes. The 1-inch (2.5 cm) bright green leaves are nearly circular.

ADDITIONAL READING

Arthurs, Kathryn (ed.). 1974. *How to Grow House Plants*. Menlo Park, CA: Lane Publishing Co.,

Bailey, L.H. and E.Z. Bailey. 1976. *Hortus Third*. New York: Macmillan Publishing Co. Inc.

Chase, A.R. 1985. Diseases of foliage plants— Revised list for 1985. *Foliage Digest* 8(6):3-8.

Conover C.A. and R.T. Poole. 1981. Guide for fertilizing foliage plant crops. *ARC-Apopka Research Rpt*. RH-81-1. University of Florida.

———. 1984. Light and fertilizer recommendations for production of acclimatized potted foliage plants. *Foliage Digest* 7(8):1-6.

Crockett, J.U. 1977. *Foliage House Plants*. Revised. Alexandria, VA: Time-Life Books.

P

Pilea microphylla

pee-lee-a
mik-ro-*fil*-la

Everett, T.H. 1980. *The New York Botanical Garden Illustrated Encyclopedia of Horticulture*. New York: Publishing Inc.

McConnell, D.B., R.W. Henley and R.L. Biamonte. 1981. Commercial foliage plants. J.N. Joiner (ed.). *Foliage Plant Production*. Englewood Cliffs, NJ: Prentice-Hall Inc.

Osborne, L.S., A.R. Chase and R.W. Henley. 1986. Pilea. *Foliage Digest* 9(11):3-6.

P

Pittosporum tobira

pi-*tos*-po-rum
to-*bi*-ra

Family Name: **Pittosporaceae**
Common Name: **Japanese Pittosporum, Mock Orange**

Originated in China and Japan.

PITTOSPORUM TOBIRA

Production factors

Light. Use production light levels of 3,000 to 6,000 fc (32.4 to 64.8 klx) for acclimatized plants.

Temperature. Greenhouse temperatures maintained above 55°F (13°C) assure continuous growth, but cooler temperatures are tolerated well.

Nutrition. At recommended production light levels for acclimatized plants, fertilize with 34.5 pounds per 1000 square feet per year (lb/1000 sq. ft/yr) or 168.4 kilograms per 1000 square meters per year (kg/1000 sq. m/yr) of N-P-K. A N-P-K ratio of 3:1:2 is suggested for use with soilless media, while 1:1:1 is recommended for soil-based media. Most media require the addition of micronutrients either by preplant incorporation of a

granular source or as part of a liquid fertilization program.

Irrigation. Keep the potting medium moist but not wet. Watering needs are more moderate in winter.

Media. Use a potting medium with good drainage characteristics.

Problems.

Diseases: Blight—*Corticium salmonicolor, Pellicularia koleroga, Rhizoctonia ramicola, Sclerotium rolfsii;* canker—*Diaporthe* sp.; dieback—*Coniothyrium* sp., *Physalospora rhodina;* crown gall—*Agrobacterium tumefaciens;* stem gall—*Leptosphaeria* sp., *Nectria* sp., *Volutella* sp.; leaf spot—*Alternaria tenuissima, Cercospora pittospori, Gloeosporium* sp.; rot—*Diplodia* sp., *Clitocybe tabescens, Pythium* sp., *Rhizoctonia solani;* virus—rough bark virus.

Pests: Mealybugs; mites; scale.

Postproduction factors

Light. Transport of plants under dark conditions is currently the most common method of shipping. If immediate delivery is not possible, place plants in a holding greenhouse or room with at least 150 fc (1.6 klx) of light. Higher levels of 200 to 500 fc (2.2 to 5.4 klx) are required to maintain typical growth habit when longterm maintenance is necessary. Variegated Japanese pittosporum requires an additional 100 fc

P

(1.1 klx) of light to preserve prime condition.

Temperature. Acclimatized plants can be shipped without damage for extended periods when held at 50° to 65°F (10° to 18°C).

Gases. Injury due to ethylene is generally not a problem when plants are shipped within the recommended temperature range. Ethylene may reach damaging levels if plants are shipped with produce or held in prolonged storage above the maximum listed temperature.

Lasting qualities. Under appropriate storage conditions acclimatized plants retain good quality when shipped within 4 weeks. Maintain temperatures near the upper end of the recommended range when transport requires only 1 to 7 days.

Care and grooming. Good storage preparation improves quality retention during transit. Moisture content of the potting medium should approximate 50% of soil capacity when plants are packed. Maintain high relative humidities of 80% to 90% during storage to retard desiccation, especially when shipping time exceeds 7 days.

Retail handling

Light. Upon delivery provide plants with sufficient light to recuperate from the stresses of dark storage. A specially designed holding greenhouse or room is ideal. When such a facility is unavailable, maintain plants with at least 150 fc (1.6 klx) of light. Japanese pittosporum tolerates low light to 75 fc (.8 klx), but 150 fc (1.6 klx) is enough light to sustain emergence of new growth. Higher levels of 200 to 500 fc (2.2 to 5.4 klx) are required to maintain the typical bushy growth habit. Variegated Japanese pittosporum is less tolerant to low light and requires 300 to 600 fc (3.2 to 6.5 klx) to keep a normal form.

Temperature. Japanese pittosporum is more tolerant to cool temperatures than most interior foliage plants and is often used outdoors in mild temperate zones. Winter night temperatures of 40° to 55°F (4° to 13°C) will not damage plants; however, normal interior temperatures of 65° to 80°F (18° to 27°C) assure growth and quality. If humidity is very low in the holding area, maintain interior temperatures near the lower end of the recommended range.

Irrigation. Keep the potting medium moist but not wet. Watering needs are more moderate in winter compared to warm seasons. Avoid excessively dry media and locations that are bright, hot and dry. When a greenhouse is used to hold plants before installation, maintain 40% to 60% relative humidity for acclimatization to lower interior humidity levels.

Disorders. Leaf abscission is stimulated by water stress.

Consumer care

Temperature. Japanese pittosporum is more tolerant of cool temperatures than most interior foliage plants and is often used outdoors in mild temperate zones. Winter night temperatures of 40° to 55°F (4° to 13°C) will not damage plants; however, normal interior temperatures of 65° to 80°F (18° to 27°C) will assure growth and quality. If humidity is very low, maintain interior temperatures near the lower end of the recommended range.

Location. Japanese pittosporum thrives

Pittosporum tobira

in areas with bright indirect light or some daily sunlight, but also maintains quality under interior lighting to 150 fc (1.6 klx). Plants tolerate low light to 75 fc (.8 klx), but 150 fc (1.6 klx) is enough light to sustain emergence of new growth. Higher levels of 200 to 500 fc (2.2 to 5.4 klx) are required to maintain the typical bushy growth habit. Variegated Japanese pittosporum is less tolerant of low light and requires 300 to 600 fc (3.2 to 6.5 klx) to keep a normal form.

Irrigation. Keep the potting medium moist but not wet. Watering needs are more moderate in winter compared to warm seasons. Avoid excessively dry media and locations that are bright, hot and dry.

Grooming. Prune and repot overcrowded plants in early spring before new growth emerges. Fertilize in early spring and early summer.

Disorders. Leaf abscission is stimulated by water stress.

Cultivars. *Pittosporum tobira* 'Variegata' (variegated pittosporum) is similar in size and growth habit to the species type, but leaves are marked with shades of cream, gray-green and green.

ADDITIONAL READING

Arthurs, Kathryn (ed.). 1974. *How to Grow House Plants.* Menlo Park, CA: Lane Publishing Co.,

Bailey, L.H. and E.Z. Bailey. 1976. *Hortus Third.* New York: Macmillan Publishing Co. Inc.

Conover, C.A. and R.T. Poole. 1981. Guide for fertilizing foliage plant crops. *ARC-Apopka Research Rpt.* RH-81-l. University of Florida.

———. 1984. Light and fertilizer recommendations for production of acclimatized potted foliage plants. *Foliage Digest* 7(8):1-6.

———. 1987. Factors influencing shipping of acclimatized foliage plants. *Foliage Digest* 10(4):1-5.

Crockett, J.U. 1977. *Foliage House Plants.* Revised. Alexandria, VA: Time-Life Books.

Everett, T.H. 1980. *The New York Botanical Garden Illustrated Encyclopedia of Horticulture.* New York: Publishing Inc.

Manaker, G.H. 1981. *Interior Plantscapes: Installation, Maintenance, and Management.* Englewood Cliffs, NJ: Prentice-Hall Inc.

McConnell, D.B., R.W. Henley and R.L. Biamonte. 1981. Commercial foliage plants. J.N. Joiner (ed.). *Foliage Plant Production.* Englewood Cliffs, NJ: Prentice-Hall Inc.

Poole, R.T. and C.A. Conover. 1980. Influence of light and fertilizer levels on production and acclimatization of *Pittosporum* spp. *HortScience* 15:201-203.

P

Platycerium bifurcatum

pla-tee-*ke*-ree-um
bi-fur-*kah*-tum

Family Name: **Polypodiaceae**
Common Name: **Common Staghorn Fern**

Originated in Australia and Polynesia.

PLATYCERIUM BIFURCATUM

Production factors

Temperature. Provide greenhouse minimum night temperatures of 50° to 55°F (10° to 13°C) to promote good growth.

Irrigation. Keep the potting medium evenly moist but not wet.

Media. Choose an organic, porous, water-holding medium. A suggested rooting mixture consists of osmunda or treefern fiber, composted oak leaves (or a suitable substitute) and a small amount of crushed charcoal. These ferns are epiphytic and grow well when potted in hanging containers or mounted on water-holding slabs such as cork bark, treefern trunk, or rot resistant woods (locust, cedar, cypress or redwood).

Problems.

Diseases: Blight—*Rhizoctonia solani*; leaf spot—*Pseudomonas cichorii, Pseudomonas gladioli.*

Pests: Brown scale.

Postproduction factors

Light. Transport of plants under dark conditions is currently the most common method of shipping. If immediate delivery is not possible, hold under at least 200 to 300 fc (2.2 to 3.2 klx) of light.

Retail handling

Light. Provide plants with sufficient light upon delivery to recuperate from the stresses of dark storage. Maintain under at least 200 to 300 fc (2.2 to 3.2 klx) of light.

Temperature. Common staghorn fern prefers fairly cool temperatures of 50° to 72°F (10° to 22°C), although higher temperatures are tolerated if high humidity levels are present.

Irrigation. Keep the potting medium evenly moist but not wet.

P

Platycerium bifurcatum

pla-tee-*ke*-ree-um
bi-fur-*kah*-tum

Consumer care

Temperature. Common staghorn fern prefers fairly cool temperatures of 50° to 72°F (10° to 22°C), although higher temperatures are tolerated if high humidity levels are present.

Location. These ferns thrive when placed under bright indirect or curtain-filtered sunlight, although plants also maintain quality if interior lighting of at least 200 to 300 fc (2.2 to 3.2 klx) is available.

Irrigation. Keep the potting medium evenly moist but not wet.

Grooming. Provide even moisture in the porous medium or plant support. Suggestions include soaking the entire basket, container or slab weekly in a sink or pail. Wash the foliage with tepid water during this soaking. In spring, carefully pry old, deteriorated media from around the soil mass and replace with fresh, porous material. Avoid damage to the roots or fronds. Small plantlets that have developed their own covering of sterile fronds can be moved successfully from the parent mass. Feed plants with a foliar-applied fertilizer.

ADDITIONAL READING

Bailey, L.H. and E.Z. Bailey. 1976. *Hortus Third.* New York: Macmillan Publishing Co. Inc.

Chase, A.R. 1985. Diseases of foliage plants— Revised list for 1985. *Foliage Digest* 8(6):3-8.

Crockett, J.U. 1977. *Foliage House Plants.* Revised. Alexandria, VA: Time-Life Books.

Everett, T.H. 1980. *The New York Botanical Garden Illustrated Encyclopedia of Horticulture.* New York: Publishing Inc.

P

Plectranthus australis

plek-*tranth*-us
ow-*strah*-lis

Family Name: **Labiatae**
Common Name: **Swedish Ivy**

Originated in Southeast Australia.

PLECTRANTHUS AUSTRALIS

Production factors

Light. Use production light levels of 3,000 to 4,000 fc (32.4 to 43.2 klx).

Temperature. Provide greenhouse temperatures above 55°F (13°C) to promote continuous growth, although Swedish ivy can tolerate occasional exposure to cooler temperatures.

Nutrition. At recommended production light levels, fertilize with 27.5 to 34.4 pounds per 1000 square feet per year (lb/1000 sq. ft/yr) or 134.5 to 168.1 kilograms per 1000 square meters per year (kg/1000 sq. m/yr) of N-P-K.

Irrigation. Keep the potting medium moist but not wet.

Media. Use a potting medium with good drainage characteristics.

Problems.
Pests: Aphids; mealybugs; mites; nematodes; scale; whitefly.

Postproduction factors

Light. Transport of plants under dark conditions is currently the most common method of shipping. If immediate delivery is not possible, hold Swedish ivy under at least 200 fc (2.2 klx) of light. Plants tolerate low light to 100 fc (1.1 klx), but quality is improved with better lighting.

Temperature. Recommended temperatures for shipping are 55° to 60°F (13° to 16°C). Decrease the production watering frequency slightly to reduce the amount of injury-prone, succulent growth if exposure to short-term cold temperatures are expected during storage. Careful monitoring of water use is necessary to balance this hardening process with the need for high-quality, unstressed growth.

Gases. Injury due to ethylene is generally not a problem when plants are shipped within the recommended temperature range. Ethylene may reach damaging levels if plants are shipped with produce or held in prolonged storage above the maximum listed temperature.

Lasting qualities. Under appropriate storage conditions acclimatized plants retain good quality when shipping time does not exceed 2 weeks. Maintain storage temperatures near the upper end of the recom-

172

Foliage Plants *Plectranthus australis*

Plectranthus australis

plek-*tranth*-us
ow-*strah*-lis

mended range when transport requires only 1 to 7 days. Severe quality loss is expected when plants require more than 2 weeks to reach their destination.

Care and grooming. Good storage preparation improves quality retention during transit. Moisture content of the potting medium should approximate 50% of soil capacity when plants are packed. Maintain high relative humidities of 80% to 90% during storage to retard desiccation, especially when shipping time exceeds 7 days.

Retail handling

Light. Provide plants with sufficient light upon delivery to recuperate from the stresses of dark storage. A specially designed holding greenhouse or room is ideal. When such a facility is unavailable, maintain plants under at least 200 fc (2.2 klx) of light. Plants tolerate low light to 100 fc (1.1 klx), but quality is improved with better lighting.

Temperature. Keep interior daylight temperatures of 60° to 75°F (16° to 24°C) with night temperatures of 50° to 55°F (10° to 13°C) for growth and quality retention. Swedish ivy is fairly cold-hardy and can tolerate exposure to 35°F (2°C) without injury. When a greenhouse is used to hold plants before installation, maintain 40% to 60% relative humidity for acclimatization to lower interior humidity levels.

Irrigation. The medium surface should dry slightly between waterings.

Disorders. Check leaf nodes and axils especially for the presence of mealybugs. Quick detection and treatment can avert serious quality loss from this pest. Severe water stress produces pale green foliage and loss of older leaves.

Consumer care

Temperature. Keep interior daylight temperatures of 60° to 75°F (16° to 24°C) with night temperatures of 50° to 55°F (10° to 13°C) for growth and quality retention. Swedish ivy is fairly cold-hardy and can tolerate exposure to 35°F (2°C) without injury. Moderate humidity levels of at least 25% are needed for best quality maintenance; therefore, hold interior temperatures near the lower end of the recommended range if humidity is very low.

Location. Swedish ivy thrives when placed under bright indirect or curtain-filtered sunlight, but also maintains quality under interior lighting of at least 200 fc (2.2 klx). Although plants tolerate a range of 100 to 4,000 fc (1.1 to 43.2 klx), quality is best sustained when interior lighting provides 200 to 1,000 fc (2.2 to 10.8 klx) for 10 to 12 hours per day.

Irrigation. Allow the medium surface to dry slightly between waterings.

Grooming. Pinch long stems to promote a bushy appearance. Overcrowded plants can be repotted at any time of the year. Fertilizer ratios of 20-10-10 or 10-5-5 are suggested for interior feeding of Swedish ivy. Apply one-third the recommended yearly rate every 4 months. Annual fertilizer rates for a typical size 8-inch (20-cm) pot are one-half gram for plants under 75 to 150 fc (.8 to 1.6 klx), .8 gm for plants under 150 to 250 fc (1.6 to 2.7 klx), and 1.3 gm for plants under 250 to 500 fc (2.7 to 5.4 klx) of light. Nitrogen delivered at the rate of one-half gram is equivalent to one-half teaspoon of 20-10-10 or 1 teaspoon of 10-5-5 fertilizer.

Disorders. Plants located in bright, hot, dry areas suffer from marginal burning and

P

173

Foliage Plants *Plectranthus australis*

Plectranthus australis

loss of older leaves. Inadequate light causes chlorosis and abscission of older foliage. Severe water stress produces pale green foliage and loss of older leaves.

ADDITIONAL READING

Bailey, L.H. and E.Z. Bailey. 1976. *Hortus Third.* New York: Macmillan Publishing Co. Inc.

Conover, C.A. and R.T. Poole. 1987. Factors influencing shipping of acclimatized foliage plants. *Foliage Digest* 10(4):1-5.

Crockett, J.U. 1977. *Foliage House Plants.* Revised. Alexandria, VA: Time-Life Books.

Everett, T.H. 1980. *The New York Botanical Garden Illustrated Encyclopedia of Horticulture.* New York: Publishing Inc.

McConnell, D.B. and R.W. Henley. 1986. Swedish Ivy. *Foliage Digest* 9(12):7.

McConnell, D.B., R.W. Henley and R.L. Biamonte. 1981. Commercial foliage plants. J.N. Joiner (ed.). *Foliage Plant Production.* Englewood Cliffs, NJ: Prentice-Hall Inc.

Poole, R.T. and C.A. Conover. 1983. Factors influencing chilling damage of foliage plants. *Foliage Digest* 6(8):3-4.

P

Polyscias balfouriana 'Marginata'

po-*lis*-kee-as
bal-for-ree-*ah*-na
mar-gi-*nah*-ta

Family Name: **Araliaceae**
Common Name: **Variegated Balfour Aralia**

Originated in New Caledonia. This plant was previously named *Aralia balfouriana*.

POLYSCIAS BALFOURIANA 'MARGINATA'

Production factors

Light. Use production light levels of 1,500 to 4,500 fc (16.2 to 48.6 klx) for acclimatized plants.

Temperature. Keep greenhouse temperatures of at least 65°F (18°C) to sustain continuous, uniform growth. Root zone temperatures of 70° to 75°F (21° to 24°C) are required during establishment of the directly stuck terminal cuttings or cane. Avoid sudden temperature reduction to 55°F (13°C) or less. Maintain constant environmental conditions during production, and regularly inspect heating systems for adequate venting and maintenance.

Nutrition. At recommended production light levels for acclimatized plants, fertilize with 30 to 36 pounds per 1000 square feet per year (lb/1000 sq. ft/yr) or 146.5 to 175.8 kilograms per 1000 square meters per year (kg/1000 sq. m/yr) of N-P-K. A N-P-K ratio of 3:1:2 or 2:1:2 is suggested. Most media require the addition of micronutrients either by preplant incorporation of a granular source or as part of a liquid fertilization program. Adjust the ph to 6.0 with dolomite.

Irrigation. Keep the potting medium moist but not wet. Quality loss from disease is curtailed if plants are protected from rainfall and overhead irrigation is eliminated.

Media. Use a clean potting medium that has high water-holding capacity and good drainage characteristics.

Problems.
Diseases: Anthracnose—*Glomerella cingulata,* (*Colletotrichum gloeosporioides*); blight—*Rhizoctonia solani, Sclerotium rolfsii;* leaf spot—*Alternaria panax, Cercospora* sp., *Colletotrichum peregrinum; Pseudomonas cichorii, Xanthomonas*

P

Polyscias balfouriana 'Marginata'

po-*lis*-kee-as
bal-for-ree-*ah*-na
mar-gi-*nah*-ta

campestris pv. *hederae*; rot—*Pythium* spp.
Pests: Mealybugs; mites; scale.

Disorders. Variegated Balfour aralia is subject to rapid leaf abscission whenever sudden changes occur in the environment. Chlorosis and abscission of older leaves are induced by changes in humidity and light, exposure to temperatures of 55°F (13°C) or less, or increased ethylene concentration within the greenhouse. Plants demonstrate slow growth and eventual decline when potted in poor-quality media. Poor establishment and growth are also caused by potting plants too deep. Variegated Balfour aralia develops a distinctive phytotoxic response to Vydate. Clusters of small shoots ("bird's nest"-type growth) develop around damaged terminal buds.

Postproduction factors

Light. Transport of plants under dark conditions is currently the most common shipping method. If immediate delivery is not possible, maintain Variegated Balfour aralia under minimum light levels of 100 to 150 fc (1.1 to 1.6 klx). Plants tolerate low light to 75 fc (.8 klx), but better lighting sustains a more healthy appearance during extended holding.

Temperature. Maintain temperatures above 55°F (13°C) to prevent chilling injury.

Gases. Variegated Balfour aralia is sensitive to ethylene.

Retail handling

Light. Provide plants with sufficient light upon delivery to recuperate from the stresses of dark storage. Maintain Variegated Balfour aralia under minimum light levels of 100 to 150 fc (1.1 to 1.6 klx). Plants tolerate low light to 75 fc (.8 klx), but better lighting improves appearance. Lower foliage is retained under 150 to 250 fc (1.6 to 2.7 klx) of light.

Temperature. Maintain interior temperatures of 65° to 85°F (18° to 29°C) to sustain growth and quality. Provide moderate levels of humidity in the holding area.

Irrigation. Keep the potting medium moist but not wet.

Disorders. Either chilling injury or ethylene toxicity can induce leaf abscission. Check for the presence of spider mites, a common problem of variegated Balfour aralia. Quick detection and treatment averts serious quality loss from this pest.

Consumer care

Temperature. Maintain interior temperatures of 65° to 85°F (18° to 29°C) to sustain growth and quality. Provide moderate levels of humidity.

Location. Variegated Balfour aralia thrives in areas with bright indirect light or some daily sunlight, but quality is also maintained with interior lighting of at least 100 fc (1.1 klx). Plants tolerate low light to 75 fc (.8 klx), but better lighting improves appearance. Lower foliage is retained under 150 to 250 fc (1.6 to 2.7 klx) of light.

P

Polyscias balfouriana 'Marginata'

po-*lis*-kee-as
bal-for-ree-*ah*-na
mar-gi-*nah*-ta

Irrigation. Keep the potting medium moist but not wet.

Grooming. Check plants regularly for any infestation of spider mites. Quality loss from foliage damage is severe if pests are left untreated. Prune and repot overcrowded plants in early spring before new growth emerges. Increase humidity by placing pots on trays filled with moist gravel. Fertilize every 3 to 4 months.

Disorders. Leaf abscission is a symptom of chilling injury. Lower canopy leaf abscission is aggravated by water stress.

Cultivars. *Polyscias fruticosa* (Ming aralia) has bright green, finely divided leaves.

ADDITIONAL READING

Bailey, L.H. and E.Z. Bailey. 1976. *Hortus Third.* New York: Macmillan Publishing Co. Inc.

Chase, A.R. 1985. Diseases of foliage plants— Revised list for 1985. *Foliage Digest* 8(6):3-8.

Conover, C.A. and R.T. Poole. 1981. Guide for fertilizing foliage plant crops. *ARC-Apopka Research Rpt.* RH-81-1. University of Florida.

———. 1984. Light and fertilizer recommendations for production of acclimatized potted foliage plants. *Foliage Digest* 7(8):1-6.

Crockett, J.U. 1977. *Foliage House Plants.* Revised. Alexandria, VA: Time-Life Books.

Everett, T.H. 1980. *The New York Botanical Garden Illustrated Encyclopedia of Horticulture.* New York: Publishing Inc.

Gaines, R.L. 1977. *Interior Plantscaping: Building Design for Interior Foliage Plants.* New York: Architectural Record Books.

Henley, R.W., L.S. Osborne and A.R. Chase. 1986. Polyscias. *Foliage Digest* 9(3):6-8.

McConnell, D.B., R.W. Henley and R.L. Biamonte. 1981. Commercial foliage plants. J.N. Joiner (ed.). *Foliage Plant Production.* Englewood Cliffs, NJ: Prentice-Hall Inc.

Poole, R.T. and C.A. Conover. 1987. Foliage variety determines heat. *Greenhouse Grower* 5(1):21-22.

P

Rhapis excelsa   *ra*-pis eks-*kel*-sa

Family Name: **Palmae**
Common Name: **Slender Lady Palm**

Originated in South China.

RHAPIS EXCELSA

Production factors

Light. Use production light levels of 2,500 to 6,000 fc (27 to 64.8 klx) for acclimatized plants.

Temperature. Maintain greenhouse temperatures of at least 60°F (16°C) to assure continuous growth.

Nutrition. At recommended production light levels for acclimatized plants, fertilize with 27.5 to 34.4 pounds per 1000 square feet per year (lb/1000 sq. ft/yr) or 134.5 to 168.1 kilograms per 1000 square meters per year (kg/1000 sq. m/yr) of N-P-K.

Irrigation. Keep the medium moist but not wet.

Media. Use a potting medium with good drainage characteristics.

Problems.

Diseases: Anthracnose—*Gloeosporium* sp., *Glomerella cingulata (Colletotrichum gloeosporioides);* black spot—*Catacauma palmicola;* leaf spot—*Alternaria* sp., *Bipolaris setariae, Cercospora* sp., *Curvularia lunata, Cylindrocladium scoparium; Cytospora* sp., *Didymella phacidiomorpha, Didymopleella* sp., *Diplodia* sp., *Exoserohilum rostratum, Exosporium palmivorum, Gloeosporium* sp., *Helminthosporium* sp., *Leptothyrium* sp., *Monilochaetes* sp., *Pestalotia palmarum, Phomopsis* sp., *Phyllachora* sp., *Phyllosticta* sp., *Physalospora rhodina, Stigmina palmivora;* microplasma—lethal yellowing; bud rot—*Cytospora palmarum, Fusarium* sp., *Phytophthora palmivora;* root rot—*Ceratocystis paradoxa, Clitocybe tabescens, Endoconidiophora paradoxa, Ganoderma sulcatum, Pythium* sp., *Rhizoctonia solani;* wood rot—*Ganoderma* spp.; false smut—*Graphiola phoenicis.*

Pests: Saddleback caterpillars; chewing beetles; leaf skeletonizer; mealybugs; mites; nematodes; scale; seed weevils; thrips.

Disorders. Provide adequate micronutri-

R

ents during production as slender lady palm is susceptible to minor element deficiencies.

Postproduction factors

Light. Transport of plants under dark conditions is currently the most common shipping method. If immediate delivery is not possible, maintain slender lady palm under at least 75 to 100 fc (.8 to 1.1 klx) of light. Plants tolerate low light to 75 fc (.8 klx), but better lighting sustains quality during extended holding.

Temperature. Acclimatized plants can be shipped without damage for 1 to 14 days when held at 50° to 55°F (10° to 13°C). Hold plants at 55° to 60°F (13° to 16°C) when transit requires 15 to 28 days.

Gases. Injury due to ethylene is generally not a problem when plants are shipped within the recommended temperature range. Ethylene may reach damaging levels if plants are shipped with produce or held in prolonged storage above the maximum listed temperature.

Lasting qualities. Under appropriate storage conditions acclimatized plants retain good quality when shipped within 4 weeks. Maintain temperatures near the upper end of the recommended range when transport requires only 1 to 7 days.

Care and grooming. Good storage preparation improves quality retention during transit. Moisture content of the potting medium should approximate 50% of soil capacity when plants are packed. Maintain high relative humidities of 80% to 90% during storage to retard desiccation, especially when shipping time exceeds 7 days.

Retail handling

Light. Provide plants with sufficient light upon delivery to recuperate from the stresses of dark storage. A specially designed holding greenhouse or room is ideal. When such a facility is unavailable, maintain slender lady palm under at least 75 to 100 fc (.8 to 1.1 klx) of light. Plants tolerate low light to 75 fc (.8 klx), but better lighting increases longevity and improves appearance. Light levels of 250 to 300 fc (2.7 to 3.2 klx) are ideal for long lasting quality.

Temperature. Slender lady palm prefers cool conditions. Maintain interior temperatures of 50° to 72°F (10° to 22°C) for ideal growth and quality retention, although exposure to 45°F (7°C) is tolerated. When a greenhouse is used to hold plants before installation, maintain 40% to 60% relative humidity for acclimatization to lower interior humidity levels.

Irrigation. Keep the medium moist but not wet.

Consumer care

Temperature. Slender lady palm prefers cool conditions. Maintain interior temperatures of 50° to 72°F (10° to 22°C) for ideal growth and quality retention, although exposure to 45°F (7°C) is tolerated.

Location. Plants flourish when installed under bright indirect or curtain-filtered sunlight but also maintain quality with interior light levels of 75 to 100 fc (.8 to 1.1 klx). Slender lady palm tolerates low light to 75 fc (.8 klx). However, better lighting increases longevity and improves appearance. Light levels of 250 to 300 fc (2.7 to

R

3.2 klx) are ideal for long lasting quality.

Irrigation. Keep the medium moist but not wet.

Grooming. Slender lady palm is a durable plant and will maintain quality indefinitely with good care. Repot overcrowded plants in early spring. Feed actively growing plants monthly during the warmer seasons but discontinue during winter. This palm grows slowly; therefore, keep fertilizer rates low. Use a houseplant fertilizer that contains micronutrients to sustain long-term health.

Cultivars. *Rhapis humilis* (reed rhapis) stems are more slender, and the plant in general is smaller and more compact than *R. excelsa*.

ADDITIONAL READING

Bailey, L.H. and E.Z. Bailey. 1976. *Hortus Third.* New York: Macmillan Publishing Co. Inc.

Chase, A.R. 1985. Diseases of foliage plants—Revised list for 1985. *Foliage Digest* 8(6):3-8.

Conover C.A. and R.T. Poole. 1987. Factors influencing shipping of acclimatized foliage plants. *Foliage Digest* 10(4):1-5.

Crockett, J.U. 1977. *Foliage House Plants.* Revised. Alexandria, VA: Time-Life Books.

Everett, T.H. 1980. *The New York Botanical Garden Illustrated Encyclopedia of Horticulture.* New York: Garland Publishing Inc.

Gaines, R.L. 1977. *Interior Plantscaping: Building Design for Interior Foliage Plants.* New York: Architectural Record Books.

McConnell, D.B., R.W. Henley and R.L. Biamonte. 1981. Commercial foliage plants. J.N. Joiner (ed.). *Foliage Plant Production.* Englewood Cliffs, NJ: Prentice-Hall Inc.

R

Rhoeo spathacea

ro-ee-oh spa-*thah*-kee-a

Family Name: **Commelinaceae**
Common Name: **Moses-in-the-Cradle, Purple-Leaved Spiderwort**

Originated in West Indies, Mexico and Guatemala. Previous names were *Rhoeo discolor* and *Tradescantia discolor*.

RHOEO SPATHACEA

Production factors

Light. Use production light levels of 4,000 to 6,000 fc (43.2 to 64.8 klx).

Temperature. Maintain greenhouse temperatures of at least 55°F (13°C) to sustain continuous, uniform growth.

Nutrition. At recommended production light levels for acclimatized plants, fertilize with 27.5 pounds per 1000 square feet per year (lb/1000 sq. ft/yr) or 134.5 kilograms per 1000 square meters per year (kg/1000 sq. m/yr) of N-P-K.

Irrigation. Keep the potting medium moist but not wet.

Media. Use a potting medium with good drainage characteristics.

Problems.
Diseases: Anthracnose—*Colletotrichum*

sp.; leaf spot—*Curvularia eragrostidis;* root rot—*Pythium* spp.; virus—Commelina mosaic virus, tobacco mosaic virus, Tradescantia virus.

Pests: Mealybugs; mites.

Disorders. —Moses-in-the-cradle is moderately sensitive to atmospheric fluoride. Symptoms include marginal scorch and tipburn. Elevated fluoride concentration darkens the purple coloration of lower leaf surfaces.

Postproduction factors

Light. Transport of plants under dark conditions is currently the most common shipping method. If immediate delivery is not possible, hold Moses-in-the-cradle under at least 300 to 600 fc (3.2 to 6.5 klx) of light. Higher light levels are preferred for best plant appearance.

Retail handling

Light. Provide plants with sufficient light upon delivery to recuperate from the stresses of dark storage. Maintain Moses-in-the-cradle under at least 300 to 600 fc (3.2 to 6.5 klx). Higher light levels are preferred for best plant appearance.

Temperature. Average interior tempera-

R

Rhoeo spathacea

ro-ee-oh spa-*thah*-kee-a

tures of 65° to 75°F (18° to 24°C) are recommended for growth and quality retention, but plants also tolerate cool temperatures to 50°F (10°C) without damage.

Irrigation. Allow the medium surface to dry slightly between waterings.

Disorders. Moses-in-the-cradle is moderately sensitive to atmospheric fluoride.

Consumer care

Temperature. Provide average interior temperatures of 65° to 75°F (18° to 24°C) for growth and quality retention, although plants also tolerate cool temperatures to 50°F (10°C) without damage.

Location. Moses-in-the-cradle thrives in areas with bright indirect or curtain-filtered sunlight, but maintains quality if 300 to 600 fc (3.2 to 6.5 klx) of light is available. Higher light is preferred for best plant appearance.

Irrigation. Allow the medium surface to dry slightly between waterings.

Grooming. Moses-in-the-cradle is an undemanding plant and tolerates some neglect. Repot if desired in early spring. Old plants can be rejuvenated by root divisions, suckers or easily rooted cuttings. Fertilize every 3 to 4 months.

Disorders. Moses-in-the-cradle is moderately sensitive to atmospheric fluoride.

Cultivars. *Rhoeo spathacea* 'Concolor' leaves are uniformly green.

Rhoeo spathacea 'Variegata' leaves are striped with pale yellow on the upper leaf surface.

ADDITIONAL READING

Bailey, L.H. and E.Z. Bailey. 1976. *Hortus Third.* New York: Macmillan Publishing Co. Inc.

Chase, A.R. 1985. Diseases of foliage plants—Revised list for 1985. *Foliage Digest* 8(6):3-8.

———. 1988. Diseases of foliage plants—1988 updated listing. *Foliage Digest* 11(6):5-8.

Conover C.A. and R.T. Poole. 1981. Guide for fertilizing foliage plant crops. *ARC-Apopka Research Rpt.* RH-81-1. University of Florida.

———. 1984. Light and fertilizer recommendations for production of acclimatized potted foliage plants. *Foliage Digest* 7(8):1-6.

Crockett, J.U. 1977. *Foliage House Plants.* Revised. Alexandria, VA: Time-Life Books.

Everett, T.H. 1980. *The New York Botanical Garden Illustrated Encyclopedia of Horticulture.* New York: Garland Publishing Inc.

McConnell, D.B., R.W. Henley and R.L. Biamonte. 1981. Commercial foliage plants. J.N. Joiner (ed.). *Foliage Plant Production.* Englewood Cliffs, NJ: Prentice-Hall Inc.

Woltz, S.S. and W.E. Waters. 1978. Airborne fluoride effects on some foliage plants. *HortScience* 13:585-586.

R

Sansevieria trifasciata

san-sev-ee-*e*-ree-a
tri-fas-cc-*ah*-ta

Family Name: **Agavaceae**
Common Name: **Snake Plant, Mother-in-Law's-Tongue**

Originated in arid Africa, southern Asia.

SANSEVIERIA TRIFASCIATA

Production factors

Light. Use production light levels of 1,500 to 6,000 fc (16.2 to 64.8 klx) for acclimatized plants.

Temperature. Maintain greenhouse temperatures of at least 60°F (16°C) to assure continuous growth. Snake plant should be protected from temperatures of 50°F (10°C) or less.

Nutrition. At recommended production light levels for acclimatized plants, fertilize with 20.7 pounds per 1000 square feet per year (lb/1000 sq. ft/yr) or 101.1 kilograms per 1000 square meters per year (kg/1000 sq. m/yr) of N-P-K. A N-P-K ratio of 3:1:2 is suggested for use with soilless media, while 1:1:1 is recommended for soil-based media. Most media require the addition of micronutrients either by preplant incorporation of a granular source or as part of a liquid fertilization program.

Irrigation. Allow the potting medium to dry moderately between thorough waterings. Do not overwater.

Media. Use a coarse, somewhat heavy potting medium with good drainage characteristics.

Problems.

Diseases: Anthracnose—*Colletotrichum* sp.; blight—*Botrytis cinerea, Pythium* sp., *Sclerotium rolfsii;* leaf spot—*Cephaleuros virescens, Fusarium moniliforme;* rot— *Aspergillus niger, Erwinia carotovora* subsp. *carotovora, Rhizoctonia solani.*

Pests: Root knot nematodes—*Meloidogyne incognita;* thrips.

Disorders. Plants exposed to temperatures of 32° to 50°F (0° to 10°C) develop foliage lesions in response to chilling injury.

S

Sansevieria trifasciata

Postproduction factors

Light. Transport of plants under dark conditions is currently the most common shipping method. If immediate delivery is not possible, hold snake plant under at least 50 to 75 fc (.5 to .8 klx) of light. This species tolerates low light better than most foliage plants but also retains excellent quality under bright conditions.

Temperature. Snake plant is sensitive to cold and should be protected from temperatures of 50°F (10°C) or less.

Retail handling

Light. Provide plants with sufficient light upon delivery to recuperate from the stresses of dark storage. Maintain snake plant under at least 50 to 75 fc (.5 to .8 klx) of light. This species tolerates low light better than most foliage plants but also displays excellent quality at much higher levels, even under hot, dry conditions.

Temperature. Maintain interior temperatures of 65° to 85°F (18° to 29°C) to sustain growth and quality. Do not expose plants to temperatures of 50°F (10°C) or less.

Irrigation. Allow the potting medium to dry moderately between thorough waterings. Do not overwater.

Disorders. Foliage lesions develop in response to chilling injury.

Consumer care

Temperature. Maintain interior temperatures of 65° to 85°F (18° to 29°C) to sustain growth and quality. Do not expose plants to temperatures of 50°F (10°C) or less.

Location. Snake plant is a most accommodating species and thrives in locations ranging from full sun to sunless north windows. Minimum lighting of 50 to 75 fc (.5 to .8 klx) maintains quality, but plants also display healthy growth even under bright, hot and dry conditions.

Irrigation. Allow the potting medium to dry moderately between thorough waterings. Do not overwater.

Grooming. Plants survive crowded conditions well but can be repotted at any season if necessary. Fertilize plants every 3 to 4 months during active growth.

Disorders. Snake plant is a very durable plant whose only major problems stem from overwatering and exposure to cold.

Cultivars. *Sansevieria trifasciata* 'Hahnii' (birds-nest) leaves are shorter than the species type and display a rosette growth habit.

Sansevieria trifasciata 'Laurentii' leaves have distinctive gold-yellow marginal stripes. Propagation is by division only, as these markings are derived from somatic mutation.

Sansevieria zeylanica (Ceylon bowstring hemp) leaves are long, narrow and concave at the middle. Leaf markings include light green crossbands and lines that run down the outer side. The leaves grow upright, but also lean outward to form a more spreading growth habit than *S. trifasciata*. Cultural requirements are similar.

S

ADDITIONAL READING

Bailey, L.H. and E.Z. Bailey. 1976. *Hortus Third.* New York: Macmillan Publishing Co. Inc.

Chase, A.R. 1985. Diseases of foliage plants— Revised list for 1985. *Foliage Digest* 8(6):3-8.

Conover, C.A. and R.T. Poole. 1981. Guide for fertilizing foliage plant crops. *ARC-Apopka Research Rpt.* RH-81-1. University of Florida.

————. 1984. Light and fertilizer recommendations for production of acclimatized potted foliage plants. *Foliage Digest* 7(8):1-6.

Crockett, J.U. 1977. *Foliage House Plants.* Revised. Alexandria, VA: Time-Life Books.

Everett, T.H. 1980. *The New York Botanical Garden Illustrated Encyclopedia of Horticulture.* New York: Garland Publishing Inc.

McConnell, D.B., R.W. Henley and R.L. Biamonte. 1981. Commercial foliage plants. J.N. Joiner (ed.). *Foliage Plant Production.* Englewood Cliffs, NJ: Prentice-Hall Inc.

S

Saxifraga stolonifera

saks-*if*-ra-ga
sto-lo-*ni*-fe-ra

Family Name: **Saxifragaceae**
Common Name: **Strawberry Geranium**

Originated in east Asia, this plant was previously named *Saxifraga samentosa* L.

SAXIFRAGA STOLONIFERA

Production factors

Light. Use production light levels of 3,000 to 5,000 fc (32.4 to 54 klx).

Nutrition. At recommended production light levels, fertilize with 20.7 to 27.5 pounds per 1000 square feet per year (lb/1000 sq. ft/yr) or 100.9 to 134.5 kilograms per 1000 square meters per year (kg/1000 sq. m/yr) of N-P-K.

Irrigation. Keep the potting medium moist but not wet.

Media. Use a neutral to slightly acidic organic potting medium with high moisture-retaining capacity and good drainage characteristics.

Problems.

Diseases: Blight—*Botrytis cinerea;* leaf spot—*Cercosporella saxifraga, Phyllosticta saxifragarum, Septoria albicans, Ramularia* sp.; powdery mildew—*Sphaerotheca macularis;* rust—*Melampsora artica, Puccinia leucherae, Puccinia pazschkii.*

Pests: Mealybugs; whitefly.

Postproduction factors

Light. Transport of plants under dark conditions is currently the most common shipping method. If immediate delivery is not possible, place strawberry geranium in an area with filtered sunlight. Provide moderate to high humidity levels.

Retail handling

Light. Provide plants with sufficient light upon delivery to recuperate from the stresses of dark storage. Place strawberry geranium in an area with filtered sunlight.

Temperature. Plants prefer fairly cool temperatures. Keep interior temperatures of 55° to 75°F (13° to 24°C) for ideal growth and quality retention. Provide moderate to high humidity.

Irrigation. Keep the potting medium moist but not wet.

S

Saxifraga stolonifera

saks-*if*-ra-ga
sto-lo-*ni*-fe-ra

Consumer care

Temperature. Plants prefer fairly cool temperatures. Keep interior temperatures of 55° to 75°F (13° to 24°C) for ideal growth and quality retention. Provide moderate to high humidity.

Location. Strawberry geranium thrives when placed under bright indirect or curtain-filtered sunlight.

Irrigation. Keep the potting medium moist but not wet.

Grooming. New plants can be started from the plantlets formed on stolons. Increase humidity by double potting, placing pots on moist pebble filled trays, or planting in terrariums.

Cultivars. *Saxifraga stolonifera tricolor* is a selection of the species type that has leaves variegated with green, cream and rose colors.

ADDITIONAL READING

Arthurs, Kathryn (ed.). 1974. *How to Grow House Plants*. Menlo Park, CA: Lane Publishing Co.,

Bailey, L.H. and E.Z. Bailey 1976. *Hortus Third*. New York: Macmillan Publishing Co. Inc.

Everett, T.H. 1980. *The New York Botanical Garden Illustrated Encyclopedia of Horticulture*. New York: Garland Publishing Inc.

McConnell, D.B., R.W. Henley and R.L. Biamonte. 1981. Commercial foliage plants. J.N. Joiner (ed.). *Foliage Plant Production*. Englewood Cliffs, NJ: Prentice-Hall Inc.

Orans, M. 1973. *Houseplants and Indoor Landscaping*. Barrington, IL: A.B. Morse Co.

Wright, M. (ed.). 1979. *The Complete Indoor Gardener*. Rev. ed. New York: Random House.

S

Schefflera arboricola

shef-*le*-ra ar-bo-*ri*-ko-la

Family Name: **Araliaceae**
Common Name: **Dwarf Schefflera**

Originated in Taiwan.

SCHEFFLERA ARBORICOLA

Production factors

Light. Use production light levels of 3,000 to 5,000 fc (32.4 to 54 klx) for acclimatized plants. Dwarf schefflera performs well under low interior lighting when produced under a light range of 1,380 to 2,070 fc (14.9 to 22.4 klx).

Temperature. This species tolerates short exposures to cool temperatures; however, avoid temperatures below 50°F (10°C) for protection against possible chilling damage. Maintain greenhouse temperatures of at least 60°F (16°C) to assure continuous growth.

Nutrition. At recommended production light levels for acclimatized plants, fertilize with 48.3 pounds per 1000 square feet per year (lb/1000 sq. ft/yr) or 235.8 kilograms per 1000 square meters per year (kg/1000 sq. m/yr) of N-P-K. A N-P-K ratio of 3:1:2 is suggested for use with soilless media, while 1:1:1 is recommended for soil-based media. Most media require the addition of micronutrients either by preplant incorporation of a granular source or as part of a liquid fertilization program.

Irrigation. Allow the potting medium to dry partially between waterings. Water thoroughly when irrigating but avoid a constantly wet condition.

Media. Provide a potting medium with good drainage characteristics to avoid root rot.

Problems.

Diseases: Anthracnose—*Colletotrichum* sp., *Gloeosporium* sp.; blight—*Sclerotium rolfsii;* leaf spot—*Alternaria* sp., *Cephaleuros virescens, Cercospora* sp., *Corynespora* sp., *Erwinia chrysanthemi, Pseudomonas cichorii, Xanthomonas campestris* pv. *hederae;* root rot—*Pythium sp.;* stem rot—*Rhizoctonia solani.*

Pests: Leaf miners; nematodes; scale; spider mites; thrips.

S

Disorders. Plants can be damaged from exposure to temperatures below 50°F (10°C). Stems lose rigidity under drought conditions and rewatering does not restore former growth habit. Conversely, overwatering destroys roots.

Postproduction factors

Light. Transport of plants under dark conditions is currently the most common shipping method. However, if extended holding is necessary before sale or installation, dwarf schefflera can be maintained indefinitely under interior lighting of 150 fc (1.6 klx) or more.

Temperature. Dwarf schefflera ships well at reduced temperatures of 50° to 55°F (10° to 13°C) for extended periods without loss of quality.

Gases. Injury due to ethylene is generally not a problem when plants are shipped within the recommended temperature range. Ethylene may reach damaging levels if plants are shipped with produce or held in prolonged storage above the maximum listed temperature.

Lasting qualities. Under appropriate storage conditions acclimatized plants retain good quality when shipped within 4 weeks. Maintain temperatures near the upper end of the recommended range when transport requires only 1 to 7 days.

Care and grooming. Good storage preparation improves quality retention during transit. Moisture content of the potting medium should approximate 50% of soil capacity when plants are packed. Maintain high humidity levels of 80% to 90% during storage to retard desiccation, especially when shipping time exceeds 7 days.

Retail handling

Light. Provide plants with sufficient light upon delivery to recuperate from the stresses of dark storage. A specially designed holding greenhouse or room is ideal. When such a facility is unavailable, provide light levels of 75 to 250 fc (.8 to 2.7 klx). Dwarf schefflera maintains quality better than the closely related Australian umbrella tree when held under low light. Natural light locations with partial shade to bright indirect light are recommended for quality retention.

Temperature. Hold plants at day temperatures of 65° to 75°F (18° to 24°C) for optimum growth and quality. Keep night temperatures above 60°F (16°C) for best plant health. Avoid prolonged exposure to cold even though dwarf schefflera can tolerate interior temperatures as low as 45°F (7°C) for a short time. When a greenhouse is used to hold plants before installation, maintain 40% to 60% relative humidity for acclimatization to lower interior humidity levels.

Irrigation. Water plants thoroughly at each irrigation but allow the potting medium to dry somewhat between waterings.

Disorders. Plants suffer damage from prolonged exposure to low temperatures. Roots are prone to injury when held in a constantly saturated condition. Stems lose rigidity under drought conditions and rewatering does not restore former growth habit.

S

Schefflera arboricola

shef-*le*-ra
ar-bo-*ri*-ko-la

Consumer care

Temperature. Hold plants at day temperatures of 65° to 75°F (18° to 24°C) for optimum growth and quality. Keep night temperatures above 60°F (16°C) for best plant health. Avoid prolonged exposure to cold even though dwarf schefflera can tolerate interior temperatures as low as 45°F (7°C) for a short time.

Location. Plants prefer natural light locations with partial shade to bright indirect light. Interior lighting of 75 to 250 fc (.8 to 2.7 klx) is recommended. Dwarf schefflera maintains quality better than the closely related Australian umbrella tree when held under low light.

Irrigation. Water plants thoroughly at each irrigation but allow the potting medium to dry somewhat between waterings.

Grooming. Remove dead or damaged growth when needed. Less fertilizer is required when plants are held under low light. Dwarf schefflera maintains good quality indoors when fertilized at a level of 200 mg nitrogen per pot per week. This plant is durable and long lasting with good care.

Disorders. Plants suffer damage from prolonged exposure to low temperatures. Roots are prone to injury when held in a constantly saturated condition. Stems lose rigidity under drought conditions and rewatering does not restore former growth habit. Accumulation of high soluble salts in the potting medium causes leaf burn and yellowing.

ADDITIONAL READING

Braswell, J.H. and T.M. Blessington. 1981. Effects of production shade levels and subsequent dark storage on interior quality retention of *Brassaia* species. *HortScience* 16:290.

———. 1982a. Influence of production and postharvest light levels on the interior performance of two species of schefflera. *HortScience* 17:48-50.

———. 1982b. Influence of cultural practices on postharvest interior performance of two species of schefflera. *HortScience* 17:345-347.

Chase, A.R. 1985. Diseases of foliage plants— Revised list for 1985. *Foliage Digest* 8(6):3-8.

Conover C.A. and R.T. Poole. 1981. Guide for fertilizing foliage plant crops. *ARC-Apopka Research Rpt.* RH-81-1. University of Florida.

———. 1983a. Environmental factors influencing long-term shipping of tropical foliage plants. *Foliage Digest* 6(6):3-5.

———. 1983b. Handling and overseas transportation of acclimatized foliage plants in reefers. *Foliage Digest* 6(5):3-4.

———. 1984. Light and fertilizer recommendations for production of acclimatized potted foliage plants. *Foliage Digest* 7(8):1-6.

———. 1986. Factors influencing shipping of acclimatized foliage plants. *ARC-Apopka Research Rpt.* RH-86-11. University of Florida.

———. 1987. Factors influencing shipping of acclimatized foliage plants. *Foliage Digest* 10(4):1-5.

Everett, T.H. 1980. *The New York Botanical Garden Illustrated Encyclopedia of Horticulture.* New York: Garland Publishing Inc.

Holstead, C.L. 1985. *Care and Handling of Flowers and Plants.* Floralife Inc., Society of American Florists, Alexandria, VA.

McConnell, D.B., R.W. Henley and R.L. Biamonte. 1981. Commercial foliage plants. J.N. Joiner (ed.). *Foliage Plant Production.* Englewood Cliffs, NJ: Prentice-Hall Inc.

Staby, G.L., J.L. Robertson and D.C. Kiplinger. 1978. *Chain of Life.* Columbus, OH: Ohio Florists' Association.

S

Spathiphyllum cvs.

spa-thi-*fil*-lum

Family Name: **Araceae**
Common Name: **White Anthurium, Peace Lily**

Genus originated in the tropic regions. Cultivars are of complex hybid origins.

SPATHIPHYLLUM 'MAUNA LOA'

Production factors

Light. Use production light levels of 1,500 to 2,500 fc (16.2 to 27 klx) for acclimatized plants.

Temperature. Maintain greenhouse temperatures of at least 65°F (18°C) to assure continuous growth. Avoid temperatures below 55°F (13°C).

Nutrition. At recommended production light levels for acclimatized plants, fertilize with 34.5 pounds per 1000 square feet per year (lb/1000 sq.ft/yr) or 168.4 kilograms per 1000 square meters per year (kg/1000 sq. m/yr) of N-P-K. A N-P-K ratio of 3:1:2 is suggested for use with soilless media, while 1:1:1 is recommended for soil-based media. Most media require the addition of micronutrients either by preplant incorporation of a granular source or as part of a liquid fertilization program.

Irrigation. Keep the potting medium evenly moist. Place white anthurium on easily drained raised benches and avoid pooled water near or under pots. This will reduce the severity of several soil-borne diseases.

Media. Use an organic potting medium with good drainage characteristics.

Problems.

Diseases: Anthracnose—*Colletotrichum* sp.; blight—*Phytophthora* sp., *Rhizoctonia solani, Sclerotium rolfsii;* green scurf—*Cephaleuros virescens;* leaf spot—*Cercospora* sp., *Myrothecium roridum, Pseudomonas cichorii;* root rot—*Cylindrocladium spathiphylli, Pythium* sp.; virus—Dasheen mosaic virus.

Pests: Mealybugs; mites; scale.

Postproduction factors

Light. Transport of plants under dark conditions is currently the most common shipping method. If immediate delivery is

S

not possible, maintain white anthurium under minimum light levels of 75 to 150 fc (.8 to 1.6 klx). Plants tolerate low light to 50 fc (.5 klx), but better lighting sustains a more healthy appearance. Provide light levels of at least 100 to 150 fc (1.1 to 1.6 klx) to stimulate flowering.

Temperature. Acclimatized plants of the cultivar 'Mauna Loa' can be shipped without damage for 1 to 14 days when held at 50° to 55°F (10° to 13°C). Hold plants at 55° to 60°F (13° to 16°C) when transit requires 15 to 28 days.

Gases. Injury due to ethylene is generally not a problem when plants are shipped within the recommended temperature range. Ethylene may reach damaging levels if plants are shipped with produce or held in prolonged storage above the maximum listed temperature.

Lasting qualities. Under appropriate storage conditions acclimatized plants retain good quality when shipped within 4 weeks. Maintain temperatures near the upper end of the recommended range when transport requires only 1 to 7 days.

Care and grooming. Good storage preparation improves quality retention during transit. Moisture content of the potting medium should approximate 50% of soil capacity when plants are packed. Maintain high relative humidities of 80% to 90% during storage to retard desiccation, especially when shipping time exceeds 7 days.

Retail handling

Light. Provide plants with sufficient light upon delivery to recuperate from the stresses of dark storage. A specially designed holding greenhouse or room is ideal. When such a facility is unavailable, maintain white anthurium under minimum light levels of 75 to 150 fc (.8 to 1.6 klx). Plants tolerate low light to 50 fc (.5 klx), but better lighting sustains a more healthy appearance. Provide light levels of at least 100 to 150 fc (1.1 to 1.6 klx) to stimulate flowering.

Temperature. Keep interior temperatures of 65° to 75°F (18° to 24°C) to sustain growth and quality. When a greenhouse is used to hold plants before installation, maintain 40% to 60% relative humidity for acclimatization to lower interior humidity levels.

Irrigation. Keep the potting medium evenly moist.

Disorders. —Marginal necrosis and tipburn are caused by fluoride toxicity in several closely related cultivars.

Consumer care

Temperature. Keep interior temperatures of 65° to 75°F (18° to 24°C) to sustain growth and quality. Moderate to high humidity levels are preferred, especially when temperatures are high.

Location. White anthurium thrives when installed under bright indirect or curtain-filtered sunlight, particularly when humidity is high. However, light levels of 75 to 150 fc (.8 to 1.6 klx) maintain quality. Plants tolerate low light to 50 fc (.5 klx), but better lighting sustains a more healthy appearance. Provide light levels of at least 100 to 150 fc (1.1 to 1.6 klx) to stimulate flowering.

Irrigation. Keep the potting medium evenly moist.

Grooming. Repot overcrowded plants at any season. Fertilize every 2 to 3 months.

Disorders. Marginal necrosis and tipburn

S

Spathiphyllum cvs.

are caused by fluoride toxicity in several closely related cultivars.

Cultivars. *Spathiphyllum* 'Clevelandii' is a graceful mound of glossy green, lanceolate leaves with blades to 1 foot long and 2.5 inches wide. Under good conditions, long-lasting flowering structures consisting of white spadices with showy white spathes emerge from the plant base on thin stalks.

Spathiphyllum 'Mauna Loa' has a vigorous and compact growth habit with dark green, glossy foliage. Spathes are slightly concave. The overall plant size is larger than *S.* 'Clevelandii.'

Spathiphyllum wallisii is a strong grower with lustrous, wavy-edged leaves. The overall plant size is smaller than *S.* 'Clevelandii.'

ADDITIONAL READING

Bailey, L.H. and E.Z. Bailey. 1976. *Hortus Third.* New York: Macmillan Publishing Co. Inc.

Chase, A.R. 1985. Diseases of foliage plants— Revised list for 1985. *Foliage Digest* 8(6):3-8.

————. 1985. Watch for these fungal diseases on Spathiphyllum. Greenhouse Grower 3(1):16-18.

Conover C.A. and R.T. Poole. 1981. Guide for fertilizing foliage plant crops. *ARC-Apopka Research Rpt.* RH-81-1. University of Florida.

————. 1984. Light and fertilizer recommendations for production of acclimatized potted foliage plants. *Foliage Digest* 7(8):1-6.

————. 1987. Factors influencing shipping of acclimatized foliage plants. *Foliage Digest* 10(4):1-5.

Everett, T.H. 1980. *The New York Botanical Garden Illustrated Encyclopedia of Horticulture.* New York: Garland Publishing Inc.

Florists' Transworld Delivery Association. 1985. *The Indoor Gardener.* Southfield, MI.

Gaines, R.L. 1977. *Interior Plantscaping: Building Design for Interior Foliage Plants.* New York: Architectural Record Books.

McConnell, D.B., R.W. Henley and R.L. Biamonte. 1981. Commercial foliage plants. J.N. Joiner (ed.). *Foliage Plant Production.* Englewood Cliffs, NJ: Prentice-Hall Inc.

Poole, R.T. and C.A. Conover. 1986. Growth of foliage plants at infrequent low night temperatures. *Foliage Digest* 9(2):7-8.

————. 1987. Foliage variety determines heat. *Greenhouse Grower* 5(1):21-22.

S

193

Foliage Plants *Spathiphyllum* cvs.

Syngonium podophyllum

sin-*gon*-ee-um
po-do-*fil*-lum

Family Name: **Araceae**
Common Name: **Nephthytis, Arrowhead Vine**

Originated in Mexico to Panama.

SYNGONIUM PODOPHYLLUM

Production factors

Light. Use production light levels of 1,500 to 3,000 fc (16.2 to 32.4 klx) for acclimatized plants.

Temperature. Provide greenhouse temperatures of 65°F (18°C) or more to promote continuous growth. Recent tests with *S. podophyllum* 'White Butterfly' indicate that this cultivar tolerates high summer temperatures of at least 106°F (41°C) without problem.

Nutrition. At recommended production light levels for acclimatized plants, fertilize with 34.5 pounds per 1000 square feet per year (lb/1000 sq.ft/yr) or 168.4 kilograms per 1000 square meters per year (kg/1000 sq. m/yr) of N-P-K. *S. podophyllum* 'White Butterfly' grows well over a wide range of fertilizer rates. Slightly higher rates may be appropriate for this cultivar under certain production conditions of light and temperature, although luxury feeding to enhance the cultivar's foliage coloration can result in a reduction of overall plant quality. Generally a N-P-K ratio of 3:1:2 is suggested for use with soilless media, while 1:1:1 is recommended for soil-based media. Avoid phosphorous deficiency problems in nephthytis by using a 3:1:2 fertilizer or by incorporating superphosphate into the medium at the rate of 3 pounds per cubic yard (1.8 kg per cubic m). Most media require the addition of micronutrients either by preplant incorporation of a granular source or as part of a liquid fertilization program.

Irrigation. Allow the surface of the potting medium to dry slightly between thorough waterings. Protect plants from rainfall and avoid overhead irrigation to reduce quality loss from disease. Space pots sufficiently to allow for quick drying of foliage after irrigation. Regulate water temperature to that of surrounding air and control greenhouse condensation.

Media. Use an organic potting medium with good drainage characteristics.

Problems.

Diseases: Blight —*Ceratocystis fimbriata, Erwinia chrysanthemi, Rhizoctonia solani, Sclerotium rolfsii;* leaf spot—*Acremonium crotocinigenum, Cephalosporium cinnamomeum, Cercospora* sp., *Colletotrichum* sp., *Erwinia* spp., *Myrothecium roridum, Pseudomonas cichorii, Xanthomonas campestris* sp., *Xanthomonas campestris* pv. *dieffenbachiae, Xanthomonas vitians;* root rot—*Pythium* spp.; soft rot—*Erwinia carotovora* subsp. *carotovora;* stem rot—*Sclerotium rolfsii;* rust—*Uromyces* sp.

Pests: Aphids; mealybugs; burrowing nematodes—*Radopholus similis;* scale; thrips.

Disorders. Phosphorous deficiency causes necrotic spots on lower foliage and reduced growth. Exposure of foliage to cold water produces lesions similar in appearance to those caused by bacterial infection.

Postproduction factors

Light. Transport of plants under dark conditions is currently the most common shipping method. If immediate delivery is not possible, maintain nephthytis under at least 100 to 150 fc (1.1 to 1.6 klx) of light. Plants tolerate low light to 75 fc (.8 klx), but better lighting sustains a more healthy and typical appearance.

Temperature. Recommended temperatures for shipping are 55° to 60°F (13° to 16°C). Exposure to temperatures below 55°F (13°C) can cause chilling injury.

Gases. Epinasty develops when plants are exposed to ethylene for several days. The response is temporary and leaves resume a normal appearance after several days under good holding conditions. Injury due to ethylene is generally not a problem when plants are shipped within the recommended temperature range. Ethylene may reach damaging levels if plants are shipped with produce or held in prolonged storage above the maximum listed temperature.

Lasting qualities. Under appropriate storage conditions acclimatized plants retain good quality when shipping time does not exceed 2 weeks. Maintain storage temperatures near the upper end of the recommended range when transport requires only 1 to 7 days. Severe quality loss is expected when plants require more than 2 weeks to reach their destination.

Care and grooming. Good storage preparation improves quality retention during transit. Moisture content of the potting medium should approximate 50% of soil capacity when plants are packed. Maintain high relative humidities of 80% to 90% during storage to retard desiccation, especially when shipping time exceeds 7 days.

Retail handling

Light. Provide plants with sufficient light upon delivery to recuperate from the stresses of dark storage. A specially designed holding greenhouse or room is ideal. When such a facility is unavailable, maintain nephthytis under at least 100 to 150 fc (1.1 to 1.6 klx) of light. Plants tolerate low light to 75 fc (.8 klx), but better lighting sustains a more healthy appearance.

Temperature. Average interior temperatures of 65° to 85°F (18° to 29°C) sustain growth and quality. When a greenhouse is used to hold plants before installation, maintain 40% to 60% relative humidity for acclimatization to lower interior humidity levels.

S

Syngonium podophyllum

sin-*gon*-ee-um
po-do-*fil*-lum

Irrigation. Allow the surface of the potting medium to dry slightly between thorough waterings. Use room temperature water.

Disorders. Epinasty is a symptom of ethylene exposure. Stem elongation and lower leaf loss gradually distort typical growth habit under marginal lighting. Chilling injury can occur if plants are exposed to temperatures below 55°F (13°C).

Consumer care

Temperature. Average interior temperatures of 65° to 85°F (18° to 29°C) sustain growth and quality.

Location. Nephthytis thrives when placed under bright indirect or curtain-filtered sunlight, but also maintains quality under interior lighting of 100 to 150 fc (1.1 to 1.6 klx). Plants tolerate low light to 75 fc (.8 klx), but better lighting sustains a more healthy appearance.

Irrigation. Allow the surface of the potting medium to dry slightly between thorough waterings. Use room temperature water.

Grooming. Pinch long stems to encourage bushy growth and to retain the colorful markings of juvenile leaves. Overcrowded plants can be repotted at any time of the year. Fertilize every 2 months with half-strength solution.

Disorders. Chilling injury can occur if plants are exposed to temperatures below 55°F (13°C). Stem elongation and lower leaf loss gradually distort typical growth habit under marginal lighting.

ADDITIONAL READING

Bailey, L.H. and E.Z. Bailey. 1976. *Hortus Third.* New York: Macmillan Publishing Co. Inc.

Chase, A.R. 1985. Diseases of foliage plants— Revised list for 1985. *Foliage Digest* 8(6):3-8.

Chase, A.R. and R.T. Poole. 1985. Effects of temperature on growth of *Syngonium* 'White Butterfly'. *Foliage Digest* 8:6-7.

———. 1987. Effect of fertilizer, temperature, and light level on growth of *Syngonium podophyllum* 'White Butterfly'. *J. Amer. Soc. Hort. Sci.* 112:296-300.

Conover, C.A. and R.T. Poole. 1981. Guide for fertilizing foliage plant crops. *ARC-Apopka Research Rpt.* RH-81-1. University of Florida.

———. 1984. Light and fertilizer recommendations for production of acclimatized potted foliage plants. *Foliage Digest* 7(8):1-6.

———. 1987. Factors influencing shipping of acclimatized foliage plants. *Foliage Digest* 10(4):1-5.

Crockett, J.U. 1977. *Foliage House Plants.* Revised. Alexandria, VA: Time-Life Books.

Everett, T.H. 1980. *The New York Botanical Garden Illustrated Encyclopedia of Horticulture.* New York: Garland Publishing Inc.

Manaker, G.H. 1981. *Interior Plantscapes: Installation, Maintenance, and Management.* Englewood Cliffs, NJ: Prentice-Hall Inc.

Marousky, F.J. and B.K. Harbaugh. 1978. Deterioration of foliage plants during transit. *Proc. 1978 Natl. Tropical Foliage Short Course,* University of Florida, IFAS Coop. Ext. Serv., Orlando, FL.

McConnell, D.B., R.W. Henley and R.L. Biamonte. 1981. Commercial foliage plants. J.N. Joiner (ed.). *Foliage Plant Production.* Englewood Cliffs, NJ: Prentice-Hall Inc.

Poole, R.T. and A.R. Chase. 1987. Syngonium guide. *Greenhouse Grower* 5(1):28-29.

S

Tolmiea menziesii

tol-*mee*-a
men-*zeez*-ee-ee

Family Name: **Saxifragaceae**
Common Name: **Piggyback Plant, Pickaback Plant**

Originated in northwestern America.

TOLMIEA MENZIESII

Production factors

Light. Use production light levels of 3,500 to 4,000 fc (37.8 to 43.2 klx).

Nutrition. At recommended production light levels, fertilize with 20.7 to 27.5 pounds per 1000 square feet per year (lb/1000 sq.ft/yr) or 100.9 to 134.5 kilograms per 1000 square meters per year (kg/1000 sq. m/yr) of N-P-K.

Irrigation. Keep the potting medium moist but not wet.

Media. Use an organic potting medium with good drainage characteristics.

Problems.

Disease: Root rot.

Pests: Mealybugs; mites; whitefly.

Postproduction factors

Light. Transport of plants under dark conditions is currently the most common shipping method. If immediate delivery is not possible, place plants in a location with bright indirect light or under 400 to 500 fc (4.3 to 5.4 klx) for best quality retention. Piggyback plant tolerates low light to 50 fc (.5 klx), but extended holding under marginal conditions produces weak, loose growth.

Retail handling

Light. Provide plants with sufficient light upon delivery to recuperate from the stresses of dark storage. Place plants in a location with bright indirect light or under 400 to 500 fc (4.3 to 5.4 klx) for best quality retention. Piggyback plant tolerates low light to 50 fc (.5 klx), but better lighting preserves typical appearance.

Temperature. Provide cool conditions of 40° to 55°F (4° to 13°C) at night and 55° to 70°F (13° to 21°C) during the day.

T

Tolmiea menziesii

tol-*mee*-a
men-*zeez*-ee-ee

Higher temperatures are bearable with good light and high humidity.

Irrigation. Keep the potting medium moist but not wet.

Disorders. Prolonged holding under marginal lighting produces weak, loose growth.

Consumer care

Temperature. Provide cool conditions of 40° to 55°F (4° to 13°C) at night and 55° to 70°F (13° to 21°C) during the day. Higher temperatures are bearable with good light and high humidity.

Location. Plants thrive in areas with bright indirect or curtain-filtered sunlight, or under light levels of 400 to 500 fc (4.3 to 5.4 klx). Piggyback plant tolerates low light to 50 fc (.5 klx), but better lighting preserves typical appearance.

Irrigation. Keep the potting medium moist but not wet.

Grooming. Plants can be repotted at any time of the year. Fertilize every 2 months.

Disorders. Prolonged holding under marginal lighting produces weak, loose growth.

ADDITIONAL READING

Bailey, L.H. and E.Z. Bailey. 1976. *Hortus Third*. New York: Macmillan Publishing Co. Inc.

Crockett, J.U. 1977. *Foliage House Plants*. Revised. Alexandria, VA: Time-Life Books.

Everett, T.H. 1980. *The New York Botanical Garden Illustrated Encyclopedia of Horticulture*. New York: Garland Publishing Inc.

McConnell, D.B., R.W. Henley and R.L. Biamonte. 1981. Commercial foliage plants. J.N. Joiner (ed.). *Foliage Plant Production*. Englewood Cliffs, NJ: Prentice-Hall Inc.

Orans, M. 1973. *Houseplants and Indoor Landscaping*. Barrington, IL: A.B. Morse Co.

T

Zebrina pendula

ze-breen-a
pen-dew-la

Family Name: **Commelinaceae**
Common Name: **Wandering Jew, Inch Plant**

Originated in Mexico and Guatemala. This plant was previously named *Tradescantia zebrina*.

ZEBRINA PENDULA

Production factors

Light. Use production light levels of 3,500 to 4,500 fc (37.8 to 48.6 klx) for acclimatized plants.

Temperature. Provide greenhouse temperatures of 50°F (10°C) or higher to assure continuous growth.

Nutrition. At recommended production light levels, fertilize with 27.5 to 34.4 pounds per 1000 square feet per year (lb/1000 sq.ft/yr) or 134.5 to 168.1 kilograms per 1000 square meters per year (kg/1000 sq. m/yr) of N-P-K.

Irrigation. Keep the potting medium moist but not wet.

Media. Use a potting medium with good drainage characteristics.

Problems.

Diseases: Leaf spot—*Cercospora zebrina, Chaetoseptoria* sp.; rust—*Uromyces commelinae;* virus—tobacco mosaic virus, Tradescantia mosaic virus.

Pests: Aphids; mealybugs; mites; nematodes; scale.

Disorders. Wandering Jew is slightly sensitive to atmospheric fluoride. Tipburn symptoms are slow to develop.

Postproduction factors

Light. Transport of plants under dark conditions is currently the most common shipping method. If immediate delivery is not possible, hold plants under bright indirect light or at least 150 to 250 fc (1.6 to 2.7 klx). Wandering Jew develops elongated internodes and dull foliage under marginal lighting.

Z

Zebrina pendula

Retail handling

Light. Provide plants with sufficient light upon delivery to recuperate from the stresses of dark storage. Place in a location with bright indirect light or under at least 150 to 250 fc (1.6 to 2.7 klx).

Temperature. Keep average interior temperatures of 65° to 85°F (18° to 29°C) to sustain growth and quality.

Irrigation. Keep the potting medium moist but not wet.

Disorders. Wandering Jew develops elongated internodes and dull foliage under marginal lighting. Chilling injury occurs indoors if plants are exposed to temperatures below 55°F (13°C). Tipburn occurs under conditions of high temperature, low humidity, water stress, high soluble salts or fluoride toxicity.

Consumer care

Temperature. Average interior temperatures of 65° to 85°F (18° to 29°C) sustain growth and quality.

Location. Wandering Jew thrives when placed under bright indirect or curtain-filtered sunlight, but also maintains quality under interior lighting of 150 to 250 fc (1.6 to 2.7 klx).

Irrigation. Keep the potting medium moist but not wet.

Grooming. Plants can be repotted at any time of the year. Fertilize every 2 months with half-strength houseplant formula.

Disorders. Chilling injury occurs indoors if plants are exposed to temperatures below 55°F (13°C). Plants develop elongated internodes and dull foliage under marginal lighting. Tipburn occurs under conditions of high temperature, low humidity, water stress, high soluble salts or fluoride toxicity.

Cultivars. *Zebrina pendula* 'Purpussii' leaves are solid red green or dark red.

Zebrina pendula 'Quadricolor' has metallic green leaves striped with green, red and white.

ADDITIONAL READING

Bailey, L.H. and E.Z. Bailey, 1976. *Hortus Third.* New York: Macmillan Publishing Co. Inc.

Chase, A.R. 1985. Diseases of foliage plants—Revised list for 1985. *Foliage Digest* 8(6):3-8.

Chase, A.R. 1988. Diseases of foliage plants—1988 updated listing. *Foliage Digest* 11(6):5-8.

Crockett, J.U. 1977. *Foliage House Plants.* Revised. Alexandria, VA: Time-Life Books.

Everett, T.H. 1980. *The New York Botanical Garden Illustrated Encyclopedia of Horticulture.* New York: Garland Publishing Inc.

McConnell, D.B., R.W. Henley and R.L. Biamonte. 1981. Commercial foliage plants. J.N. Joiner (ed.). *Foliage Plant Production.* Englewood Cliffs, NJ: Prentice-Hall Inc.

Woltz, S.S. and W.E. Waters. 1978. Airborne fluoride effects on some foliage plants. *HortScience* 13:585-586.

Z

CROP INDEX

CROP INDEX

CROP INDEX